THE QUIET VET

By ROD WOOD.

The Quiet Vet

Book Printing UK

Remus House

Coltsfoot Drive

Woodston

THE QUIET VET

ROD WOOD

Book Printing UK

Peterborough

2022

Peterborough

PE2 9BF

www.bookprintinguk.com

A CIP catalogue record for this book is available from the British Library.

Other books by Rod Wood

Kilimanjaro. My Goal. My Story.
(republished as Kilimanjaro. My Story)
Fishing the Net. (with Jane Reeves).
Kenya. A Mountain to Climb.

Dedicated in memory of my late father, Anthony Wood,
Without whom this career may not have happened.

Contents

Prologue

Author's Biography

Since my early teens I had decided on a veterinary career and qualified from Bristol University in 1977. That was the start of a career spanning forty five years until I retired 1n 2022.

I am a dairy farmer's son so my interest was always in farm practice, and that has been my main speciality throughout my career, mainly in the South-West and Shropshire. I have always loved the outdoors and the countryside. There have been the odd dabbles at small animal work, but for the last seventeen years of my career I have had the pleasure of working solely on farm.

It has been a career with its ups and downs, including working through two epidemics, and experiencing the affects this can have on ones well-being. But throughout, it has been a pleasure to be involved with the farming community, and offer what help I can.

Married twice and with two children, now well grown-up, but neither of whom wanted to follow in father's footsteps. Jane and I will now pursue our interests in retirement but hopefully nearer the coast where I can indulge in my walking, gardening and hopefully golf again. In the later part of my life, I have found that I enjoy writing, especially on East Africa, an area I have been privileged to visit on three occasions so far, but is certainly on my wish list to return again, maybe even to climb one of its mountains again.

A largely happy career that I hope I may have conveyed in this book, along with the changing times in farm practice.

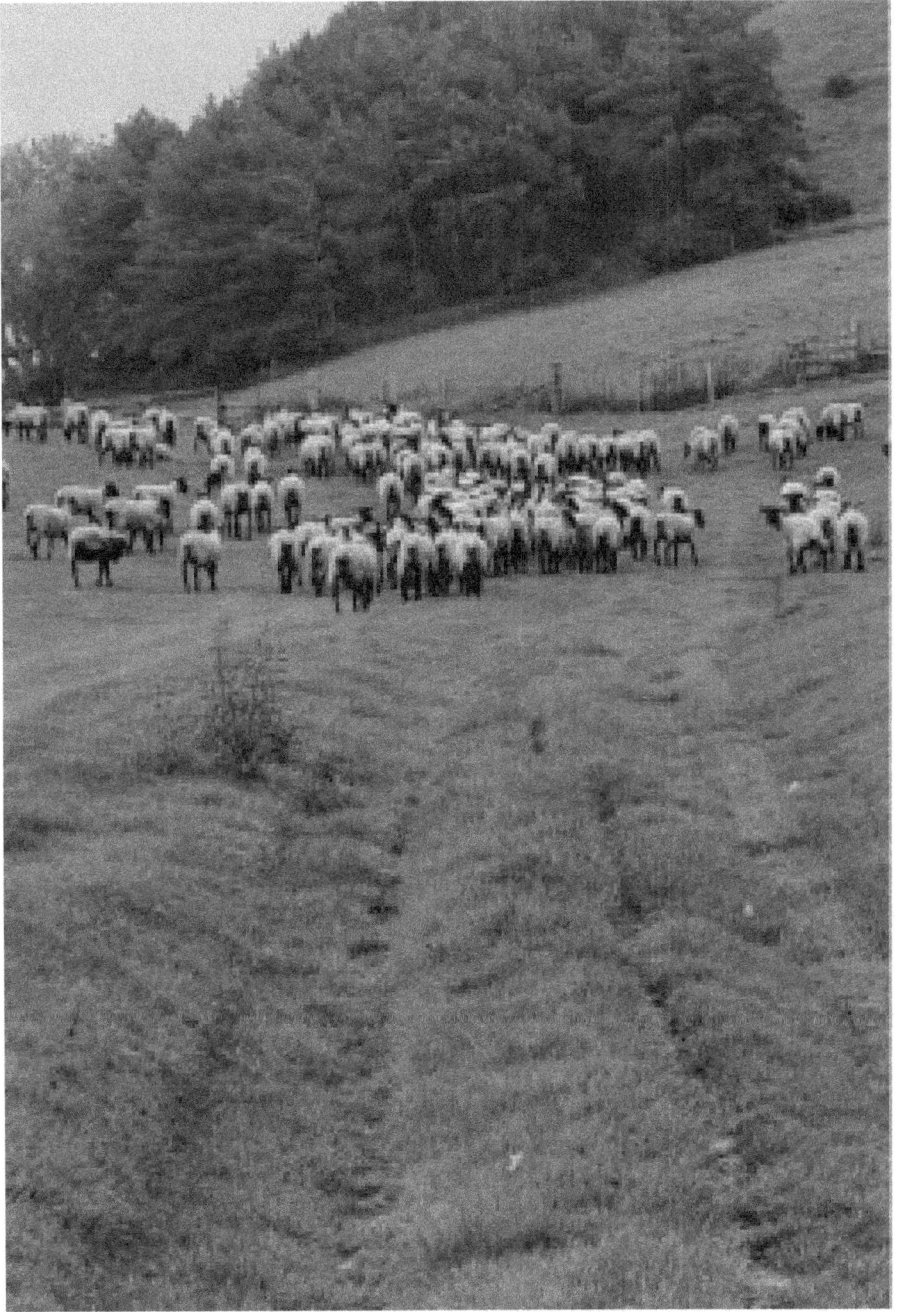

PROLOGUE

It is 1978 and I am lying in bed as the dawn breaks on a peaceful sunny morning. The birds are starting to sing outside in the Devon air as I start to stir, ready to begin another day of my veterinary career, still in its infancy. I have been on call for the night, my duty is nearly over, if all is quiet then another couple of hours in bed before getting up to begin the day afresh.

For once the night has been quiet, but then summer is generally a bit quieter as not so many cows are calving, that will all change in a month or two as we move into autumn, along with spring a more seasonal time for calving cows.

My peace is disturbed by the phone ringing, on these quieter nights it is almost a rude awakening from a whole night's sleep. I come to my wits to answer the phone.

"Traille here at Yarde. I have a cow with her bed out", a voice says in a deep Scottish accent.

This was something new to me, had I heard him right, a cow with her bed out. I asked him to repeat what he had just said. With his accent, I needed to be sure that what he said was what I thought he had said.

"Traille here and I have a cow with her bed out".

"Her bed out?" This was a mystery to me, something I had never heard of despite being a farmer's son, or I had misheard him through his accent.

"Yes. Her bed out. I need a vet as soon as possible".

"Okay, I'll be along as soon as I can, should be with you in less than half an hour."

I had a fifteen-minute drive after getting dressed, along the Culm Valley before crossing the river and following it along another mile to the farm I was going to. A journey where I was wondering what I was going to see. A cow with its bed out! I had no idea.

I was soon to be enlightened as I drove into the yard to be directed towards a ford across the river. Lying in the river was a cow and even from a distance I could see an enormous red bag hanging behind here. Her bed was her uterus, she had prolapsed her uterus after calving and there it was inverted and now outside her body, inside out, engorged with blood.

In all my days as a student, and at home with Dad, I had never come across one, now in real life I was going to have to sort this out. Experience, nil! All I knew was from my university lectures, that cows usually had Milk Fever (hypocalcaemia) if they did this so they couldn't stand, and if they did then with the weight of this engorged sack hanging behind them, there was a chance that it could cause the rupture of the uterine artery and the cow would soon bleed to death.

I was going to have to try and put the uterus back from where it came from, inside the cow, in the river where she was lying, luckily on her sternum, rather than being flat out on her side.

In those days of my fledgling career, I wore waders which were appropriate in the river, but luckily being the ford, although some ten yards across, it was only six inches deep, with a stony bottom, but even in summer, cold!

I entered the water to assess what we were going to do, how to approach this. University notes said give an epidural injection so the cow would stop straining. Then what? The placenta was still attached, and the job would be made easier if I could remove this. There is an old wives tale about putting sugar on the engorged uterus to make it go smaller and support its weight with a sheet to lift it higher, resulting in some of the blood running out, back through the uterine veins and back into the body of the cow. Or was it something to do with osmosis?

"Don't think the sugar is going to stay around too long with all this water!"

I thought to myself," I may have to make this up as I go along". Having administered the epidural, all I could do was kneel in the water behind the cow and support the uterus in my arms while trying to manipulate it back through the vulva, back into the vagina and then invert in to how it should be. This had to be the most tiring thing I had ever done as a vet in my short career, as I pushed one bit in, the bit I had just pushed back would pop out again. This was hard work.

Here I struggled for a long time, thirty minutes, then forty. But at last the thing felt as if it was getting smaller and with that, I was finally making some progress until eventually I had managed to pop it all back from whence it came. Success!

"What do I do now," I thought to myself, "I have to make sure it is inverted fully". Somewhere in my memory was something about using a wine bottle to act as an extension of my arm to reach right into the tips of the uterine horns to make sure I had achieved this.

"I don't suppose you have a bottle a bottle of Riesling?" (How times change, loved the stuff then, wouldn't touch it now). Too early for a drink the farmer thought, but no, empty would do fine. Upon the arrival of the bottle, I was able to use it for the purpose I had required it for, though a drink would have been good.

I was knackered, but at last success. I was happy the uterus was now where it should be and how it should be. I would give some Oxytocin to make the uterus contract, then some Calcium to treat the Milk Fever, cover with antibiotics and I would be done.

I didn't want to leave the cow lying in the river, and back in those days giving Calcium in the vein worked almost instantaneously, so she was soon on her feet and staggering slowly out onto dry land.

Thankfully, even if I was exhausted, we had achieved a successful outcome and I was rewarded with a cup of coffee and a cooked breakfast. No worries about cholesterol levels then, the rasher of bacon was nearly a centimetre thick, a real treat.

I was pleased, and surprisingly, still dry, my waders had worked a treat in covering enough of my legs to keep the water out.

Forty plus years on and I had finished doing night and weekend duties. I was having my breakfast before waiting to start my day, remote working because of Covid. My phone went and a good friend, a local farmer, Paul, was on the end of the line. He had a heifer who had prolapsed her uterus (no local terms here, he described just the condition that a vet was needed for). He had called the duty vet who was some forty minutes away, was I free to come now?

I was there in less than fifteen minutes and soon getting ready to do the job I had been called out for. Over those forty years, experience had shown me how to make this job less onerous. If the cow was down, one would stretch her hind legs out behind her to put her in a far easier position to correct the prolapse. I also knew not to rush trying to put the engorged organ back in. Patience, just holding it up while some of the blood drained back out of the uterus, then gently pushing, kneading it back to its original position. Others hold the cow up by her back legs, using a tractor and loader, letting gravity do some of the work for you: we all have developed our own techniques.

Here, the heifer was still standing, but in a cattle crush and well secured. Again, an epidural anaesthetic was important. Once I had given that, with just a little patience over the next few minutes whilst holding the uterus up, cleaning it with warm water and removing the remains of the placenta, I was ready to try putting it back in from where it had come from, inside the heifer. With experience and a refined technique (and its one of those things I find it difficult to explain to anyone else how to do it, I just do it) it was a matter of minutes before the uterus was replaced and I now used my long, thin plastic bottle (when did I last have a Riesling) to use as my arm extension to reach to the tips of the now inverted uterus.

Success, and after the necessary injections the heifer needed, we were soon able to return her to her calf who was awaiting his first colostrum. A good outcome and I was not even tired.

Sadly, no bacon this time. But a condition that has not changed over all those years, though I have seen many of them in between, but experience had shown me how to deal with it in a far quicker and less onerous way. For years I thought it was the most tiring job I could get called out to. Now it does not bother me at all, as long as I have enough water to clean myself up with when done, as especially as I am not very tall, I can look a bit of a mess when finished.

I now find a "cow with her bed out" a challenge to get it replaced as efficiently as possible, rather than the laborious job it used to be. It would probably be one of the few jobs as I vet that I do where the tools of the trade haven't changed over all those years, but experience has changed the way I approach them.

In those long-gone days in Devon I soon found out what a cow with her bed out was, a term which I have found in the various places I have worked throughout the country.

I would soon afterwards be challenged with a cow with her "reed out" (she had prolapsed her vagina), where that term came from, I would be intrigued to know!

Has anything changed here? Yes, I guess the benefits of experience!

1

THE PROFESSION

The Veterinary profession has always held a special place in the eyes of the general public, animal doctors who look after beloved pets and serve the farming community in looking after their animals as they seek to produce food to feed our population. A profession, that in the latter part of the twentieth century, became ever popular with school leavers who saw the career as the job they wanted to do, university places became harder to find, entrance became stricter and that was even after a significant increase in places available at all the sites of teaching. Now courses are available at new universities, at Keele and Surrey, but there is still the ever-increasing demand for places at university to become a Vet.

We have been around for years, but the books of James Herriot and the tv series that followed, certainly popularised the profession. A common talking point on a Monday morning back in the late seventies, early eighties when I started. "Did you see the vet program on Saturday night?" with the latest exploits of Trickie Woo, or that young Veterinary?

 Other programmes have followed such as Animal Hospital, Supervet and now The Yorkshire Vet, all showing the work of my profession both in large, small and exotic animal work. And we now have a return of "All Creatures Great and Small" from another production company. The general public are shown what now can be done using ever more sophisticated techniques of treatment. These programs have also shown the emotional side of our work, the ups and downs for both vet and owner, whether of a dog or of a cow, and of course the old-fashioned treatments and remedies.

We have seen practice on the Yorkshire Moors, in Central London, in Scotland and on farms in Countryfile, in fact over much of our country. We have become an open book, though these programs may be very selective in what they want to show the public, glamourizing us while hiding some of the mundane day to day bread and butter work that keeps us busy. The profession, certainly on television but also I think in the vast majority of the eyes remains popular and looked up to. People admire the amount of hard work that goes into our training after achieving top grades in school exams to even get into university. A lot of people think our training harder than a medic's, that probably is not quite correct. We are qualified straight after leaving university, once we have sworn our hypocritic oath then we are free to practice, let loose on a world of unsuspecting animals. A doctor is not quite there yet, with time spent as housemen while they continue their learning and gaining valuable experience. Us vets, though now very often working some sort of apprenticeship, internships, are the real thing from day 1. As demands increase it is now not uncommon that our learning will continue under the tutelage of more experienced members of the profession, working in the same Practice. Changing times and something I'll return to later, have certainly meant that the profession I entered into all those years ago is vastly different from the one a new graduate would experience now.

But as was then, I think most who enter the profession have chosen it from a young age. They will have the high demands of school and seeing practice for work experience well and truly encrusted in their minds even as young as entering secondary school. Myself, I was a farmer's son and if my first ambition was to become a Zoologist so that I could pursue my love of East Africa and its wildlife, then I guess it was when I was about fourteen that I decided that I wanted to become a farm vet. With farming parents there was a lot of encouragement for me to follow this line, this profession, even after my first experience of going out with the local vet at that tender age. I was then but a small lad not carrying an ounce of flesh more than I needed and it was a cold, very cold winter's day when my parents had arranged for me to go out with the senior vet in the local practice. As it happened, I would spend the first part of the day at our neighbour's farm Tuberculin testing. Government policy had started TB testing not long before in an attempt to eradicate Tuberculosis in the cattle population. I was picked up by our vet and taken on this test and it was my job to record the skin measurements of each cow when it was tested. In those days in the mid-sixties, each cow was tied in its stall in the cow shed. I was a very quiet and shy lad, so it did help me that I knew the farmer and his son, but that didn't make me any warmer and as the morning progressed, I got colder and colder and colder, shivering away under my winter clothing. Needless to say, it did not put me off the profession though I will never forget that day, my first experience of a farm vets life. Little would I know then how much Tuberculin testing would play such a major role in my life fifty years on as my time in the profession drew to a close.

From those early days I knew the part of the profession that interested me was farming and especially cattle. That is what I wanted to do, so all I had to do was to work hard at school to ensure I achieved the required grades at A level in the subjects very much chosen by the Universities. These were not necessarily my best subjects and from a personal point of view, I felt a great shame to give up Geography and even Latin which I very much enjoyed. We, in those days were asked to specialise too soon, so it was straight science, science and more science. I enjoyed Chemistry and the

Zoology part of Biology, so it was only Physics that was a bore. But with ample amounts of sport, especially running and hockey I did just scrape into a place at Bristol University to undertake my training and get my degree. It was my chosen University though I did try or was asked to try Oxbridge exams by my school, a place at Cambridge would have been the reward but the course was a year longer there and the only real reason to choose Cambridge over Bristol was the thought of getting a hockey Blue. Bristol it would be!

Those distant days when I loaded my little Austin A30 with my trunk of possessions and set off to the big city for the first time as a naïve country boy. None of my other friends from school who tried to get into Bristol on other courses succeeded, a new world with no friends, a new beginning.

That was my beginning into this profession that I have devoted my life to. Five years at Bristol to get my degree and then through the years, until now as my career reaches into its dying embers. Time spent in Buckinghamshire, in Devon, in Gloucestershire and last, but not least, the thirty plus years I have spent in Shropshire, as a partner in two practices before finishing in a farm only practice for the last seventeen years of my career. I had come full circle back to why I started the job in the first place. If Buckinghamshire was just a short beginning, then my move to Devon, to an almost completely large animal practice was the place I started my love affair with the Southwest, also meeting some of those friends who remain friends for life. It was a place I learned a lot in terms of Farm Practice which I have carried through my career, a great place to live and some great times were spent down there. Ironically, it is my son who has now settled there, the area I have always longed to return to.

Through those years until my last job outside Shrewsbury, I have been involved in some small animal work, some equine work but my first love has always been farm, and especially cattle work. Cows can be so placid and curious animals, they like an easy life, traits I find in myself as well, but they also can be moody and stubborn, again like me!

But I think, at least with farm animals, you are treating the animal and not to some extent the owner as you do in small and equine work. I think that is why from my farming background, then it was farm work I had always wanted to do. The joy of working with cattle and farmers, helping in animal welfare and in the country's food production.

There were times when my enthusiasm waned, even looking into the possibility of swopping into financial services at one stage when I had a young family and saw little of them. But I stuck at it until I reached the point now where I am at now, retirement.

As I now look back on those years, I ask myself if things have changed? Is the profession I started in all those years ago the same one I finish in? Forty plus years, how different is it now from then? I have often looked back, and thought were they the good old days or is what my colleagues have now just as good as that of my memories?

For me, I wanted to go back and compare then and now but almost entirely from my perspective as a farm vet. Change intermixed with joy, sadness, dark times and good times.

If it was not entirely the end of my career, then what brought a lot back to me and made me want to record some of it was back in 2017, when us 1977 Bristol graduates held our fortieth anniversary graduation dinner. So, that will be where my story begins.

2

FORTY YEARS ON

We left Telford after breakfast, heading down to Bristol for my University forty-year re-union. It was mid-September, myself and my wife of a mere two months, Jane. We would arrive in Bristol just before lunch, going direct to the hotel which we would be staying at and where the re-union was taking place that evening. It would consist of a formal three course set meal, and then retire to the bar to renew old acquaintances after all those years. Some of us were still involved in our veterinary careers, like myself, others had taken different courses in their lives. Some had gone into industry, pharmaceuticals, others teaching, lecturing at Vet Schools in the country (one or two who had never actually left Bristol). They were now retired on nice final salary index linked pensions. That was something I could only dream of. Some were bringing their partners; others would arrive alone. I was looking forward to meeting up again after all those years with the group of people I had spent five years of my life with, studying. I guess as a class, and it was a small class compared with Vet school intakes these days, thirty-six who started, a couple less who finished. Though we lost a few and gained one or two others on the way, but in the summer of 1977, we all graduated to pursue our chosen profession. We were probably not the most sociable of groups. Entry into vet school had suddenly become harder, with high academic standards required. This resulted in the swats, the country boys who fancied a beer after a hard day's work, and those that crossed between both groups, and mixing was not that great. We also had a couple of mature students, four I seem to remember, that lived away from the University, their lives already established in the outside world having pursued other careers to begin with.

For that reason, whereas I had heard of some re-unions that took place from other Faculties and from other vet years on a regular basis, it was only our third. One at ten years, one at twenty-five and this one now, forty years. How it had flown! I had not made the first one, although I worked closest to where it took place. In those days, I worked in a two-man practice on the edge of the Cotswolds, working seven nights on then seven nights off, and with a young family, it fell in the wrong week for me. Twenty-five years, again meeting up in a hotel in Bristol. It was a good catch up with those that attended, a fun evening when we were all still working in some form in our chosen profession. It was a shame the whole year could not make it there, but the majority did, and it was great to catch up after so long. Some who attended I had not seen since I had left Bristol in 1977.

This time, I wanted to make the effort because it would almost certainly be the last reunion we would have, the Bristol year of '77. We were not getting any younger and we were not guaranteed eternal immortality.

Forty years, although to be precise forty-five, it was a similar time in September that I had set off from the family farm in Oxfordshire to begin my career. Then, a naïve country boy, not used to the city. In fact, other than the odd day out, I had never stayed in a large town or city. It was quite intimidating for the shy lad I was then. I had packed my trunk into the back of my old car, a cream Austin A30, and had headed down the M4 to begin my university career, which would end up with, hopefully, a Veterinary degree, and a chance to follow my love of working with animals, especially farm animals, cows.

I had gone through the boy phases of wanting to be in the Blues and Royals. I rode a lot in those early days, and then as I developed an interest in Africa, the great plains of the Rift Valley, and its wildlife, a Zoologist was the next aim. But as I got older, going through my teen years, I got more and more interested in Dad's farm, his cows, and working in the countryside, somewhere I was happy to spend all my free hours there sharing it with my love of sport. I would become a farmer, but no. The farm wasn't large enough to support the active minds of both me and my father, plus a twin brother who would also go into farming and who knew that was his course many years previously. In those days, tenancies (county council small holdings) couldn't be passed on from father to son, so there was no certainty that a business could continue as a family concern.

A large animal vet was as close as I could see I would get. In my mid-teens I had spent a few days out with Ken Day, a local farm vet practitioner in the neighbouring village. Despite the cold, for there was not much of me in those days, I had not been dissuaded that this was what I wanted to do. So when I reached my Upper Sixth at school and had to choose Universities, I knew that with the difficulty of getting a place that my first choice was the only likely offer I would get. My first choice was Bristol, I did get an offer. Despite a small hiccup with grades, thankfully with the persistence of my father, I got my place to start in 1972.

So, in mid-September there I was heading to Bristol, slightly early. I would be involved in pre-season hockey training, a sport which was my real strength, and a sport in which by mid-term I had forced my way into the University first team. My university career had started; a full lecture timetable, many exams, much practical work and then seeing practice in the vacations, where we would be sent into general practice to get more experience. Great days under the guidance of Ian Baker in Aylesbury, he taught me far more than I ever learnt in Bristol, a practical approach which suited me more than the academic learning of a lecture theatre. The drought year of '76, where he would plan our day so as to end up at a farm with a swimming pool, or we would be excavating his old well in his garden. Happy times, he taught me a lot. So that in 1977, I graduated and though still shy and lacking in self-confidence (except on a hockey pitch), I was about to begin my chosen carer in earnest. A career which would take me briefly to the Bucks, Beds border before spending five very happy years in Devon, then five years either side of the Severn in Gloucestershire before ending up in Shropshire for nearly three decades.

So here I was, forty years on, heading back to Bristol to meet up with my fellow graduates, to catch up, hear about their lives, careers, families, and to reminisce on those university days now so long ago. Forty years, they had seen a vast change in myself from that shy and quiet lad setting foot in the big city and starting out on a daunting career. Now to the confident though still quiet (most people would say) person that I am today. As Jane and I drove down to the re-union, it was time for me to reflect on my career, and the changes that had taken place in that time in vetting, and in farming. The funny times, also sad times, there had been many of those, especially the Foot and Mouth outbreak of 2001. Being able to experience the countryside on a day-to-day basis, being able to help people, especially farmers when they were down, the joie de vie it had given to me over those years.

Those thoughts that I guess have made me put pen to paper now. I had found not many years ago that I enjoyed writing. Something that until I had wanted to record my experience of climbing Kilimanjaro, I had always hated. I hated writing essays at school, at university and through my career, writing articles for Newsletters, or, well anything. But even then, I said I would never write a vet book!

So, in December of 2016, I received an e-mail from one of my fellow graduates that our year leader, and Janet always was our leader, was trying to get in touch with the whole year of '77 to arrange the big one. The fortieth-year re-union! She did not have everyone's contact details, so those she did, she asked to forward her details to those which she didn't. Although Janet and I chatted for a long time fifteen years earlier, sharing the personal difficulties we had had in our lives, and promising to keep in touch, we didn't actually in the end swop details. Though I guess somewhere she must have contacted me for me to have gone to that reunion, our twenty fifth.

But thanks to a good old friend, Graham, I was able to contact her. If the date was suitable (she had talked of summer or September and I knew I was going back to Africa in the summer to climb Mount Kenya), then I was keen to go. I was also very keen to see Graham again after so long, we had always exchanged Christmas cards with a catch up note of what was happening in our lives.

Janet was wonderful in her efficiency, as she always had been over the years, even when representing the year as a student. I don't know how many of us she did manage to contact, but she came up with the date, booked the hotel and arranged the meal. She also arranged a trip to the Field Station at Langford where we had spent our final two clinical years, then to the new vet school for the pre-clinical students in Bristol itself. I had decided to give these a miss, and just attend the dinner.

She sent out a list of those that would be attending, a smaller number than I had hoped. Looking down the list, one or two names that I had hoped would come wouldn't be attending, Graham for a start. But I was happy to accept and take Jane along as well. Janet had also asked if any of us going had any old photographs of our student days. Did we even have cameras in those days? Certainly not the digital phone cameras of today, snap and retain or snap and delete. I certainly had no pictures, other than the group photograph of the class taken on our final day at Vet School, just before we were about to be dressed down for who was responsible for raising a pair of the Langford House Warden's underpants up the flagpole on the roof of the main building. He was not amused and was threatening to fail us all in our finals! I also had a few photos from a hot summers day that Janet and I spent on Exmoor in search of the Doone Valley, but I don't think they were what she had in mind.

So, all was arranged, paid for and we were on our way. My son had moved to Bristol a couple of years previously and I had seen that the city had changed somewhat since my student days. He lived in Cotham which in my day was a big student lodging area, but now seemed to have gone rather up market. The docks had been developed, no longer the hole that I remembered. Even when I had gone to the twenty-fifth-year re-union, that area had changed so much for the better. The sites such as the S.S Great Britain were now a worthwhile trip. Just wandering around the developed waterside areas was both relaxing and exhilarating with the new, vibrant area that has been created.

Even as we now drove into the city, all had changed. The route in, the shopping centres, Broadmead the new centre in my day now redundant as newer out of town centres such as at Cribs Causeway were developed. I thought I knew where I was going, but as I said, all change. Thank heavens for Jane's phone Sat Nav to take us to our hotel.

It had been so long. I said to Jane how I wondered how everyone would look after all these years, and whether I would recognise them, because some of them I hadn't seen since I left. Some of the faces I would know, who like me would not have changed that much since leaving and from the photograph that I had that was taken on our last day, I could recognise them from that. But what about the others, the ravages of time, how would they look now?

We parked the car and checked in, finding our room before deciding it was time for lunch. We took the lift down to reception, and there sitting in the window was one of us, like me completely unchanged from fifteen years earlier, probably more as I think I last saw him at his house years before that, when my children were still little. He didn't look any different than he did at university all those years ago and didn't sound any different when I called across the reception area to greet him, and his lovely wife who I had also met years before. Pete was no different from the person I had worked with so often at university, for our names were both so close together at the end of the alphabet, that we would always be in the same group. We were on the same floor in Hall in our first year. It was good to see him again. We had enjoyed happy times together, and it was often his encouragement when I was struggling academically that got me through.

"Don't let the bastards grind you down" he would often say to me.

When we had both worked in the West Country in our early days in practice, me in Devon, him in Dorset, and I had visited him in Sherborne before we set off to try and find a meal. We eventually ended up in Weymouth on the sea front where we procured fish and chips, Pete was really starving, but he promptly dropped his portion all over the pavement. It took him many seconds to decide whether to pick them off the dirty walkway or not, before his better judgement decided he wouldn't.

So, it was nice to see a friendly face to start with, but they were going to look at the new faculty. We said we would see them later and went in pursuit of lunch, which coincidentally was fish and chips, but in a Wetherspoons. Pete and Anne did pass by as we ate.

We ate and then wandered around the docks, exploring the new waterside paths and cafes before returning to the hotel where Jane wanted a rest. I took myself back into the city, but this time towards the old haunts of my student days. The Wills Memorial Hall was as distinctive as ever, though it struck me how much Park Street and the Triangle had changed, like so many inner-city shopping areas, mostly now just cafes and charity shops. The old Vet School which had been in an old garage on the corner of Park Row no longer existed but had instead been replaced with some university office building. Once a place where we would dissect dogs, a horse, and a cow, was no longer suited for that purpose. The big department stores like Habitat, so distinctive in my day, were gone. Pete and I had decided we would get Janet some flowers for organising everything, but could I find a florist!

But some things in Bristol never change. I had set off without a coat, as I walked around the Triangle, it began to rain, in fact it chucked it down, just like in those good old days forty plus years ago when I would be walking down from Clifton to lectures.

I wandered back down Park Street towards the hotel. The same street that all those years ago, Pete and I had wandered down. On one occasion stopping traffic, dressed as a panto horse on the way to the Mandrake Club at the bottom for a party. Sadly, that didn't seem to exist any longer either.

I did eventually manage to find Janet some flowers, but from an unlikely source. I was then straight back down into the City Centre, exploring those places I never had the bravery as a naïve country lad to do in my student days. The Colston Hall, the theatre, the Arnofini, and one or two of the old pubs I did used to get to on occasions. The Llandoger Trow, and The Old Duke, which was always a great haunt if one wanted to listen to jazz live.

It was a brief exploration of the city I studied in, finding out how much the city had changed. It was now a far more vibrant, an exciting place to be. My son, on his journey through life, had attended University in Exeter. He then worked in the City, London, and seemed to have a plan of where he was going to spend parts of his life. Once he had undertaken some travelling, South America and Costa Rica, he had decided Bristol was the next exciting place, so he ended up buying his first house there with his lovely girlfriend.

But that was all I would see of the city for now. I had a dinner to get ready for, and a catch up with Mrs Wood. These were very fond memories and I wish I had seen more of Bristol when I was there for five years as a student. My life then was study, and playing hockey for first the University, and then for Swindon where I would have to drive to most weekends to play. Strangely enough, away games would often be just down the road outside Bristol playing the likes of Bristol, Long Ashton, Old Bristolians and Firebrands. I will no doubt see more when visiting my son, and I very much look forward to that.

Jane and I wandered down to the hotel reception to be directed to the suite our dinner was to be held in. How many faces would I recognise? By coincidence, after having already met them earlier, the first faces we did see were Ann and Pete again. They had gone on the organised trip that afternoon, so were able to tell me of the "new" Vet School they had seen. I was able to fill them in on my walk. But soon the room was filling with the assembled guests, some familiar, completely identical to those forty years ago bar a few marks from the ravages of time, one or two I hardly recognised at all. Our conversation was soon on what news there was of others who qualified with us, where they were now, and what they were doing. But more pertinently was the news of those who were no longer with us, and there were a number sadly. Stories of them and their demise soon turned to the happy memories that we had of them, and some of their antics. One of them I had shared a flat with in my fourth year, but we had lost touch a long time ago, and I knew nothing of his death.

There were one or two who nobody knew of their whereabouts these days, characters then who now seemed to have disappeared off the face of the earth, with the odd rumour attached to their history. But we had a laugh amongst ourselves remembering them and some of the mishaps they got up to when they were students with us. We spoke of some of the others who hadn't made it through the course for one reason or another and what had happened to them.

Even after forty years, it was like as if we had seen each other yesterday. Straight into conversations with everybody, in fact some of them were now easier to talk to than when we were fellow students.

Time to eat. As we went into our dining room for our meal, it occurred to me that it was a shame we couldn't all be on the same table. But we stuck to the seating plan and we neatly sat around the three tables provided. Though we probably divided into those cliques that we had been in all those years ago.

Janet had asked us for photos, I don't know where they came from, but on one of those ever-lasting loops, she had set up shots of us in our final year pantomime, our final Langford Games, and what I presume was the first re-union, the one that I was unable to attend.

There was a sight for Jane, Rod the student, thin, long-haired and bearded. I looked very young and innocent in the frames I had been captured in. But some of those things I had long forgotten.

The Langford Games is now a part of Bristol Vet School history. In all the jobs that I have worked in, my final employment in Shropshire was where I worked with the greatest number of ex-Bristol students. Fellow Alumni I suppose but from different times. None of them had partaken in these Games because they were now discontinued for Health and Safety reasons. Bureaucracy gone crazy; it was all a bit of fun. The Games were always organised by the fourth year. Various events which took place between the respective years, but it was always a poor show if the organisers didn't win overall as they had the advantage of knowing the events. In such events as the donkey race, they could "dope" everyone else's donkey.

But the highlight of the Games was always the "Ha Ha". Now, because of my hockey commitments, I had never actually participated in the Games until my final year. This was when I was picked for the "Ha Ha" team, and for a Sack Race. The latter of which I had quite forgotten. But there on the wall in the sequence of photos was myself and a fellow fifth year, looking in a compromising position laid on the ground inside our sack. She was a very pretty girl and one of those who was unable to attend our re-union. She was also one where no-one seemed to now know her present whereabouts.

How would I best describe the "Ha Ha"? It is a game of five-aside rugby played on a short pitch in what is a garden. The garden would be surrounded by a dry ditch with a stone wall on one side, the ditch sloping down to the wall, and usually grassed. There was such a feature at Langford House and that was where the event took place. Except....

The day before the games, some lucky person would be given the task of removing the turf from the "pitch" and loosening the earth underneath. Then making it as wet and muddy as possible. How wet the pitch was usually depended on how drunk the "groundsman" was when preparing it, but in our final year it was a quagmire.

The game was played with a deflated rugby ball, partly filled with sand. The rules, well the first years didn't know, but basically there weren't any. Except that the poor unsuspecting first years always played first against the organisers, the fourth years, and the first years were led to believe it was a simple game of rugby. They had never seen it played so would try to play an attractive attacking game, only to find anything went. Inevitably they were always knocked out Round 1!

Which would mean semi-finals comprised of second year against final year. This gave the second years a chance of revenge from their experience the previous year as first years, and third year would play against fourth.

But we were a small year, our two biggest members were the mature students and there was no way they were going to participate in this "bit of fun". So our side consisted of Neil, the largest of us, two rugby players, myself (a hockey player who did play rugby), and a farmer's son. We would have to devise new tactics against these second years bent on revenge.

We did. We would have three "grapplers", and two "players". When the ball was thrown in, the grapplers would grab any member of the opposition they could, preferably all of them in whatever hold they could. In the mad muddy scramble of flaying bodies then the players, Pete and I would find the ball and either go for the line or pass to one another, if all the other bodies weren't subdued, and score a try. The second years had a plan to beat us but became unstuck by our "new" tactics. Perhaps unstuck is the wrong word because in that mud they were well and truly stuck. When they thought they would try those same tactics on us, they found they couldn't get hold of us because we had covered ourselves with Paraffin Wax. We won that game easily, and the final too. We spent the time in between matches sitting in a hot basin of water in the changing rooms to keep warm. A late October afternoon isn't the ideal for standing around too long bare-chested waiting for the next game. It did take along shower though to remove all the mud and wax. Again, in Janet's photos, some great shots of us merry band of five, winning our games, covered in mud. Looking at the opposition held down in the mud then maybe gives an indication as to why these games no longer takes place for Health and Safety reasons. No-one ever drowned, but I suppose there may have been a chance! But still, great pictures and happy memories of our student days.

The panto as well, always just before Christmas, done again by the Final Year for anybody who wanted to come and watch. This included our dinner ladies, the cleaners in hall, and the lecturers. Neil, myself and one other who I can't remember, volunteered to write and produce our show. Many evenings were spent coming up with ideas to present to a rather apathetic year, who once we got them on board, really excelled themselves in putting together a great show. "Alice through Vet School", our version of Alice in Wonderland as she entered Vet School through to qualifying. The hidden talents that our year had, singers (though I wouldn't include my version of "Doctor, I'm in trouble" as the greatest solo ever sung), dancers, groupies, belly dancing soldiers, and Neil on his Sax. We brought the house down, very well received and no repercussions from the staff members we took the piss out of.

I had never seen any photos of this, I didn't know anyone had taken them, but it was marvellous to see them and reminisce on what was a great night.

The meal with this background was very good, and we soon forgot about our careers to concentrate on university memories. This is where I found out things I never knew about fellow students including their musical tastes, very diverse and some's tastes were quite unexpected. Those that I thought were quiet like me, were heavy rock fans, frequently drunk and having to be rescued by their colleagues. The mischief we got up to at Association of Vet School trips, again being weekends I missed when playing hockey.

I found we were not quite the goody two shoes year I thought we were.

The meal was finished off by one of our former lecturers giving a speech on how the organisation of the schools has changed so much, funding, curriculums, so different from our day. But, as it had turned out, he and several of our now retired lecturers had now settled close to each other in the Southwest. A fascinating talk, with of course any changes that Brexit may have brought to aspiring vets as well.

But like all good thing, they come to an end. Having thanked Janet for her organisation of the evening, and presenting her with her flowers, like most Veterinary and certainly cattle Veterinary evenings, it was time to retire to the bar, to drink and chat to those that weren't on our table for dinner. Jim, a classmate I hardly knew in five years, but here I chatted to for ages, while Jane spoke to his wife. Also, Pete and Janet (didn't have long enough to catch up with her as much as we would like), but it was good to relive old memories, and renew friendships that would continue into the future.

I had enjoyed it all and was a little sad that this would be the last. But I was very glad I had made the effort to attend, and that Jane had gotten the chance to meet some of my past. It was late and time to retire to bed. Then in the morning to return home again to get ready to prepare for another trip to the South-west, to a cottage we had rented on the edge of Exmoor for what would be our time together.

Driving home I reflected on just how much had changed in those forty years, for me as a person, but also my role as a vet. A variety of things, different medicines etc, probably more so in small-animal work, but my role as a farm vet was quite different now. I have had some great memories, sad times, harrowing times, but I had been given the opportunity to work all those years in the countryside that I love so much and grew up in. I had worked with some wonderful people, real characters, salt of the earth. At times I had thought I had made the wrong choice in my career, and asked myself if I had my time again, would I have done the same? I guess the answer would be probably not. But there have been many good times and changes that I thought would be good to record. A changing world but my life has always been farming, in a friendly hardworking community that endeavours to put food on our table. A sometimes-maligned industry where people perceive money, rich landowners, expensive cars, big subsidies to produce the food that goes on our table, and an industry which is always moaning about the price they get paid for their produce. The people I have met over these years as a vet would contradict this perception. The farmers who work every hour of the day, feel the loss of their animals, have faced disasters like Foot and Mouth Disease where their livelihood had been wiped out in a moment. An industry marred by high rates of mental illness and suicide, and top of the list for accidents at work. Yes, I came from the same background but when I have hooked up my gown for the last time, put my wellies away, they are a group of people that I will very much miss. A group I have shared pain with but have also shared laughter, joy and success.

My time left in this profession was nearing its end but there have been great memories in changing times. It would finish and then it would be my time to retreat to the country again. To enjoy the life of a rural community, with no more nights on call, every weekend to be my own, and to observe from a distance what further changes occur to the rural landscape, farming and vetting. Our green and pleasant land.

So where does one start, I suppose the best place is at the beginning.

3

IN THE BEGINNING

If I have already given a brief description for the reasons behind my chosen career, then it is clear what has driven me through my forty plus years career as a vet. Essentially being a love of the countryside and all things to do with it. A hundred and thirty-acre farm had been the location of my upbringing. A farm with streams, woodland, wetland, meadows and pastures. A farm dominated by massive Elm trees before being ravaged by Dutch Elm Disease to the extent that the farm I grew up on is not the farm it was then. I gather that the farm is now completely changed, the fields now pony paddocks. The buildings now a centre for conferences, for wedding receptions, and other hospitality events. Finally, my home, the farmhouse no longer there at all. Changing times!

Mum and Dad would both start as townies. Mum growing up in Ealing, a London girl. She started her love of animals by going to work in the pet's department of Harrods, her love of the land developed when she joined the Land Army. A career on the land was about to begin which would take her to agricultural college to learn farming. Dad went through his school years living in Leamington Spa, where his father ran a garage, and where in her time his mother would eventually become a civic dignitary, becoming Lady Mayoress. I wonder if it were her frequent visits to see dad's brother in Southern Rhodesia as was then, now Zimbabwe, which kindled an interest in East Africa and its wildlife in me. Certainly, from the age of eight or nine it was a fascination to me, one that has never left me and one that at last I have had the chance to explore.

Through dad's school years he only had one interest and that was to be a farmer. I think somewhere in his ancestry which means mine as well, some of his family were landowners, farmers in Sussex, and this was a vocation he was also determined to follow. School finished, and he applied to go to agricultural college as well, Northampton Agricultural College at Moulton. Here he met mum, they fell in love and got married. After well over seventy years they are still there to look after one another.

My parents, after working with a Jersey herd near Chester where I was born, managed to get the tenancy of a small holding in Berkshire. From there a long career in farming was on its way. My parents and us three boys, their sons (though until right up to my birth the doctor had sworn mum was only expecting one baby, if it were twins, he would eat his hat, I hope it was tasty) were about to start a new beginning. They bought a tractor, twelve cows, a couple of pigs and the farm was on its way. We would come home from school and sit on a bale of hay in the cowshed to eat our supper out of an Oxo tin while mum and dad did the milking. The cows got more in numbers, the pigs less. This was in time was going to be solely a dairy farm.

The school holidays would see us helping where we could. Earning extra pocket money by mucking out calf pens, helping with the harvest but in all these times I would love to go and explore what nature provided close by. Catching sticklebacks in the stream, even once a trout that must have taken a wrong turn somewhere down our watercourse. Watching spring unfold, the pussy willow, the cowslips on the stream banks, orchids growing in the wetlands. A real experience, enjoying all that nature threw at me. All while going through school, firstly in a nearby village and then to a public school in Abingdon, without which I wouldn't be where I am today. But through those days my interest in animal and in farming developed more and more. I would help milk the cows; the herd now comprised of well over a hundred high yielding animals. I would be interested in their milk records; their pedigrees and dad would involve me a lot in what he planned to do. He was very innovative in a lot that he did, a very good farmer.

My school years would also see me go through a Foot and Mouth outbreak, the smell of disinfectant as we left the farm every day to go to school, crossing the straw disinfectant mat at the end of our farm drive would be a smell that stuck with me for years. But although it got very close, we were spared the ravages of this disease. Sadly, it would return later in my career and have a prolonged effect on my well-being.

My career path was set. The farm wasn't big enough to occupy both my father and my active minds, and my twin brother was also very much into farming, although he was more into machinery and arable farming, not a livestock man at all. His career path would follow these interests, firstly in working the land, working on a couple of large arable farms before he settled on the farm machinery sales side of the industry. A job he still pursues.

I had a choice to make! I would be a vet, as close to farming as I could get. It would be a career working for farmers and their livestock, a career I have stuck at until my time has come to call it a day, that day soon approaching. But all through that time, in the places I have worked, Devon, Gloucestershire and in Shropshire. It has been that love of the countryside that has driven me on to stick with it. There have been times when I have looked at pastures new, a career away from farming, but in the end, it has always had a hold on me, through changing times.

The land, the countryside, farming in general and vetting as well has changed so much even in my years in the profession, and that is what I want to write about. Some has been progress, some perhaps not but what I do know is that right up to my end whenever that may be, the love of all things rural will stay with me forever. One day soon I hope I will get to live again in a more rural community and enjoy again the pleasures of it 24/7 other than just in my working time. I have lived in a town far too long and the pull of the countryside gets stronger and stronger as my career nears its end.

But in September 1972 it was time to leave home and begin my career in the profession I had chosen. My dear little Austin A30, a car which had caused me more than a little grief with the police. I had bought it from the local doctor's wife for the huge sum of £35 and the police stopped me so many times because they thought I had stolen it! It was loaded with my big trunk of worldly goods, all necessary items for a life at university when I drove out of the farmyard and headed towards Bristol. A new beginning, the start of Veterinary Medicine which would be my life for the next nearly fifty years. I can admit now that when that career started all those years ago, there was no way that I thought that I would be still working as a vet as I neared my retirement age. They were supposed to be well paid and so work I imagined would have ceased by the time I was fifty-five. Like so much in my time, how things change!

A naïve country boy heading for a big city, the start of a new adventure in my life, time to accept manhood and begin a career, time to leave the comfort of my parental home to step out into the big wide world out there.

Those days were good, a struggle but good. I settled down in a Hall of residence in Clifton, finding that on my floor, a shared it with two other vet students, and a lady vet student on the floor above. Thirty-six in our year, and four of us were so close together. But I was out of my comfort zone, a shy lad without a lot of self-confidence suddenly cast amongst all these fellow students. A lot were street wise from living in towns, a completely new experience for me. But I had one asset that would get me to meet people quickly and get in a team, I was a hockey player and a fairly good one at that. I had been at the university less than a couple of weeks and I was already captain of the University Third XI. After six weeks I was playing in the seconds where I met an ex-school colleague (not that I knew him at school but soon got to know him as an OB) who nurtured me so that it was only a few weeks later that I was playing for the University First XI. That did my confidence no end of good and got me away from spending all my time with vet students as we would travel across the West Country for our games. I even ended up playing against a couple of England Internationals. One game playing against the then England Under 21 captain, a big stocky lad, going into a tackle with him, thinking this is going to hurt, but finding him crumpled on the floor afterwards. I guess in our contact I must have hit him below his centre of gravity. Another time playing against an England winger who gave me the only real run around I have ever had on a hockey pitch, but when in the second half I finally managed to tackle him and win the ball. His inside centre took a dislike to my kneecap and that was the end of my game.

The first couple of years were relatively easy, one subject, Animal management being a breeze for anyone with any farming knowledge. First year revision consisted mainly of getting around to reading "Lord of the Rings" and then "War and Peace" as well as exploring some of the pubs just outside Bristol. A tough Animal Management oral exam, where our dear Professor had a like for testing you on thirty-five plus different sheep breeds. First looking at the picture then showing you and asking you to name the breed. Being at the end of the alphabet and going into oral exams last, I had usually been forewarned what we may be asked and had been told how others had struggled with these pictures. Perhaps the Professor was getting bored when I came in, but one by one I got them all right, so he would ask another and then another. He was holding the picture up to look, and there written on the back was the name of the breed. This was a doddle to the extent that out of the thirty-six he asked me, I thought I ought to get one wrong deliberately.

But as the course went on, it got harder and we lost one or two of my fellow students along the way, failing their end of year exams. I myself found a couple of the exams a struggle, but I persevered and got through in the end.

We had some good times, fun times, some of which I really should not describe. There were some naughty boys in my year, and we had a laugh when they got up to mischief. Parties, dances in the clubs of Bristol where it would be nothing to find more than one female student prancing around with nothing on. That was new for a country boy! The party that I have already mentioned, where we walked through the middle of Bristol dressed as a pantomime horse. Our attire created much frivolity amongst both pedestrians surprised by a horse suddenly appearing around the corner and with traffic who stopped to hoot their horns at the sight of a horse crossing the zebra crossing in front of them.

It was also the time that Mum and Dad decided to give up dairy farming. After the 1976 drought, which was probably for us in the Vale of the White

Horse, our sixth drought running. We knew we had to get more land to grow more grass for the cows, or to pack up. They couldn't get more land, so the cows were sold as a herd. My parents bought a farm on Exmoor where they did sheep and beef farming, they also did riding holidays for the more experienced rider to see parts of the moor that you wouldn't normally get to see. This was another step in my love of the country as I got to explore Exmoor over time, both on horseback with dad and on foot. It was a different way of life as well, away from the pressure of dairy farming where there were things you had to do every day, essential daily chores. But on the moor, one soon realised that life moved more slowly. What you didn't do today, you could do it tomorrow, or the next day, or, well whenever you got around to doing it.

So, University took its course. Some days being fun, some hard and as I said some a struggle. I started playing hockey for Swindon and Wiltshire rather than the University. This took me away from fellow students a lot in my spare time, and my student girlfriends were also distant from Bristol. But I did meet some lovely people, fellow students from other courses who I still have some contact with. For most of them, after three years they left (no Masters in those days, you qualified and went and got a job). Whereas myself and my fellow vet students still had another two years to do at our field station at Langford, beyond Bristol Airport, way outside of Bristol. A year in a flat in the village of Wrington, over the butcher's shop, opposite the church with the constant and annoying chiming of its bell. A local pub a mere four or five hundred yards around the corner. This was the start of the gradual invasion of local villages by vet students which has increased over time as the years have got larger, but the hall of residence hasn't. Days when not studying, I would be introduced to bands and music I had never heard before, but some I still listen to now. How pleased I was when watching the film "Baby Driver" recently to be reacquainted with a band called Focus, and the track "Hocus Pocus", a real trip down memory lane to those student days in Wrington.

With long days of lectures and practicals, long exam periods in the summer and our vacations being taken up with "seeing Practice". It often felt like it was all work and no play. But there were a few of us who would make a point of ensuring we had down time, especially when back in hall for my final year. At nine we would down tools and head off to the Churchill, just down the road for a pint or two, leaving all those conscientious students still studying away in the library. I had given up hockey by then with plans to resume when I had left University. It had become too time consuming as we would work rotations in our final year. This could involve being on call at nights and weekends if medical or surgical cases were admitted to the teaching unit, our assistance would be required. In its place I started playing rugby again for the vet school, with the delight of home games at Langford played on a field in front of the refectory, usually grazed by cows and covered in patches of stinging nettles. Being a small, but skilful winger I soon learned when to sidestep as a defender approached me to tackle, but I would leave him floundering in my wake as I skipped around a cow pat, he didn't.

Fond memories of the occasional day or night out with Janet. One in our early University days, and before my parents had moved down there. A trip to Exmoor in mid-summer on a beautiful sunny day, stopping on the way at a picturesque little pub on the edge of the Quantocks. A bar with not enough room to swing a cat in and the pub used as a setting in the film "The Belstone Fox". A pleasant stop for a pint before continuing on beyond Simonsbath where we would abandon the car to cross the moor in search of the Doone Valley. A dry moor that day as we passed a few bogs but were able to see them. It almost certainly wasn't the conditions for the lady to be wearing a skimpy halter neck short dress with no sunscreen. I started our day accompanied by a beautiful redhead and returned with a rather sore beetroot. The company though, I could not fault it.

I spent most of my time seeing practice in Aylesbury very much under the tutorage of Ian Baker, as previously mentioned. A wonderful man who probably taught me so much that I carried through my career. I often stayed with him and his lovely wife, so when he was on call, then I was on call too. His philosophy was that soon I would be qualified, so there was the cow, get on with it and if I was wrong, he would tell me and put me right. First-hand experience, a real practical learning process which may not have been perfect for passing exams but stood me in good stead for when I was qualified and out on my own.

Ian was a wonderful tutor for me, and I can't say how grateful I am for him teaching me so much of what I know. Also, how to apply it, how to have a working relationship with a farmer, how to talk to him and "get him on board", and for showing such an interest in my career once I had left University. He always would find the time to chat to me at Congresses or wherever we ended up encountering each other. I spent the summer of the drought year in 1976 with him in Aylesbury. To avoid the heat of the day he would start his day early, planning it so that we would finish around lunchtime at a farm who had a swimming pool. This was experience showing itself!

When our day was done, we spent many hours in his garden trying to renovate an old well he had there. Descending a ladder to the dark depths to remove years and years of soil deposits until even, in the drought, we did at last find water. Happy memories indeed.

I remember one day we had to take a final year student with us to a farm as there were no other calls for her to go on. We went to see a calf with a swollen face, which I thought had calf diphtheria. The other student stuck her finger inside the calf's mouth to try and examine the swelling, getting bitten in the process. She withdrew her finger now covered in blood. Ian suggested I had a feel, saying," you won't get bitten, will you?". I felt the lesion inside the oral cavity just as I felt the teeth close on my finger. A young calf's premolars can be very sharp, as I had just found out. I quickly hid my finger in my pocket so that I wouldn't show I had met the same misfortune as my fellow student.

But as I have said, Ian taught me a hell of a lot. Knowledge that has stuck with me right through my career, and now when I have students with me, once I have a little confidence in them and their ability, I am quite happy for them to get on with it, only stepping in to support or take over from them on a case when I feel it is necessary. Maybe that is something to come back to later when I start talking about how much has changed during my career, and there has been a lot. The modern student would be one of those changes, but there are reasons for it.

In 1977 my university career was nearing its end, just my finals to do. Medicine was not a problem, but the Surgery exams I struggled more, being one of half a dozen of us failed for "being not practical enough". In their wisdom, they probably failed the most practical people in the year but a few weeks on we resat and passed with no problem. At last, after all that study, hours sweating over books (and the odd pint or two), doing our rotations and vacations spent either with Ian in Aylesbury, or with other types of Veterinary work, small animal clinics, an equine practice in Lambourn and seeing what the Meat Hygiene Service did, at last it was time to do the job for real.

I now had all these letters after my name, BVSc, MRCVS. Bachelor of Veterinary Science and Member of the Roya College of Veterinary Surgeons. I had qualified and was now a real vet.

This was also the time that James Herriot hit the television screens, a cult Saturday night viewing on BBC1 with Christopher Timothy in the lead role, with Robert Hardy and Peter Davidson as Siegfried and Tristan. A series closely followed by the general public after a series of successful books, and always a topic of conversation on a Monday in the surgery amongst our clientele.

But I hadn't quite got that far yet, first I had to find a job. I had always set my heart on being a farm vet. I was not that interested in small animal work and had by then discovered I was allergic to horses. It was fine when I went to university as mum had over thirty Highland ponies, but maybe it was the break from regular contact with them that desensitised me to them. I was now a vet and any regular contact with horses made me sneeze! In those days if you wanted a job then you scanned the columns of the Vet Record, the weekly journal of the British Veterinary Association, where all new and available jobs were listed. The latest ones would be at the top of the columns, the further you went down, then the longer they had been advertised. I was more than nervous about this first step into the profession, out on my own away from family and friends, a shy lad moving into an area where he would almost certainly know nobody.

My first scan of what was available took me to an interview on the Buckinghamshire/ Bedfordshire border, Olney, a small market town in a mixed rural economy of both dairy and arable. At the time I couldn't tell whether the interview went well or not, I had never had one before. But I must have made a good impression as I did now have a job.

After years of hard study both at school and at Bristol University, I had at last reached an ambition of being a qualified Veterinary Surgeon. Little time for holidays, breaks, rest, it had been a hard slog since the age of fourteen, but I was at last there. On top of that I had come out of university with no debt! I had skimped and saved where I could, maybe not bought all the textbooks that I could have done (Veterinary textbooks are extraordinarily expensive). I had worked on farms when I could to earn more money during school holidays and university vacations and finished the course still with money in my bank account, and that was despite running a car throughout my university career.

I feel sorry for the modern graduate who leaves their course with so much debt around their necks from student loans and course fees. They are burdened with it for a considerable length of time, I was lucky in my day. But on the other hand, I didn't go on some of the extravagant trips some modern graduates seem to do, and although I ran a car, it was an old banger. But these are the changing times we live in. It is somewhat surprising now, considering the debt incurred in getting their degree, that so many leave the profession at such an early stage of their career. Did those Herriot days of past over glamorise the profession? Or is it that the young of today have too many pressures put on them by a discerning public? Especially as the profession is shown more and more on television which raises expectations by a large degree. It seems to be just a job to them now, as opposed to the vocation it was deemed to be in my day.

Changing times and those pressures will be something that I will return to later, something which has affected me in my time in the profession, as it has to so many others. But pressure affects us all in different ways and the mental stress endured by so many in the profession is a big worry.

Back to the autumn of 1977, and yes, I was at last a vet with a job to go to, albeit in an unfamiliar part of the country to me. In those days, anyone with veterinary degrees was considered a bit elitist, the crème de la crème of academia as it was so hard to get into vet school. It was in those days almost taken for granted that your employment package would include accommodation being provided for you, as well as a car, and a massive salary! I think I started on three and a half thousand pounds a year. Big money! But we were expected to make a mint in our career as pillars of society, respected citizens, and hopefully retired in our mid-fifties with a sizeable pension, a massive house and success written over everything we did.

Where did I go so wrong?

So, it was with some feeling of success that I was now a vet, but some sense of trepidation that I was now going to have to put teaching into practice. I had to try and overcome my natural shyness because now I was in a people job, animals don't usually talk so any information I needed would have to come from a worried owner or a suspicious farmer. They would be worried about the ability "of young veterinary" who had just arrived on farm to try and find out what was wrong with his precious cow.

I left my parents farm, now on Exmoor, in the last of my university old bangers. It was laden with my clothes, of course all my university notes and what textbooks I still had, and most important of all, my hockey stuff because that was how I was going to meet new people. It was what I was good at, and my ability would do some of my talking for me. That was with the proviso that I would have time to play at a level I was happy with, fitting it in between on-call duties. Thankfully my new boss, Eric, had been in a similar position when he qualified (though his sport was rugby) but his boss then had given him time off to pursue his sport as much as was practical. My new boss was going to do the same for me. I could turn out every Saturday but needed to get back as soon as I could if it was my weekend to work, he would cover for me while I was playing. That was very much appreciated, and in time gave me the chance to settle a little into the new area and meet new people, giving me something of a social life.

The job was mainly on the farm side of this mixed practice, although I would be expected to do some small animal work, especially when on call. I would get the chance to do some operating, although Eric's wife and the other assistant did most of it. I could learn from them.

I arrived in this to me unknown town and to my new home, which wasn't quite ready for me when I arrived. So, to begin with, I had to stay with my new boss and his family, eat and drink with them, not something I enjoyed entirely. But in time my home was ready. The main entrance to it was through the main consultation room, direct into my kitchen and then a living room and bedroom upstairs. It was very comfortable except that I seemed to have rather a weird neighbour who if he heard me in my flat would start calling out "whooooooo" continuously until he thought I was no longer there. This almost made my living room a no-go area.

A career was about to begin which would span over the next forty plus years of my life, until my retirement whenever that would be. As I have already said, I thought when I started in 1977 that my time as a vet would have finished several years ago but the unexpected turns of life meant that I would carry on working, retirement a wish for the future, a date yet to be decided.

But over those forty years as a vet, most of them as a farm vet I have seen many changes both in the countryside, systems of farming and in the tools and drugs that I and my fellow vets have to treat those cases we see. Our day-to-day routines have changed considerably and the demands both on us and on the farming community from an ever more discerning general public. Those Herriot days of now so long ago are just memories as the face of large animal practice has changed, and even as I write this, an ever-popular television program, "The Yorkshire Vet", in my mind paints a rather romantic picture of days long past. Certainly, in the areas I have worked in I think we have rather moved on in some of our techniques compared with those shown there. It maybe that there is a greater intensification in farming in the Shropshire area I have spent my latter days in compared with Yorkshire, but my work seems greatly different from that shown on tv. Along with that, here and in a lot of the country, there is a greater specialisation in the species treated by the modern vet. I finish in a hundred percent farm animal practice, that did do some equine work until a few years ago, but that too was getting more and more specialised. The large veterinary hospitals that now exist throughout the country, a lot now owned by corporations investing in pets for what they see as a money pot. Large specialist equine practices covering vast areas in what is now a very specialised field, with like small animal work, ever more elaborate treatments and surgical routines. Large poultry and pig practices treating thousands and thousands of animals, where they tend to be more consultants than hands on vets.

Those glamorous days of mixed practice that we saw James Herriot in have largely long gone. Yes, there are still some in existence, but the days where you would do morning consultations before going out to see a few cows, sheep and then the odd horse or two before coming back to evening surgery, hoping along the way that someone else would have spayed the odd cat or two, have largely long gone. There are still mixed practices, but even a lot of them are split into their different departments.

Whether it is a better profession for it I don't know. Certainly, looking back now over all my years, would I have complained if I had never seen a dog or cat, a horse or donkey? I think the answer is almost certainly a no and if I had spent all my time as a farm vet, I would have looked back feeling quite satisfied. There have been some highs in both the equine work and the small animal work I have done. I always really enjoyed operating and would take great satisfaction in some of the orthopaedic work I did, some of the horses I have seen in the past and sorted them out. But would I have missed it, probably not.

When I qualified, there was not a vast choice of jobs to go for, certainly not specialist jobs. To be honest, how can you be a specialist when you have no experience, something that must be gained along the course of your career. Even now I am still learning, always will be even after that retirement day finally arrived, the striving for more knowledge that keeps the mind active. It was therefore a mixed practice that I started in and would return to several times before I arrived in my last position in what is a specialised farm animal practice outside Shrewsbury.

Times have changed. They have changed a lot and the profession I started in, the daily routines of forty years ago will almost certainly never return. The glamour of being a vet has largely gone. It is still said that us farm vets are still entering a job as a vocation, like me most have a great love of the land, the countryside and of farming. But for many now it is just a career, they do not want the out of hours work, the weekends on call, and the now relatively low pay for what is such a long training. When qualified, veterinary work is a very demanding job both physically and mentally, the affect it has had on the modern vet is considerable. I have suffered from depression, not entirely from the pressures of the job, but there are many who have qualified and suddenly have to face the pressures of ever demanding clients. Alongside clients there are the emotional attachments that you make in some of the cases you treat. Could you have done better? Was something your fault? In those times of pressure, sometimes it can be a very lonely job with things building up inside you, wanting support, help, a shoulder to cry on. Too often these emotional problems are not met and is this more so as we see an ever-increasing number of females in the profession. That is not being sexist, it is a matter of fact that there are more females now. What they all need, men and women is support. In the male dominated profession of old, perhaps a man's outlet was drink but now it is becoming more and more essential in our ranks that we can spot and support those members who are starting to suffer mental strife from their work. Well-being is the in-vogue word for the workplace, but in this profession, it is becoming more and more important to look after our colleagues.

Yes, a changing profession. I shall try and give an account of those changes, good and bad, that I have seen through the course of my career.

4

A LIFE A VET

In the latter part of 1977, I started my career as a vet in Olney, Buckinghamshire. A novice vet with a lot of dairy farming knowledge which I had learnt from my father and from Ian when seeing practice in Aylesbury. Was that going to be enough for a guy fresh out of college, on the shy side and probably lacking a bit in confidence? Olney was a pleasant little town with all the basics there; bank, pubs, post office and a supermarket, not dissimilar to the town I had grown up near in the Vale of the White Horse. It was a beginning and ticked the box for most of my requirements. What it didn't, well then Bedford was not far away to offer more shopping, cinemas and of course hockey.

I made a couple of friends in Olney, but most of my social life revolved around Bedford Hockey Club. It wouldn't be long until when I wasn't working I would be training, playing for the club or the county, or just socialising with other members of the team. I became firm friends with one of the other single and eligible men in the team, Simon Smith (at least he wasn't John Smith). When we were not playing we would spend much time together especially at weekends, if there was a party on, then one of us would know about it and we would be there. Nights spent sleeping in the car when he had picked up some lady and taken her back to his flat where I was supposed to be sleeping as well, only to find in the morning that he had left the door unlocked for me.

We had a lot of laughs, and with the hockey going so well, it probably glossed over what my first experience of work was like. I know I was new to the job, but for each case I went out to I would be told what I was going to treat it with before I went, even if that was not the correct treatment. Mental stimulation and experience gained, very little! But I had a job which was something. I was happier when I moved out of the principal's house into my flat, despite the constant whoooooooo, but I had to admit I wasn't enjoying my first experience as a vet.

It was a largely forgettable time, even with one of my university colleagues in the next practice so we could discuss cases and our lot, but he wasn't happy either. The practice was reported to the Royal College for some perceived misdemeanour by a disgruntled dog breeder. The complaint only involved me because I was part of the practice despite the fact that I had never seen or spoken to the people. It was dismissed, and I was exonerated but it did nothing for my confidence.

I went to do a Brucellosis blood test on a farm, which was going well. Having taken blood from most of the cattle, I turned around in horror to see a cow munching away at the plastic bag which contained all my needles.

What should I do?

Keep quiet and hope all would be okay? Or say what had happened while young veterinary was on his first visit to this particular farm. That would go down well. I opted to say nothing and thankfully no harm was done to the cow with the strange appetite.

Then there was the incident when one evening after hockey. I had driven down to see my brother who lived on the edge of Battersea Park and upon entering London I had the arse of my car dented by Mr Lin of whom we will hear more of later. Improvising, I managed to return back home with what I started with, less the bandage used to tie down the car boot, but my boss was not pleased when we found Mr Lin did not exist!

I was happy to leave Olney after such a short stay. I was after only five months very disillusioned with life as a vet. I felt I had wasted that time and learnt very little except perhaps not to trust a Chinaman! I had had enough and despite the fact that I didn't have another job to go to, I was happy to return back to my parents on Exmoor and take stock of my life again.

I have very little recollection of that job other than it being a bad experience. Life could only get better. I would bide my time, help dad on his Exmoor farm and find the right job next time. I packed up my NSU car and headed back to the West Country, a chance to spend a little time on the moor, something I hadn't managed since my parents had moved down there. A quiet departure from the job, only stopping in Newport Pagnell to wish my other work or ex-work colleague the best of luck for the future.

My hockey friends I would miss but I would be seeing them at Weymouth Easter hockey festival, and I would drive up to Bedford for the last couple of league games to stay with Simon and complete our season.

A journey back to Exmoor that would take me back to my past. Back through Oxfordshire and taking a slight detour to see the place of my upbringing, Coldharbour Farm, Hatford. Then on towards Swindon, through the countryside of my Young Farmer's Club days and onto the M4 to Bristol. The city of my university years and finally the M5 to the Southwest, Exmoor and to Gallon House, my parents' home.

My parents had been on the moor now for a couple of years, building up the riding holiday with accommodation side of their business while getting more experience in their new venture on the farming side. Now with just with beef and sheep rather than the dairy herd. Gallon House, formerly Red Deer Farm, was the highest farm buildings on the moor. Perched above the main Exford, Simonsbath road, isolated, sometimes desolate with moorland allotments either side of the farm. On reaching the highest point at the top of the farm, it rapidly descended into the bleak but beautiful Exe valley. Beyond that was open moorland for miles.

This would be home for the next best part of three months while I tried to regain my confidence in myself and made sure that my next job would be the right one. I would search the pages of the Vet Record for possible jobs. Sending off applications, to some sending letters requesting more information, some I would call, speaking to the practice principle and then on what he told me, arranging an interview or not. No CVs or anything like that in those days, getting veterinary employment was a very informal affair. What you ended up with after a phone call and interview carried out with the boss, you hoped it would turn out okay. Our graduate grapevine had told us where to avoid, which bosses were bastards!

I spent my time helping dad, and at the end of the week I would try and arrange any interviews. This would take me on my way to Bedford and hockey on the Saturday and Sunday. My confidence was shot, and there were one or two of these interviews that I would set off to, but on the way would lose confidence in myself, then would ring up and cancel.

But dad was a pillar of strength, giving gentle words of advice when he thought it necessary, but otherwise just letting me bide my time. He was lambing, and I was only to willing to help, especially if he was taking guests out on the moor on horseback. Sometimes I would go with them as well, other times I would potter on the farm, learning some of those moorland skills. Laying hedges, turning those tall beech hedges into a manicured fence to keep stock in. I learnt how to rebuild Exmoor banks, the barriers between fields, which had the beech hedges on their top. That I really enjoyed, restoring some of the moor to its former glory.

I dug mum and dad a vegetable patch although unsure how successful it would be at that altitude. I chose artichokes to grow first, I don't know why I chose them as my first attempt at vegetables.

I was very content, very happy spending this time unwinding. It almost certainly did me a lot of good, at last having some time to myself after all those hard years at school, university and working through my vacations. I learnt to relax for the first time.

I got to know a few of the local farmers, some who would ring up dad knowing he was a dairy farmer, to ask him if he could help to calve a cow. Also knowing I was a vet, they would say

"Bring your son as well, an extra pair of hands may be useful."

So, I would go and calve the neighbour's cows for them, and they didn't pay a penny, they thought it great. It was good experience, gave me confidence but for no reward other than they would buy me a beer down the pub when they next saw me in there. They knew that wasn't going to happen!

My trip to Weymouth Hockey Festival was memorable, from what I can remember of it. Bedford sent down a strong squad, most of the First XI had signed up to it. There was a festival party on the first night we got there, and it would not be an exaggeration to say that the beer flowed. We got seriously pissed. A ladies and gents' tournament, so plenty of both sex at this event it was a really good evening, except...

We were given the first game slot the following morning and with our heads as they were, we were not in a state to try and play hockey. We were not very good! In fact, it was a bit embarrassing watching us. Our next game that afternoon was against a strong visiting Dutch side. We decided that maybe a lunchtime drink was not the best idea if we were to try and regain some of our dignity. We had to play on the show pitch in front of a crowd, this could be embarrassing. But from somewhere, we found our form and we beat them much to everyone's surprise, including our own. A close but skilful game in which we prevailed with strong defence and a single goal.

They stood in line when we had finished, shook all our hands, and then presented us with a bottle of Schnapps which was soon gone. A smart move as we then had to reciprocate and buy them a round, sixteen pints of lager, they did a lot better out of the deal than we did!

The rest of the tournament passed, and we did okay in our last two games, we even managed to have one player in the festival side. Then it was back to Exmoor and sadly the last time I played for Bedford. It was also the last time I played high level hockey in my life, something I had to sacrifice for my career. I was good but never had the chance to reach my full potential on a pitch. Work and later family life would take over and prevent me from playing at the level I had reached again.

That is something I have always regretted, never finding out how good I could have been in an environment I felt so confident in. Those are the sacrifices we had to make, which maybe the modern graduate doesn't have to. Changing times. It will be interesting to see how a modern athlete like

Laura Muir manages to combine a vet career with her running career, being at such a high standard.

What Weymouth had done was to drive me to that job I was looking for. It so happened that shortly afterwards, a job came up less than forty miles away, in Devon. It was comprised almost entirely of farm work and right up my street. Exactly what I had been looking for! It was the type of job that sounded as if it was why I had decided to go to vet school, farm work with a smidgen of equine and small animal.

A phone call was made, an interview arranged and after a couple of days, a job offer arrived. I was only too keen to accept with a start date being arranged. In the interview the three partners had been so friendly, it was so relaxed that there was something that told me, "This is right".

My own car had given up the ghost by now, so dad kindly took me down to start my new job where I would get another car provided by the practice. While going off to one of my hockey games I travelled from home into Exford. You had to descend down a hill, turn sharp right, then sharp left and over the stone bridge that traverses the Exe, a humpback bridge. As I broached its summit, there was a bump, and the steering suddenly became hard work. There seemed a pull one way and the rear end seemed to have dropped. Luckily just the other side of the bridge in those days there was a garage which I was able to pull in at. We inspected the car, one of the rear wheels had come off but was wedged under the wheel arch. Would it be worth repairing? I left the car there and continued my journey after a little re-organisation by bus then hire car.

Cullompton is a small market town in East Devon, set amongst the rolling hills of that part of the country. Cow country. The town in those days was one of those towns mainly set along the main road that went through it on the way between Wellington and Exeter. Quaint in its own way, light industry at either end with traditional shops lining either side of the road in the centre of the town. Situated with its own junction off the M5, it would soon become a fast-expanding town, probably now almost unrecognisable from the town I knew forty years ago. I often pass it on the motorway while travelling down to Graham in Stokeinteignhead, but it is a long time since I have diverted to take a look at my old haunt. Now, much housing has been added, started when I was there, and with its position just off the motorway, a site for industrial development.

I was to have a flat above the practice office, but when I started it wasn't quite ready. The vet I was replacing hadn't moved out, so I spent my first couple of weeks in digs. It was the same place one of the partners had stayed in when he had arrived in this beautiful part of the country a few years previously. It was owned by a lovely elderly couple who looked after me well for my short stay with them. My practice car was waiting for me there, ready for me to turn up for work the next day. Unfortunately, as well as having not vacated my accommodation yet, the previous vet had also managed to seriously damage "my" car. It was in the garage awaiting repairs, more strictly some major body work. More on my Vauxhall Viva later, but this would be the start of a love hate relationship with both Vauxhalls and my Viva.

Dad left, and I was on my own again, warmly welcomed in my temporary home but about to start the next chapter of my life, my veterinary career. They fed me, then an evening of television and finally bed ready to start day one at Griffiths and Partners.

Next morning, I would turn up at the practice, sited in the middle of the town, and report to the office for duty. This was a far bigger practice that in Olney. In Cullompton I was one of a team of seven vets, soon to become eight, and we had a sister practice in Tiverton, just over the hill where there were another six vets. A large predominately farm animal practice, my role would be as a farm vet plus I would be the second horse vet. Small animal work, I would do Monday night evening surgeries and would operate once every five weeks on a Wednesday, the day we did most of our routine ops. That I thought would give me the ideal mix of what I wanted to do, mainly farm but I could pick up a little from dogs and cats just in case my career didn't quite follow the path I wanted it to.

I was greeted in the office by the office staff, Pat and Joyce who made me more than welcome and showed me how the practice worked. They took in the calls, answering the phones and recording all visits in a daybook. The daybook had seven columns at the right-hand side, one for each vet, if the call was designated for me, then a tick would go in my column. Being the new boy, mine was empty but the more senior vets would have routine visits, farms that they went to on a weekly or fortnightly basis so were pre-arranged. I was shown how to book my work and given a space on one of the large tables to do any office work, my desk! It all seemed a very relaxed atmosphere, and all the vets that passed through were only to keen to welcome me. First impressions were good.

But in those days, you were a qualified vet, so you were capable of "doing almost anything". Really! That meant after my welcome and having got together what kit I thought I needed; I was soon out on the road. These were the days of small family farms, not the large many hundred cow herds of today. Each cow would probably have a name, were part of the family and so demanded individual attention. The days of earth and stone tracks, muddy gateways and many lame cows. My first list of calls would be just that, a couple of lame cows on one farm, then onto another just up the road to do the same. Except that one or two was actually five or six. Waiting around every corner would be a number of lame cows. One soon learnt the value of having sharp hoof knifes and learning how to sharpen them.

That was my first day in practice in Devon. It was nice to get back to my roots though and be on dairy farms again.

At my interview I had been told that I wouldn't have to do any night duties until I was familiar with the area. That was a relief but on my first afternoon I was told whoever was on call that night couldn't do it so would I mind stepping in. I was in a new job and so could hardly say no, this really was going in at the deep end. I was assured it would probably be quiet so on my first night. However, I would actually end up getting called out to two calvings, both dead and smelly and one at the farm of an Olympic Three-Day eventer. That one I did find rather intimidating, but all went well. The only hiccup in the night was that I found the lights of my "new" car somewhat unreliable, driving in Devon by moonlight alone was to say the least, interesting.

It would be the next day that I found out that the brakes didn't work either as I was going up a hill only to meet a wide load coming the other way. When would I be getting my "proper" car? That day could not come soon enough!

And when I got back to the office and told them of my woe, "was there any way I could work that night as well?" Again, I couldn't say no, but this time I did have a quiet night.

Devon, I found to be a lovely place to work. We were busy, and on the whole, especially with my own farming background, I found the farmers a joy to work for. They were friendly, appreciative, and again I had fallen in love with that local accent, slightly different from the accent I had heard on Exmoor.

And some of the colloquial sayings. Things I had never heard of before.

"Can you come out, my cow or sheep has her reed out." A reminder of my incident with Mr Traille!

"What?"

"My cow has reed out."

I could only go along and find what I find. She had prolapsed her vagina.

"My cow has her bed out. She is in the river."

"Really!"

I have told you the rest.

But those early days in Cullompton I learnt a lot, we were a great team, working hard but also sharing our knowledge and experiences between us. We would socialise together a little but when I had arrived, everyone had been there a couple of years and had their own circle of friends. The job was good but after work in my flat above the office, when I was able to move into it, I was lonely. I wouldn't see anyone from the minute I finished work until the start of work the next morning. Weekends were easy if I wasn't on call, I could just make the short drive over the border into Somerset and back to Gallon House and mum's cooking.

In my evenings of solitude, I did make myself quite an accomplished cook. Let's face it I had plenty of time on my hands. I read a lot, watched TV and wondered how I could get myself out and about. Cooking became a good release as I could plan new recipes with what I could buy in the town. The occasional pheasant came my way, either from a farmer from his shoot, or from a bird brought in after being hit by a car. One, with no hope of a return to the wild with a broken wing, I thought would make a nice supper. I took it up into my kitchen and having had to wring many necks in my past had no qualms about dispatching this one. A sharp tweak of its neck, but unfortunately its head came off in my hand. It should be dead, or so I thought laying it on the work surface only for it to come back to life, running around the kitchen headless pumping blood all over the walls.

It was a spacious flat, a large kitchen, massive living room and two large bedrooms as well as a bathroom. What little furniture I had accumulated easily fitted in it, as well as piles and piles of university notes, my knowledge bank to begin with before I discovered the first-hand experience of my work colleagues was far more valuable.

I met one or two people from my equine calls, one the head "lad" of the local stud, she was a lovely girl but a bit Amazonian. Another, young lady who took rather a shine to me and in time we did go out once or twice, but she smoked, a definite no -no for me. Another lady who I would frequently have to visit, but I'm not sure if there was anything wrong with the horse. Every time I visited though, there seemed to be another button of her blouse undone. I would have to admit, East Devon did have some wonderful views, refreshingly open. This young lady was very pleasant but probably a bit young and though I considered asking her out, I was worried if I did, I may be taking mum and dad out as well. There was also a very pleasant lady in my bank and if it was quiet when I went in there, we would often chat for ages, until the next client came in.

A shy country boy, yes, I was enjoying my work, but I was getting more and more lonely. I decided one day that the next time I saw one of these ladies, which ever it was, I would ask her out. Though where to go? I had no local knowledge. I had been in Cullompton for over three months and hadn't been out once.

It turned out to be the stud "lad", Christine. A date was arranged, and we headed off over the hill to a village called Silverton, and into The Three Tuns. A pub that over the coming years would be a regular stop for me, somewhere I did meet a lot of people, some who have become lifelong friends and to whom I owe a great deal to for advice and help. Those type of friends that are few and far between, but you know you can rely on to stand by you. Anthony, Ian and Graham certainly became them.

Christine took me to this pub, which was largely deserted, other than two men sitting at one end of the bar. Chris knew them and as I would find out over time, she seemed to know most of the local men. Because of that I was christened "Hot Rod" by those two men, it was Ian and Tony! A name I acquired from the reputation that had gone before from this lady of whom I was spending my first "Devon date" with. I knew nothing of it, I just heard over the course of time who else she had been with. But I am not going to knock her or her reputation, she was a wonderfully kind and interesting person who I spent many happy hours with over the course of time. I met her parents who lived locally, and would often go and help them on their small holding, once clearing a barn for them to find it inundated with adders and their eggs.

We would be frequent visitors to the "Tuns", heading over the hill through Bradninch, and into Silverton. Tony and Ian lived in the village and were frequent visitors as well, in fact they went for a pint or two of draught Bass every night. Through them I at last developed a circle of friends, and if I wasn't with Chris or on call, then I would generally be with them in the pub. They were rugby players so on Saturday nights I would see them after their game for a few pints before returning to my lonely flat.

But at last, I had a life outside work, a girlfriend until she started to see her boss and then move in with him. But through her I had met people, and as I have previously said that became lifelong friends. It was a great pub, great friendships were made, as well as sometimes bumping into some of my farmers and work colleagues there. We had a lot of fun through the "Tuns", some great evenings and adventures which could almost be a book in themselves.

It was through visiting the pub, calling into see Tony and Ian first going around to their house that I met another lady who had just moved into their spare room from lodgings next door. I knocked on the door and went in, the boys were not there and this lady in her dressing gown told me they were already in the pub. Fine, I thanked her and went on my way, only for this process to be repeated seven days later. The following week she was dressed and said she would come to the pub with me, the start of a romance even if at the time I was seeing another couple of the local ladies. Hot Rod!

Fifteen months later we would get married, not in the place of her upbringing, but in Silverton which had become almost our second home. By this time, we had bought a house together in Cullompton which she lived in until shortly before the wedding when I vacated my flat above the office. For all its drawbacks, the dust and being above the practice, it was spacious and comfortable. It had served me well as a home.

Summers passed into winters and then into spring, a really busy time for us with famers wanting to produce milk from these productive grasslands. Turnout would always bring its problems. During my second spring there we were rushed off our feet, operating on cows on a daily basis. A mixture of Caesareans, cows with twisted stomachs, and cows with wires. The latter is where a piece of metal they had consumed in their forage would penetrate the wall of their stomach, pushing forward through the diaphragm and sticking into the sac around the heart, causing infection, pericarditis. We had to remove the metal, a nail or piece of wire before it penetrated and caused too much damage. Day after day this went on, one, two, three or more ops a day. By the time Easter came and there being two Bank Holidays for some of us, a four-day break, we were exhausted. Five thirty on the Thursday came and we were done until the following Tuesday morning. We headed over the hill to Silverton to at last unwind and relax. A much-needed rest, the beer flowed, we were happy.

Strangely, after the break, the ops came to a halt as well. The wonders of nature. One particular farm on the side of the M5, we operated on many cows with wires, finding their stomachs to be full of sharp metal filings. Metal that had been left at the side of the motorway, had got into the field and been through the silage forager. It was then unintentionally chopped into these sharp fragments which were very difficult to remove from the insides of the cow's stomach as they were so sharp, cutting our hands as we proceeded. Again, a farm I pass on my way down to Graham's and often think of those days operating there.

Heady days, very enjoyable days which shaped my career over a long period. Even the horse work I enjoyed. A few colic's, lameness's, the run of the mill horse cases but I was ever increasingly starting to find that I was allergic to them. Mum had Highland ponies that do sweat up a lot, and when dried, if you stroked or patted them, a plume of dust would rise. That made me sneeze, my eyes would run, and I would desperately be seeking water to wash with before I started rubbing my eyes and exacerbating the problem.

What would the lady with the half-undone blouse think if every time she saw me my eyes started watering!!

We also in those days did some of the work for a certain Martin Pipe as he set his National Hunt racing stables and gallops up at Culmstock. Frequent visits to blood test horses that hadn't run particularly well, looking for that mysterious virus which would explain it. He did at last have success in the Triumph Hurdle at the Cheltenham Festival with Captain Christie, he was started and as time would tell, he would never look back. In time he became one of the top trainers in the country, and with that sought more sophisticated facilities than we could offer. But we were there at the beginning.

Another Saturday morning on call and I was summoned just up the road to the eventing lady. We were their farm vets, not the horse vets there, but they rang because I could get there first. Panic, I got there to find the police and many spectators hovering around this distressed Olympic rider and her horse which had what looked distinctly like it had a broken leg. Why I asked myself did it happen to me that the first horse I was going to have to shoot would 1) be an expensive event horse, and 2) would have to be in front of a crowd of people including the police.

Thankfully the horse was wonderfully placid as before I shot it, I thought I had better show some sort of clinical skill in examining it, before reaching for the gun. I bent down to look at its fetlock joint, front left. It was sticking out at a horrible angle, but I wasn't convinced it was broken, it may just (JUST) be dislocated which would mean a lot of ligament damage as well.

Horses usually have a low pain threshold, but he let me yank his joint so that I managed to manipulate the leg into its correct shape. A miracle. Looking at the leg it looked normal again. I strapped it up and advised that they get their horse vet to radiograph it for them just to check on any damage.

My attentions worked, after a period of rest the horse returned to eventing, and I had an ever-grateful client whenever I saw her.

East Devon is of course close to the Jurassic coast, the resorts of Sidmouth, Seaton, Exmouth, Lyme Regis, but it is strange how with these tourist attractions so close that one never visits them if you are a "local". Was it the thought of trying to cross the ever-busy A30 to reach the coast? Or just that we had a very enjoyable social life that we never got that far? Having said that, over time I did discover more and more the delights of my parent's home. Especially when new to the area I would make constant trips up the Exe valley to Gallon House. I would go there to rest, to walk, to ride and discover more and more of Exmoor, the hidden beauties you couldn't reach easily from the road, but on foot or especially on horseback were easily accessible. The hidden glories of the Barle valley, Cow Castle an ancient hill fort with the river running around its base, the Wheal Eliza tin mine (or what's left of it) further along. Dunkery Beacon, the highest point on the moor and Horner Woods just below. Further west, the Doone Valley, which was a great ride and even better walk, being dropped off at Malmsmead and walking across to Larkham Foot. Seeing some of the places used for shooting practice during the Second World War, history I knew nothing about. And the wild and bleakness of the Chains, that part of the moor that took so much rain to cause the Lynton flooding in the fifties. Lastly a place I have visited many times since, Tarr Steps just outside Dulverton, on the Barle just below Winsford Hill. An ancient Clapper Bridge and one of the iconic pictures of Exmoor, but also with wonderful walks through the picturesque beech woods lining the valley of the Barle as it flows from Withypool towards Dulverton. Then its junction with the Exe before flowing into South Devon and Exmouth to join the sea.

A trip I would make back home often at night, sometimes when one would have to endure the wildness of Exmoor weather. Snow covered roads, ice, rain blowing sideways, and sometimes beautiful moonlit nights where you could see for miles. The sheep on the moor, the herds of Exmoor ponies and the occasional sighting of red deer.

One time when I had gone up there, to my parents for Christmas, a year where the Bank Holiday was the day after Boxing Day, and I was due to work it on call, the snows came on Christmas night. There was a lot of snow, and our road was blocked, most roads on the moor were blocked. The snows had drifted between the hedges bordering the roads. In the fields so that there were six, seven-foot drifts around the edge of the fields, but the centres had a mere smattering of whiteness. There was no way I was getting back to Cullompton in the foreseeable future.

We got a phone call from a neighbouring farmer that he couldn't get to his sheep. Could we take a look at them on the allotment? It was the neighbourly thing to do to try and help in adversity. My father and I having checked his own sheep first, went next door to search for this farmers sheep. Nowhere to be seen. It is often the habit of sheep to seek the shelter of the hedges, which with their beech cover would often be fifteen, twenty feet high. They sought shelter and the snow drifted over the top of them. We would search the hedge rows with long sticks looking for air pockets and something soft like a sheep at the tip of our poles. We spent a long morning searching for these sheep, digging them out and chasing them out to the centre of the field away from the drifts, where they could graze safely.

A job well done while I waited for news of the snow plough trying to clear the main roads, it was lucky that we lived on one of the main roads across the moor. By mid-afternoon it was in sight having cleared the road across Winsford Hill, now it was coming towards us. Finally, it reached us and headed on towards Simonsbath and I was able to start my journey back to Cullompton on slippery roads bordered with snow piled high either side of me. But I did get back to work.

Five happy years were spent in Cullompton where I developed skills to serve me well for many years to come. But it was the ambition then of any vet to be invited into partnership, make your fortune and be retired at around fifty-five years old. That was the plan anyway! I had achieved a lot, had got some great friends, had bought a house and had got married. We were expecting our first child, but I wanted a partnership, we needed a bigger house, and it was time for big decisions. The practice had just appointed three new partners, I would be next in line but when would that be? Was it now time to move on in search of this pot of gold which would lead me to a comfortable retirement?

I decided it was time to go, with a great reluctance as I had fallen in love with this area and swore one day I would come back, in my retirement. Graham had moved to Cheltenham, Ian to Stroud. I had been offered a job in Blandford Forum which was ideal except again there was no immediate offer of partnership. I turned it down after much heart ache, something in hindsight that may have been a big mistake with my now love affair with Dorset. At the time it was Devon I was in love with, Dorset was yet to be discovered and wouldn't be for many years. A job came up in the Forest of Dean with prospects, yes, the chance of a partnership so we moved up to Lydney, loading all our worldly goods into the back of dad's horse lorry to move to a rented house while we found a house to buy. The Cullompton practice had bought our home there from me for my replacement.

They had decided not to have a Christmas party that year, but my colleagues wanted to give me a send-off, so my leaving do became the Christmas party. Very kindly one of the partners who had wanted a party, coughed up for the lot of it.

Devon was a fantastic experience and I fell in love with the County. For many years I had a strong desire to return, as I have said, to retire. The draw grew stronger as Graham moved back to work in Torquay and over time I discovered the South Hams, more of Exmoor, and having taken up golf later, some of the great courses Devon had to offer, East Devon at Budleigh Salterton still being one of my favourites in the whole of England that I have played so far. Exmoor always had an attraction, a draw back for me whenever I could get back there, and in later years would have a significant part in my recovery from depression. The wildness, the openness yet so many secluded valleys, the rivers, the whole place was a fascination for me. Whenever I had the urge I would be back. When mum and dad decided to move closer to my twin brother and I in their later years, not only was there a sadness in their hearts for leaving the moor, but also in mine that visits wouldn't be so frequent. I returned for the first time in three years in September 2017 to spend a week in a cottage near Blackmoor Gate, the trip I mentioned after our reunion. A trip down memory lane, to visit parts of the moor I missed and to find parts I had never been to before. It was lovely to talk to so many locals who still remembered mum and dad, even going into one pub and chatting to the land lady to discover that mum had taught her to ride.

It must rate as one of my better holidays, Exmoor seemed almost timeless, and it was a shame to come home. BUT as I find now, Dorset still wins for me.

Another chapter of my life was about to start, a diverse practice covering the rich pasturelands on the banks of the Severn and then extending into the Forest of Dean, with all its characters and mystery. Three hundred cow dairy farms on one hand, Forest sheep on the other, roaming free until round-up time in the autumn. Our first child was due in the March, we had arrived for New Year.

Life was about to change in many ways, and in the structure of my work. This was a mixed practice and small animal work would come back into my life, for better or for worse. A very mixed practice with intensive dairying, beef herds and fattening units, lowland sheep on the banks of the river, and the forester's sheep in the forest. We would cover an area along the river from Chepstow nearly to Gloucester, with the river and the top edge of the Forest of Dean being our north and south borders. I would do some operating, but they had a lady who came in just to do small animal work, so my involvement would be largely secondary except when on call. For some reason, though now with five years experienced, I was nervous starting a new job. Perhaps it was the thought of dogs and cats again, of operating more often, although why that should have worried me, I'm not sure. Between us we had carried out some pretty complicated operations in Cullompton, helping each other out, putting our brains together and coming out with some great success stories.

The other big change was that we were starting a family. We had accommodation provided for us in a rented house to begin with, living next door to one of the other vets in what was somewhat of a mansion for the two of us. It did give us plenty of storage space though to keep our unpacked belongings until we had found our own place.

The Forest is a fascinating place, quite oldie worldly in some respects, almost backward compared with other places in the country. A great accent accompanied the locals, and most people seemed to know everyone else if they were local. The Forest had been an areas of open cast mining in the past and there was still a tradition that if you were in born in the forest then you were allowed an allowance of coal from it each winter (if you could find it!).

There is also the tradition of the Verder's court held annually in The Speech House Hotel in the middle of the forest, where matters between the Verder's would be settled by an independent committee. If only token now, it is nice that some of these traditions still live on. It is an ancient woodland, dense with deciduous trees, some years and years old, oaks, beech, a richness of British woodland which is now being developed in a nice way to encourage tourism to the area. Woodland walks, wood art and sculpture, nature trails and so many more which shows the true joys of this natural forest.

Now, it was my new home, based in Lydney but a new area to explore. Again, it was a new area for us, and we didn't know anyone, but it is surprising what having a baby does to your social life, my wife especially soon met no-end of new people through attending antenatal classes and then through toddler groups afterwards. For me, again hockey was my saviour, one of the partner's son in law played for the local side and took me along to training one day after we had settled in. I was soon accepted into the team and again met people I have kept in touch with for a long time now, one who is a godparent to my daughter, and myself a godfather to his son. It gave me a great social life outside of work, which was a great help in settling into a new area.

We bought a house after a couple of months and had just settled in when after a few days my son arrived on the scene. I was busy constructing a new wardrobe in our bedroom when the cry for help and take me to Gloucester arrived from my wife. We rushed in late at night as she went into labour but after some hours it was obvious that nothing was going to happen imminently. She went to sleep quite happy while I lay uncomfortably in a hospital chair, unable to sleep until the nurse suggested I went home and came back later. Nearly twenty-four hours later, my son emerged into this world, I thought I should be there to comfort my wife, hold her hand, encourage her but the gynaecologist seemed more intent when he found out I was a vet that I should go down the other end and watch what he was doing while he explained it all. He was not going to take no for an answer. A Wood was born by right a forester (which coincidentally was my mother's maiden name). And what a coincidence that as they went back to the cottage hospital in Lydney, the only other baby in there had the same first name and surname. I hope we got the right one! I wouldn't change our Richard for the world! I became quite a celebrity there with the nurses, the local vet up there with his family and when England were on television playing rugby, they would set the television up in the room so I could watch while visiting.

I had experience and so was readily accepted by the farming fraternity where I could carry out routine visits on dairy herds, looking after their fertility work and dealing with whatever else came along. One thing I did find there was that if they could treat anything themselves, then they would do, often inappropriately which as we move closer to the present day would be a serious issue in the development of drug resistance.

But essentially while I was there, I was getting the impression my career was standing still. Any promises of a partnership seemed a long way off, and I don't think I would have taken it if it were offered. I suppose I started to get a little bit disillusioned with what I was doing, and even started looking at different careers, especially in the finance industry. I suppose the grass is always greener, and I was quite away down the road into taking this drastic decision to change my career when two things happened. Firstly, an element of self-doubt crept in and secondly a financial crash which rather knocked the whole idea on the head anyway. I was caught not knowing what to do. Again, I had some great friends here and Graham and Ian were only an hour away but was that enough to keep me in a place where I could see no future. My wife if the decision was hers would have stayed put but I reached the stage that for our future security I needed to move and so took the short step across the Severn to work in Dursley. As the crow flies, literally only a few miles, but by road one had to traverse the river, either at Chepstow on the Severn Bridge or at Gloucester, a good hour drive either way.

Baby number two was on the way and arrived shortly before my move, so I went ahead to our again rented cottage to get it ready for the arrival of now a family of four. We were again given a rented cottage on one of the local farms until we had sold our own house in Lydney and then found somewhere to buy for ourselves. The housing market was poor then and although we soon had a buyer, they had to sell theirs which was proving more problematical.

Our new home on the farm was an old mill cottage with its own mill pond just outside our backdoor, with a small waterfall which flowed into it. This would have been a lovely cottage to buy if it was available, but it wasn't, and as we entered the winter still in it, we found it to be hard to heat and keep dry. I would be forever cleaning the bathroom walls trying to remove the black mould, only for it to reappear a few days later. We lived in a gorgeous kitchen or huddled around the wood burning stove in the sitting room. The rest of the house was too cold although we would have to retreat upstairs at bedtime and cover ourselves with blankets. No doubt if it were ours, we could have changed things to make it warmer, but as a summer holiday cottage it was fine.

My fourth job was about to begin on the Monday morning having travelled over myself on the Sunday afternoon. It was autumn, but with the leaves still on the trees, I settled into the cottage thinking what an idyllic place it was. An old cottage next to the millstream and the constant sound of falling water as it entered the mill pond before heading down into a stream and away eventually into the Severn. A beautiful willow leaning over the pond and the delight of seeing the last rays of sunlight falling on this Cotswold stone building.

I had not given myself much time to organise what I had taken over with me and so had decided for that first night I would sleep downstairs in an armchair. I was about to find out how cold these old houses can be as I curled up in the chair to sleep. But with the cold that was one thing that I was not going to do readily as I got colder and colder and colder. I found more coats and blankets to wrap myself in, but I was not getting any warmer. Eventually I did manage to reverse the temperature gradient, and with a little warmth did manage to drop off.

But, for the first time in my life I overslept. I awoke to find I should have been in for my first day's work in my new job half an hour ago. How embarrassing! There was no time to have any breakfast, I just had to rush out and be so apologetic when meeting my new work colleagues. Luckily it was quiet, no calls had come in yet.

I haven't overslept on a workday since that day some thirty-five years ago, in fact it is rare that I even need an alarm clock.

In looking for somewhere to settle and with partnership prospects I had taken the risk of going to a two-man practice where I would do the farm work, my boss the small animal work. A small crossover in terms of I would have to do some evening surgeries and would be on call every other night and every other weekend. When not doing evening surgeries I would be home to see the children for a couple of hours before bedtime. The other downside was that when one or other was on holiday then you would be on call every night until he returned.

A surgery which was a quaint old building perched over the stream, further down from our cottage, an old building and if it rained hard then we could get flooded. It all added to the experience.

I enjoyed working with the farmers on that side of the Severn, they were reasonably progressive, and it was a nice part of the country to work in. We moved out of the mill cottage and bought our own house once we had managed to sell our house in the Forest of Dean. We moved into a lovely and spacious house with a big garden to amuse the kids in. We were reasonably content until the inflexibility of a two-man practice came to light. I needed to be able to take my young daughter to hospital as an emergency had occurred at home when I was on call, but was unable to be covered, showing me that we needed to be elsewhere. Family needs should always come first, I needed to be in a larger practice with more flexibility with duties. It was time to move on again.

Sadly, not many months previously I had met one of my old colleagues from Devon at a conference. They had just been looking for a new assistant vet again and thought about contacting me to see if I would return, but when they found out I had just moved they did not pursue the idea. If they had, I would have returned straight away without any hesitation. I would have even overturned my rule of "never go back".

I was at the stage of my career that the length of time I was qualified would have demanded a sizeable salary compared with younger vets with half my years in the profession. I wanted a partnership, they wanted a not overly expensive assistant. It took some time for me to find my next job which I hoped would be my last, the place I would settle, watch my family grow up, become a partner with the financial security that should bring and then retire.

Finally, at the end of 1988 we arrived in Shropshire, and I am still here. Different wife, different job but then who says life always runs smoothly. I would fully have to admit Shropshire was an area of England I knew very little about, I had spent two weeks in Bishops Castle in my first year at university, supposedly learning about sheep farming and getting some lambing experience. However, as soon as the farmer found out I was a dairy farmer's son, I spent most of my time looking after his calving beef suckler herd. Cathy, a close friend from Uni also lived in the town and I would get the chance to visit the infamous "Three Tuns" pub which she had told me so much about. My first experience of hill farming was invigorating, especially seeing how hard some of the shepherds worked in their lonely conditions in this harsh countryside. I was kept busy, but when I left, he was going to have to do all of what he did and what I did himself. For all my labours, I was given a fiver which is more than any other student had ever got there! That was my first introduction to Shropshire and the county was never given another thought until now, when I was seeking that perfect job and somewhere to settle down. Shropshire, somewhere west of Birmingham was about all I knew of the place so when I saw a job advertised in Wellington, Shropshire I thought I would give it ago, I have been here ever since. Back to mixed practice, a fairly equal split of farm and small animal work in a four-man practice. If all went well then after eighteen months, I would be taken into partnership. As we drove up through the Severn Valley between Kidderminster and Bridgnorth towards Wellington on the way to my interview, the scenery looked nice rural and to my liking. I guess then what we did not see and know was that Wellington was part of the new town of Telford. Wellington was like an old-fashioned market town with its cattle market, station, a cinema, and a traditional style High Street. It would only be after some time that we would discover the real Telford with its sprawling housing estates, featureless town centre and its inhospitality. After nearly thirty years I am still there but have never settled and the true friends that I have in the town I could probably count on both hands.

We were here and I still am, and in fairness I have met some lovely people in the surrounding areas of what is still a very rural county (Telford excepted). We bought a large house on one of the new estates, it was actually one of the show homes and we did eventually managed to persuade the builders to sell it to us as there was so little property available and the estate was almost completed. We had a nice new home and a view just over the horizon of partnership in a Veterinary Practice at last. Nirvana!

Thirty years on and I am still here, though there have been many changes in my working career. Wellington was a mixed practice, and I was a youngster compared with my colleagues. The practice had a good farming base along with its small animal side. Although I mainly worked on the farms, I did undertake some of the dog and cat work, and it was always remarkable that if there was any species of snake coming in, then it seemed always that I was the only vet available to see it.

Yes, after eighteen months I did obtain my partnership, buying in when interest rates were nearing fifteen percent. But even with the large repayments it did offer a light for future financial security. Another of the older partners would retire and perhaps then there became an unease in the partnership. A job did come up on the Somerset/Dorset border which I applied for and would have been very keen to accept if my fellow partners had given me the go ahead to leave the partnership. I would have returned to my beloved South-West, but the Practice there couldn't wait forever for my decision and the opportunity passed. When I told my colleagues, they said of course I could have gone but it was too late.

The practice had been built around the old market town of Wellington and although most of our farms surrounded Telford, we did have a few more distant farmers who had been moved to accommodate the development of the new town. They stayed loyal to the practice. But farming was changing and more and more of our dairy farmers were getting out of milk production, the farm side was shrinking and the small animal side growing. With another of the older partners retiring it was down to two partners and my fellow partner decided then that he didn't want to do large animal work anymore. I had enjoyed some small animal work especially surgery, but I didn't want to do only that for the rest of my life.

The partnership broke up and I took most of our farm clients with me to a neighbouring practice in the very rural town of Much Wenlock. I approached them to see if they would take on our clients to which they said yes but only if I would come for at least six months to bed them in. In my heart I was seeing this as an opportunity to move back to Devon. I went to Much Wenlock short term but ended up becoming a partner there being in charge of the farm-side of the practice but still doing some small animal work. The parts of Shropshire I was seeing in practice was expanding as we covered a greater and greater area.

Farming continued to change and with that I think there were differences in views as to which way we should progress. A big development was taken to improve our main small animal base and office facilities, money was spent on the equine side, but farming was going through bad financial times. I was getting frustrated both by the lack of support and also the stubbornness of our clients in seeing a better way forward. Foot and Mouth came along in 2001, something which would have a lasting impact on me, and this occurred at the same time as my marriage was failing. My life was spiralling downwards in the end reaching the conclusion I should be moving on again. I was a lost sheep and having left the partnership I spent three months enjoying summer but probably wasting a lot of time.

In the end I was approached by a newly formed farm practice just outside Shrewsbury to see if I would work part time for them. I was only to happy to accept and to be able just to work in farm practice which was my aim when I had set out in my chosen career all those years ago. With joining them, many of my old clients who had followed me through my last move, subsequently re-joined me now in my new employment. This fast-developing practice covered an even greater area of Shropshire and was rich in dairy farmers who were, and still are very progressive in their outlook and willingness to undertake new ideas.

My original employment was for three days a week, and I was the fifth vet working there, having grown from two originally. A fourth day was added on, then a fifth until once again I was full-time and working a full out of hours rota. As well as new farmers to meet it was fantastic to still work with those that had stayed loyal to me throughout my Shropshire career. Some of those, and some of the new farmers I would meet, I am pleased to say have become good friends and will remain so even after my retirement. The move, even if I didn't manage to sell my home in Telford and move closer to the practice base, allowed me to see what a beautiful county Shropshire is. What a wonderful town Shrewsbury is when you get to know it, something I had never done while working in Wellington and Much Wenlock.

The seeds had been sown earlier in me with Foot and Mouth, divorce and other traumas in my personal life leading to the dreaded depression catching up with me. This was something I kept to myself when I finally accepted that I had the condition. I became very withdrawn, very quiet and unapproachable. a I can't deny it did affect the way I worked, especially as I never admitted to anyone that I was suffering.

Luckily in time I found a way out of it and became a far more self-confident person, more forceful and only worrying about things that were really important and becoming able to dismiss those that weren't. Overcoming that has allowed me to enjoy far more the latter years of my career, finding myself at last. It is that which has allowed me to be writing this now because I never would have had the confidence to do so before, nor the desire.

That now has given me the chance to look back and reflect on my career as mainly a farm vet and to think about how so much has changed in those forty plus years. I suppose everyone as they get older can look back and say things are not what they were. I will reflect and maybe as I reach the end of my tale I may conclude as to whether they were the good years or whether the best years lie ahead. The life of a farm vet!

5

THOSE STUDENT YEARS

The best years of your life!

Or that's what I was told!

My first experience of being away from home and meeting the world head on. My upbringing had been quiet, brought up on a farm not quite in the middle of nowhere but from the school chosen for me for my secondary education, too far from there that once I came home then I was very much alone. My school bus journey was just over an hour long each end of the day, so I left home soon after seven in the morning, was home again at about half six in the evening. A long day with homework to do after supper. It got slightly better when I could drive in my final year so I could leave when I wanted to, usually after sport. But that distance from my friends often meant once term finished, then I didn't see them again until the next term started. My two brothers and I had little in common, so I guess when my school education finished, I was very shy and reserved, lacking a lot in self-confidence. My only outlet for expression was on a hockey field or playing cricket for the local town, Faringdon.

In those distant days ago Bristol University had offered me a place if I obtained A-Level grades of B, B and C in my chosen subjects of Biology, Chemistry and Physics. What that compares with modern grades I wouldn't be sure, but I guess probably two A's and a B. That wait for the envelope to drop through the door in early August 1972 was stressful. I had excelled in Chemistry but then I had fallen just short in Physics, but they would balance out to my necessary grades. I was pleased.

I was applying for one of thirty-six places on the Bristol course having visited the University some months earlier for one of their open days and seeing the mighty Wills Memorial building for the first time. Only one fellow applicant can I remember from that day, Kendall, one of the most beautiful women, schoolgirls you could possibly ever meet. I had ticked the boxes in terms of showing an ambition to be a vet and my farming background had stood me in good stead.

But this was the year too many people obtained the required grades. I received a letter saying I hadn't got the necessary grades, my D being held against me. Dad was immediately on the phone to the University and dragged me down there to the Senate House to meet the powers that be that very afternoon. They offered me the chance of resitting just Physics or taking the whole school year again, not what I wanted to hear. But they also did say that I was next on the waiting list, if anyone didn't accept their offer of a place then it would be mine. I guess I returned home a little disconsolate, I really didn't want to waste a year which is what it seemed was likely to happen.

I often reflect how much my life would have been different if dad hadn't made that trip. The next day I had a phone call to say that I had a place. Did anybody not take up their place or was it the fact I appeared in person to plead my case. I will wonder but will never know. But.......

I had a place at Vet School and all being well in five years I would be the real McCoy.

In September 1972 Rod Wood, a rather naïve lad left home for Bristol. For two days there and back to attend pre-season hockey training and then to go to university proper and to enter my Hall of Residence. I was away from home. The authorities did try and group fellow course students together so I did share my corridor with two other vet students, like me at the end of the alphabet so I would usually get grouped with them.

Our first week before lectures, FAFFY week, I don't know what it means now but certainly knew the meaning then as we were shown bad habits by fellow but older vet students from the years above us. Drink, pyrotechnics and the rest, these guys knew how to enjoy themselves and how to misbehave. No, I don't know who blew up the Burwalls lawn!

And there I guess would be one big change between then and now. Back in '72, as in previous years, the intake throughout the country (from memory about three sixty places) in was very much a male orientated profession and that would take a few years to change. My year out of thirty-six, only ten were female. Now, as selection is done more fairly on academic ability then the ladies put us to shame with up to eighty percent of the intake being of the fairer sex. Its implications on the profession I will come back to later.

Among those ten ladies was the beautiful Kendall!

Our lectures were split between the Vet School in Park Street, a converted garage and in the newer Medicine School further up the hill where we would share lectures with Medics, Biochemistry students and Physiologists.

Biochemistry, I had found a subject I excelled in. We would also take trips out to the University farm at Langford, a place we would spend the last two years of our five-year course and would have to lodge nearby accordingly.

A new beginning, and a scary beginning but helped by having Pete and Julian so close in Hall that there was always someone to accompany oneself to lectures. Slowly but surely as I came out of myself then a group of friends expanded up to the girl's floor above ours and then to other people in other Halls of Residence and those I met through hockey, playing for the University Thirds, and then progressing rapidly through the seconds and into the University 1st. XI. I still have my black and claret hockey shirt though whether I would ever get into now is very doubtful, well let's be honest, no, I wouldn't.

I would play for the University for two years before leaving them to play for my local big town team, Swindon, and then for the County.

Days, as they were throughout the course were full and with hardly any free time away from lectures and practicals. Our introduction into Veterinary Anatomy as we slowly, bit by bit, took a greyhound to pieces to find all its inner workings. Farm trips where my practical experience always came to the fore as it did with the other farmers offspring on the course. My first year went quickly and well, working on different farms in the vacations as a course requirement, lambing in the Shropshire Hills, a pig farm in Kings Lynn where I stayed with some lovely people who taught me how to drink! A great year weather wise with quieter times spent playing rounders on the Bristol Downs, visiting hostelries just outside the city, an advantage of having a car. This also allowed me to be able to return home now and again when hockey allowed. Heady days when I could get home and back in my little old Austin A30 for £1, thirty-four pence a gallon.

My first year was easily my least arduous, yes, I would be bored once a week starring down a microscope in Histology but other than Genetics the other subjects were interesting, and to be honest, a course in Animal Management for a farmer's son was hardly taxing. With Biochemistry passed before exam time then summer revision was when I finally got around to reading "Lord of the Rings" and "War and Peace".

As was the rest of the year, there was an interesting interlude in the Animal Management exam where our dear professor would expect us to identify a few breeds of sheep from photographs. As I have said before, a breeze when you realised the name of the breed was written in front of you!

The summer of '73 was a glorious summer and great to enjoy what Bristol had to offer A time to make friends and ease into university life which was a help to shy Rod. There was a vet student's society, the Centaur Society, where we would meet regularly, and it was a chance to meet up with vet students from the four years above ours. In this I had my first introduction to snakes as we had a talk and slides. They passed the snakes around for us to gently handle but I was not so keen when one arrived in my hands and the lights went out to facilitate the projector. Pass it on quick, but then another arrived in my lap. And at one of these meetings we would meet the great man in person, James Herriot.

My first taste of Balls, the Centaur Ball where I took my dear friend Cathy from the floor above in my Hall of Residence. We drove down to the City Centre to dine and dance the night away only to find when I had arrived back at my car that I had left the lights on, and I had a flat battery. Cath could see the funny side of it luckily as we walked back through Bristol late at night, her in her finest long dress. We still see each other from time to time with her being a native of Shropshire.

And these were briefly my "hippy" days as I decided that it was fun to walk bare foot everywhere, but perhaps it was not ideal in a dissection room! And there were the Langford Games as previously mentioned, where us naïve first years thought every contest had a strict set of rules only to find out that anything goes, especially in the Ha Ha game. Health and Safety has seen its demise, but it was an experience, as was the doped Donkey Derby and other dubious contests.

The years got harder as we went on as theory turned into more practical veterinary related topics. Our year gained one or two who had intercalated a year, and we lost a couple who either failed or again intercalated another subject to join the vet course the following year. We were a strange bunch, united but apart, some sporty, some the opposite. Some would burn the midnight oil with their course work, others like myself would down tools to get to the pub before closing time but not drinking to excess.

We had a vet's rugby team which I did play for in my final two years, an experience in itself when playing at Langford as we had to chase the cows off the pitch before we started, and with home advantage we knew where the cow pats and stinging nettles were. A little shimmy, I played on the wing, would often see your opposite number slipping in something he wished he hadn't trodden in, or looking for a Dock leaf to relieve the irritation from nettle stings. We were a successful side helped greatly by Mervyn, a beanpole who would try and did run through anybody. Another from strong farming stock!

Subjects changed to Pathology, Parasitology then Medicine and Surgery as we started to learn more and more about the profession we had chosen.

Lectures, practicals and hardly a free moment. I had to give up my beloved hockey which was getting too time-consuming travelling to Swindon for home games, most away games being in or around Bristol. But it was hard to commit to those and County games on a Sunday and to study hard. Holidays were taken up with seeing Practice, hands on experience of vetting and for me especially farm work. The first opportunities to have a go at surgery, nerve racking to begin with but at least we had an expert standing beside us to help and guide us. It was intended that we would have spayed a dog and a cat, likewise with castration of each species before we qualified. How many each of us did before we left University differed from student to student, but I was far more familiar with putting dogs' stifle joints back together than I was with neutering!

Good times and when we were out at Langford, again much mischief did take place. Dave, our poor long-suffering Houseman who would find the hinges taken off his door, local anaesthetic in his toothpaste, and even once when a fellow student was short of a weekend meal, the chicken he had purloined from the farm then plucked in poor Dave's living room. As I said, long-suffering.

The course by now I did find hard. Although so close to the end, I had to approach it as if they were going to pass me then they would. If not then I had tried my best but was not quite up to the task, although I did find the practical side of farm work when seeing practice with Ian Baker in Aylesbury quite easy and enjoyable. Exams, another story. By this time my parents had sold the cows and had moved to Exmoor to begin their new venture. We had a transition of eighteen months where we had both farms with the farm in Oxfordshire put down to corn. The times when most needed doing coincided with my vacations so between seeing Practice and term time, my brother and I would sow, harvest and do whatever else needed doing on the farm. That included the drought year of 1976, and were we so pleased to see the rains when they did arrive?

But through all this, my university career was coming to its end. Our Finals and why did it always seem, the vet course exams always were the last to take place in the whole university. Being at the end of the alphabet, when I had finished my last oral exam the rest of the University had finished and were partying hard or had gone home. I would walk out of my last exam wanting to celebrate with someone, but there was no one around until I arrived back at Hall or met friends in the pub.

We as the Final year produced the annual review as I have mentioned previously. It was a great success but it was very hard work to produce, maybe my time would have been better spent studying. But we did it, three writers and then with the rest of the year then on board, we produced a great show, a great achievement by the Year and I think what finally pulled us all together. Fond memories.

We were done, some had jobs to go to, some still looking but all of us would be going out straight away to earn a living as Vets. One final year photo on the lawns at Langford, a final inquest into who had hoisted the Warden's underpants on the Langford Hall flag staff and then we would be on our separate ways.

To meet again, our reunions as previously mentioned few and far between. Sadly, some of those colleagues of five years I would never meet up with again, now over forty years on, how many of them are no longer with us.

That was then, but what has changed, what of the modern student?

Our year's four and five timetable was full, crammed with lectures and practicals right up to our final examinations. We even had a couple of lectures after them, Jim Pinsent (a senior lecturer) realising no-one had told us about a couple of serious but common diseases of cattle, he filled in the missing blanks for us who wanted to be cattle vets!

Finals, a pass and you were qualified. Free to practice and any aspiring employer expected you to get on with it.

Times change and although I wouldn't know exactly how the course finishes now, the modern vet student has a different life to what we went through forty plus years ago. The timetable has changed, the universities now try to finish all lectures in all subjects by the end of the fourth year whereas we were still having them in both veterinary medicine and surgery right up to our final term. That means that the modern student should have all their theoretical knowledge when they enter their final year.

Their final year is now taken up doing rotations, whether that be at the university doing surgery, medicine in house with the various departments the university may have e.g., the Royal College in London have their own small animal practice in Campden Town. I would spend my vacations in my final two and a half years seeing practice away from university, mainly with Ian in Aylesbury. I learnt a lot from him, but I didn't have the theoretical knowledge from lectures to back up what I was seeing and learning practically, especially in my fourth year. I fully admit that he taught me a lot, but with that bit more knowledge perhaps it would have all meant a little bit more.

We have had many students seeing practice with us, looking to gain farm practice experience. Some have been a complete waste of time, it being obvious that they were only interested in a small animal career and were just going through the motions, ticking a necessary box. Others were excellent and came back to us on more than one occasion which was also good for us as we knew what they were capable of, and therefore what we could let them do. There were some promising farm vets amongst them.

In theory therefore the modern graduate should be far better equipped to leave university and start a job with all the knowledge and experience that they had picked up.

But in my opinion, most of them are not and that probably reflects the type of work we do these days, more operations, more fertility work on Routine visits, and less of the fire brigade work that would have been my introduction to farm practice. Seeing individual cows, examining them, learning how to handle them, seeing the normal and the abnormal gives you so much more a clinical eye. And it allows you to get to know your client better, to build up a relationship with him.

I qualified and in my first job I was expected to go out on farm and vet, the modern graduate, especially in farm practice, we have to run some sort of internship, or having the "new vet" shadowing an experienced vet for some time before it was felt that they were competent enough to manage on their own. They would start with castrations, disbuds, the more straightforward tasks and as their experience grew, they would be allowed to do more. With that they would then start going on the out of hours rota but to begin with they would always have an experienced back-up on hand.

In the middle of the night, you have to show patience with them, knowing you would like to get back to bed but they have to have the experience so though you know you could finish the job far quicker, you have to give them the time to complete the job themselves, giving advice where necessary.

The modern course is organised better for the students, but on qualifying, then the pressures on you are now far greater than in my day. Knowing how to deal with those pressures should at some stage become part of the veterinary course. Well-being, more on that later.

But for now, you have just qualified, it is time to be a vet!

You are about to join....

6

THE REAL WORLD

Yesterday I was a student, today I am a fully qualified Veterinary Surgeon and having been sworn in by the Royal College of Veterinary Surgeons (I can now add MRCVS after my name to the BVSc I had obtained from university), I am ready to be let loose on the world. I had started the course to be a farm vet but now the reality was that there were some three hundred newly qualified vets all looking for a job and in 1977/8 jobs were not that plentiful, especially if you wanted to specialise in farm work so early on.

Welcome to the real world Rod, it is time to start earning a living with the thought of work until…. Whenever!

The Final year at Bristol had been a bit of a struggle but I had got there. How much confidence I had in myself was debatable as having got through the sheltered life of a student, it was now time to face reality. The decisions made would now be mine and mine alone and I would have to justify them to both clients and my peers. The best I could find was a job in a mixed Practice in Buckinghamshire/ Bedfordshire border, and even then, not a predominantly dairy area. But Olney was a job and a start.

My first job I would have to say was not a happy one, working in this three/four-man practice with myself and the boss doing most of the farm work while the other two covered the small animal work across two surgeries. But I was largely told how I was going to treat everything before I even got to the farm, any decisions were made before I got there regardless of what I may find on my arrival. Where was clinical judgement, in my boss's eyes everything could only be treated with bottle A or bottle B. If I did any different, I was in trouble. This was something I didn't enjoy and as a learning curve it was completely non-existent.

I found sanctuary in returning to playing hockey, this time for Bedford and the County and would meet a great bunch of people who to be honest I would have to thank for keeping my morale up. It was the last time I played hockey seriously, though not the end of my hockey career. Looking back now, it has always been a sadness that I never reached my full potential in a strictly in those days, amateur sport. I had to make the choice, hockey or career and one of those choices didn't pay a penny.

There is little point dwelling on this part of my career, five long months but it was time to move on and look for a change of scenery. As I have said, I headed back home to Exmoor to my parents and spent some time searching for the right position to come up, but eventually it did and so close to home in the rural town of Cullompton in East Devon. I would be joining a seven-man team in aw hat was a predominantly all farm practice.

My interview was strange, almost like I had the job before I got there, a very informal affair. It was almost as if I was entertaining them, I made the tea. I led the discussion. Perhaps this was as sign they really wanted me there. But it did offer a new beginning and only an hour away from my parents.

The job sounded just what I wanted. There would be a small pet involvement with me taking one evening surgery a week, Monday night from five to six and I would operate once in five weeks on a Wednesday. Yes, self-doubt reappeared but was soon gone in such a friendly working environment.

I went to work on my first Monday morning, allowed to equip the car with what drugs and equipment I thought I would need, then sent out with a list of calls. A far greater variety of drugs to call upon, and a lot of experience to back me up when necessary. And I worked my first night there!

The Culm is a beautiful area, and we covered a large area of East Devon with our twin practice in Tiverton where another University colleague worked. The coast was nearby though it is strange how you never take advantage of it while it is so close but miss it when you move away. We worked with a variety of farms from Council small holdings to small family farms, and this was the time when large dairy farms were starting to be created so we had a few very progressive dairy farmers to service. The other great thing was that farms were so close to each other so driving was not tiring, often going from next door to next door to next door. How things have changed in 2020/1.

Looking back, I would have to admit that the grounding for my future career was very much started in my five years in Cullompton. After leaving, every new job I did view with some trepidation, but I think that was more down to my lack of self-confidence, shyness and difficulty or just being uncomfortable with new work colleagues and clients until I got to know them better.

When I started in Cullompton I was dropped in at the deep end, I had BVSc, MRCVS after my name so I was a vet, and I was expected to go out and do the business from day one. You weren't going to develop respect amongst the farming community if you showed no confidence and kept on asking for back-up. The farmers, if a little apprehensive at first when another new vet arrived on the farm, were always after that initial meeting both friendly and helpful. We turned into a great team, offering and exchanging ideas between the seven then eight vets, and there was a great feel of mutual respect. Even in the small animal work we did, not much, but we still managed some very complex cases and operations, leaning on each other's advice.

I have no intention about writing much of my small animal Veterinary career other than I did bits and pieces until arriving in my final job. I enjoyed operating, especially orthopaedic ops but consulting I generally found a chore. In small towns like Cullompton, or when in Shifnal in Shropshire, they were small communities and you generally saw the faces on a regular basis so there was less formality, more friendship so consultations for me tended to be far more relaxed, less pressure. That is something I will return to later and its effect on your inner soul as a vet.

But if I am not going to dwell on my life as a Small Animal vet then I would just mention one case that I had while in Cullompton which even now gives me a lot of satisfaction because of the outcome. My consultation night, Monday, and often busy after the weekend plus the numerous conversations about "*All Creatures Great and Small*" with every client asking me if I had seen the vet program.

One-night clients brought in a lovely Golden Retriever puppy, Honey, who was just over four months old. She was a happy dog, wagging her tail as she met someone new, the vet. Her owners reported that at times she seemed very unsteady on her legs, seeming to lose co-ordination of her back end. On extending her head there did seem to be some discomfort at the top of her neck. I had heard of, had lectures on something called a "wobbler" in horses but had never seen one, whether I had heard of it in dogs I wasn't sure. This condition is a sub-luxation of the axial-atlantial joint, cervical one and two vertebrae, where they don't join properly and so cause some compression on the spinal cord, hence the wobbler term because that is how the animals present.

I would admit her for an Xray and in the meantime chatted with my colleagues. Radiographs confirmed the diagnosis and Honey was such a lovely and friendly puppy, even though after much research and explaining the risks involved, we decided we would operate. I had never seen this done and now was about to try and do this op myself, stabilising the two vertebrae to stop the compression of the cord. I would use thermo-cautery to dissect down to the vertebrae, and then put in a stabilising ligature on the wings of the vertebrae to stop the luxation. Dog on one end of the operating table, textbook on the other, I embarked on the longest op I ever did in my career. Numerous stops for coffee and reassurance I was doing what I had intended, at last after four hours I sutured the skin back over the wound and hoped.

We didn't have the pain killers then that we have now but when Honey came round from the anaesthetic, she wagged her tail and was so pleased to see myself and Anne, my nurse assistant. Honey must have been so sore, but she took it all as the happy dog she was. After a couple of days, we sent her home with strict instructions on exercise, and I would see her again in a week to take the stitches out.

She returned, wagging her tail, and after those early days she seemed to be making good progress but we would only be able to evaluate that fully as she increased her exercise. I saw her from time to time and my happy ending to this tale was when the owners told me that Honey would soon start training to be a Guide Dog for the Blind. She succeeded and she was, has always been my fondest memory of Small Animal Practice.

Devon was a great experience and I always promised I would go back there when I retired. Lovely villages, beautiful countryside, I loved the Devon accent, nice pubs and a coastline nearby.

It could be that Devon showed me what I wanted in life, what sort of work I was most comfortable with and in what sort of surroundings I wanted to work in. The scenery, the farmers, my work colleagues, and yes, just the way of life that I had in that job. In those five years, everything there had been a real joy. It was a hard decision to leave but what I did and learnt there would have a profound effect on the rest of my life. And the lifelong friends that I first met down there, those that have stood by me through the rest of my life, through the good and the bad and to who I owe an eternal gratitude.

It would be ironical that now my eternal wish is to retire to Dorset, not Devon (and neither may happen), and I would have been there if I had accepted that job in Blandford Forum. But looking back on life, would I have achieved the things I have now if I had taken that job? Would I have climbed Kilimanjaro, Mount Kenya and many other things if I had gone to Dorset back in the early '80s? I doubt it.

We moved to the Forest of Dean, then across the other side of the Severn. Five years in Gloucestershire where although I was comfortable, I didn't feel my career was doing anything but standing still and that partnership was no closer on the horizon. Yes, I played hockey again, took up golf and my second child was born but there was a growing sense inside of me that I was getting disillusioned with my chosen profession. They say it is a vocation, but it seemed to be getting more and more a chore. Advice fell on deaf ears and other than a salary there seemed little reward in what I was doing. It was time to move on and so in very late 1988 we up sticks and moved to Shropshire. Although in different practices and having achieved that goal of partnership in two of those Practices, that is where I remained for my final days as a vet, and at last solely a Farm Vet. It took some time, but I finally reached my goal and can look back on a life here that I have enjoyed and with some great farm clients, some of whom will remain as friends even when I settle wherever I put my retirement roots down, which won't be Shropshire. Devon, Dorset had become too expensive for my goals, but the sea has a draw for me. North Wales may well be that place to put my feet up and build on what I have achieved in life so far.

In those forty plus years I have changed from student to vet with L plates and more latterly to teacher myself as the new generation of vets firstly as students, and then as recently qualified graduates looking to gain experience from us old "uns". The full circle but for them it has been an ever-changing game. Their requirements in academia have increased to get into Vet School but the demands on them when they have qualified have changed greatly as well. It is probably a lot harder for them to get the necessary experience like I did in that stage of my career where I just had to get on with it, I was qualified so I was a Vet and had to apply my knowledge as best I could.

Animals, our patients, have become more valuable, the owners have become more litigation conscious and the ever-increasing number of TV documentaries on the Profession mean when the public see something on the screen then they expect that treatment as well. It is not always that simple because of availability and cost. The pressures are growing and with that the mental pressure in what at times can see a lonely world. We as a profession have a high suicide rate and if well-being has very much become the buzzword in the workplace, then it has become more and more significant in the Veterinary world. But again, that is something I will return to because although I am now in a good place, then in the past the pressures of the job and life in general have taken me to dark places.

So, what is life like for the present-day new graduate, and again I am being more specific to those that want to specialise in farm work.

7

THE PERKS OF THE JOB!

That first job, how do you choose it? When I qualified and for many years surrounding then, veterinary positions were only advertised in *"The Veterinary Record".* It was our weekly journal full of adverts, research and practical papers and a couple of pages of jobs that had become available, the most recent at the top, descending to those that had been advertised for some time. A practice would generally put an advert in for three weeks, if it were there longer, then one worried that the job was not that special, and those practices struggled to retain staff. The availability of Small Animal jobs was always greater than mixed then Farm and Equine practices.

One had an idea of what one was looking for in terms of job description, so the next consideration were the "perks" of the job. Location was important to a lot of us graduating students, sorry, now vets, but also a big consideration was what else was on offer with the job. Holiday time, salary though that was often not put in the advert (generous salary and time off was the normal wording) and what was the norm in those distant days, a car and accommodation.

Salary in those early days wasn't great but there seemed to be a general scale so that was what it was, and you had to accept it, just hoping there would be regular reviews. Those that think us vets make a fortune would be sadly mistaken especially in Farm Practice and it is often thought you have started the job as a vocation rather than making a packet out of it. Perhaps when partnership comes about then income can increase greatly and you at last reap some of the rewards for your endeavours. But partnerships cost money, including that vague but expensive term called "Good Will". When I first became a partner loans were expensive to finance the buying into a practice, so one needed a good return just to pay off your loan and to live.

Holidays, one hoped one would get four weeks and Bank Holidays plus a day in lieu of any of those holiday dates that you had worked. Certainly, after busy times and especially when night duties were busy then you needed that amount of time to recuperate, though partners usually gave themselves more time off and may have reduced the number of nights and weekends that they worked compared with their younger assistants. That was their entitlement, they owned the business. Some practices included

Bank Holidays in the holiday allotment, thankfully wherever I worked that was not the case. Devon roads, especially near the coast got busy over Public Holidays so it was not uncommon for me to volunteer to work them and have time off at a later day when you could move around without being stuck in a traffic jam.

In terms of holiday, little has changed over the years though consideration is now taken into account for those nights and especially weekends worked. I have vague recollections of getting a Friday afternoon off after a weekend on call in those early days just to give a slightly longer weekend off. Now, in my last job in Shropshire, we now get a Monday off after working a weekend, and then the following Friday off as well, if you had worked the weekend on second call then the following Wednesday could be taken off. Progress in a demanding job, and the Working Time Directive and work Risk Assessments in regard to working when tired helped in achieving this end but it did take some persuading. There is a realisation that downtime is increasingly important with the mental pressures of work.

It was quite common for accommodation to be a flat above the main surgery building, often then being old, converted houses or shops. The modern surgery is often a purpose-built hospital or a unit on a retail park so that accommodation no longer exists. In my early days, money was hard to borrow, and one didn't know how long you would stay in each job until you finally settled down in a partnership. We needed a roof over our heads, and it was the norm for the Practice to provide it.

I have described my flat in Buckinghamshire before with my strange neighbour calling out if he thought I was about. It was unnerving for the few months I was there, but otherwise it was a comfortable and roomy home with a nice sized garden, if I had stayed there long enough to enjoy it. But I did have to exit my flat through the consultation room which was always a pain, and it was not uncommon to get a knock on the door to say could I just give a hand holding a dog or whatever. Living on the premises can have its disadvantages.

My flat in Devon was again above the office but there was another floor between me and the consulting rooms. Again, a roomy flat with two large bedrooms, a large kitchen where my pheasant met its demise, and a more than comfortable living room. It would only be later that at some stage I had found it had been declared unfit for human habitation as it was, on a sunny day you could see the dust rising between the floorboards and I would have to dust and hoover again. Here I am getting quite domesticated, this is when I started to enjoy cooking and entertaining the local young ladies with dinner parties for two. Again, the downside of this place was the front door. Clients knew someone lived upstairs and would often ring the front doorbell or knock if they wanted something out of office hours, I soon learnt not to answer the door unless I knew someone was coming to see me at an appointed time. If you opened the window to look down and see who, your cause was lost if it were to be a client and they looked and saw you.

I lived there for nearly two years before when getting married, then my wife and I bought a house in town.

After that, when changing jobs, we always bought a house after an initial period when we were house hunting where we would stay in a rented accommodation. In Lydney, a lovely large house but next door to one of the other vets. Crossing the river, we lived in the Mill Cottage described previously, again a lovely house in a beautiful setting. By now, dad with his lorry licence was well used to loading our worldly goods into the back of the lorry and moving us on to our next destination. Loading up the night before, freezer always in last and plugged in on an extension cable before setting off early the next day to start a new life somewhere else.

In Shropshire we moved into the house we bought straight away as it was a new build, and other than renting when going through my divorce then I have owned my own house ever since.

Changing times. Whether accommodation is provided nowadays I wouldn't be sure. Certainly, where I have worked over the past twenty years then the answer is no, it being far more likely that some sort of housing allowance would be made in your salary. In my last job in Shropshire, you would find your own accommodation, probably renting to start with but it would be true to say that most of the assistants, if they had been here for a year or two, generally bought their own property. We have not seen great turnover of staff; a lot have liked the area and have settled down and so it was logical to buy.

Why the change? The Inland Revenue decided that a house with the job was a perk and so taxable. If you could come up with an argument that like in Cullompton, where I lived above the surgery, you could justify there was a need for someone to be on the premises for twenty-four hours a day, then you may persuade the Taxman it was a necessity. But that was a hard argument to win. The days of accommodation with the job are now history.

The other big perk was the car, and when I qualified it generally was a car. I owned a car at university. It enabled me to play hockey both for the University and for Swindon, without it I would have been totally reliant on public transport and there would have been no way I could have played for the town and county at weekends. It also got me about the country in vacations when I was seeing practice, part of my training.

None of my early cars would have been suitable for Farm Practice though. For all of us new graduates we became mobile so we could do our job but also have the means to get about in our free time. However, it wouldn't be an understatement to say that the new veterinary graduate had earned somewhat of a reputation for not prolonging a car's life and so it was more than common that the vehicle provided for you in your new job was often not in pristine condition.

Having said that, in my first job in Buckinghamshire I was given a brand-new mustard coloured Ford Escort saloon. It lived on the courtyard of the Surgery and was well-cared for by me.

But one weekend while driving down to stay with my brother in Wandsworth, I had just entered north London and stopped at some red traffic lights. Unfortunately, the car behind me didn't. I minor bump caused by a Mr Lin, a Chinese gentleman who seemed to have little grasp of the English language. I was well versed in what to do so took the details of him and his car so the Insurance Company could sort it out. He drove into me so it was his fault. The main damage was to the boot of the car, it wouldn't stay closed so there I was in the middle of London for the weekend with a boot full of drugs and equipment tied in by a crepe bandage to keep the boot shut. At my brothers flat I did take my post-mortem knife into the house with me, otherwise it was fingers crossed that Londoners would leave my boot alone.

I returned to work on the Monday morning and reported the incident to my boss with the details of Mr Lin. It transpired he did not exist! Strike one!

I moved on to Devon and as I have explained earlier, the Vauxhall Viva I was supposed to use was not available for a while. The assistant I was replacing had gained a reputation for his slick and quick driving but sadly just before he was due to hand it over to me, he had decided to rearrange the shape of it a little. Well, a lot in truth, the car had become a little concertinaed and so needed pulling back into shape, I would hopefully have it in about three weeks.

In the meantime, when I arrived at the practice on a Sunday afternoon to be shown my lodgings (again I would have the flat above the surgery when my predecessor had moved out) I was given the keys to a rather classy Opel, with sleek lines of multiple dents all over. I had a little over a mile to drive to my lodgings but straight away it was a car that gave the impression that you may never reach whatever destination you were aiming for. A reluctant starter! I hoped the next morning when I had to begin my new job that the car would take me there. Luckily it did start that morning but when I was asked to work that night on call then I would certainly have to admit my biggest concerns were of the car and not of what I may have to visit. The night was negotiated and luckily the calvings I had to do were but a short drive away.

On my second day I set off on my round again. In the afternoon I had to visit a farm between Cullompton and Tiverton. My return journey would require the ascent of a steep hill. Devon roads are often not wide and if meeting a vehicle coming in the opposite direction you would frequently have to pull into the side of the road. My misfortune, going up the steep hill I did meet another car and there was no way he was going to stop. I pulled into the side of the road and put the handbrake on.

It didn't work!

Help, what do I do now, rolling backwards down a hill with a car coming the other way? I had to reverse into the bank to stop the car and then practice my hill start technique without a handbrake. By the time I got back to the Surgery my nerves were feeling a little raw. My confidence in this car was quickly evaporating.

Three weeks on and the Viva was almost ready, and my flat was about to be vacated. Things were looking on the up.

A few more calls in the Opel and I could then abandon it in the Practice yard, and it could return to its status of being "reserve "car. I had to do a call the other side of Willand, a small farm on a bad bend. Having finished my work there I cleaned myself up and set off to return to the office. I looked both ways as I pulled out of the farm entrance aiming to turn right, across any traffic that was coming from that way. All looked clear as I pulled out, but it was a blind bend, I would find out a car was coming around the corner. Crash and technically my fault. There was some damage to the front of the other car driven by a middle-aged lady, and to the front of the Opel. There was no anger exchanged, the bend was the culprit.

I had to ring the office with my good news and one of the other assistants came to pick me up. The car was a write off but that was mainly because it was in such poor condition pre-accident that it wasn't worth repairing. I got in my rescuers car to be told that everyone was told when visiting this farm to turn left out of the entrance, go down the road a little way and turn around there. Nobody told me!

I arrived back at the office feeling quite glum, three weeks and I had already written a car off. But everyone else was rejoicing and congratulating me.

Why?

They told me they had been trying to get rid of this car for months, get it off the road. I was a hero; I had managed to do it in three weeks.

I couldn't quite share their celebrations at the time. But I was relieved not to have to drive that Opel again. Strike 2.

It was time to start my Viva experience, the new remodelled model. But it was my car and I soon got used to it and its idiosyncrasies. There were three Vivas in the Practice, mine the blue one and by now I was living in the flat above the surgery so could view my car with pride out of the kitchen window. What I would say for it, once I had it organised to my satisfaction, was that with all the drugs and equipment stored inside it, I had a system of where everything was and it is probably the only car I have had where I could find anything in it, even if blindfolded.

But there was a but with it, it never had really recovered from its straightening out and I could almost judge to the day when it would next have to pop across the road to the garage to have another repair.

A new colleague, Pete joined us and was given a little Vauxhall Chevette to drive, red and obvious when approaching but that was not enough to prevent its demise. Pete was leaving a farm late one afternoon when from a hedge and bank above him, a cow suddenly appeared, jumping the hedge and landing on top of the car. Luckily, there were no casualties, only the car whose shape was considerably rearranged. The curse of the assistant's car.

My Viva struggled on, in fairness went very well when it was running but still developed various foibles. One night on the way to the pub in Silverton I was driving along the road on the hill down to the village of Bradninch when the headlights suddenly decided to stop working. Luckily, I knew the road and there was something nearing a full moon so I was able to navigate, hoping I wouldn't meet anything coming in the opposite direction. After a few seconds, just as suddenly the lights came back on again, only to go off again and then back on. It never did it again but for a short while was a little bit scary.

Another time I had picked the car up from a service and had again gone to Silverton to go out with my girlfriend. I was dropping her off late before driving up to my parents on Exmoor to spend the weekend. I pulled up outside her house, kissed her goodnight and after seeing her safely inside her door I began my journey to the moor. First manoeuvre was to turn around, so I tried to put the car in reverse which meant moving the gearstick across and then lifting it up.

It came off in my hand!

I could place it back in its socket and use the forward gears but not reverse so had to do a five-point turn where I drove forward, got out of the car to push it backwards, back into the car and first gear, out again to push it backwards again before getting in and finding first again and setting off.

I was not impressed; my parents found the gear stick sitting in the sink when they got up the following morning. Fortunately, it was a problem I was able to sort out myself in the light of day, the gear stick hadn't been screwed back in properly by the garage.

By now even my bosses were losing faith with the car and decided to replace it, I would have a brand-new Morris Marina, green, to continue my work with.

Motoring suddenly became free and easy, no worries about my regular three weekly check-ins at the garage over the road, just the regular service and running in the engine gently for the first fifteen hundred miles. This was the first new car I had ever had, and I was happy. Even watching one day from my kitchen window as in the sunshine as saw my new car gently rolling down the slope of the staff car park but I was able to reach the car before it hit anything. Luckily it had missed the gate post by centimetres and had come to rest against the curb on the other side of the road. A close shave but all turned out okay until....

It was mid-summer and at the end of the week I was supposed to be going down to St. Mawes in Cornwall with my now fiancée for our first holiday together. A couple more days at work and then we would be off.

I was sent to a farm just north of Exeter at Columbjohn to pregnancy diagnose some cows. I had been to the farm several times and the farmer and his wife, progressive in farming, were very friendly. To get there you had to turn off the A38 and head down a couple of narrow country lanes surrounded either side by tress and scenic countryside. It was a journey I always enjoyed and on this wonderful summer's day all seemed well with the world. Even when I saw a lorry coming towards me in the distance and didn't foresee any problems, I was able to pull gently into the side of the road and stop, waiting to let him pass. I was on a slight bend as I waited....... but was rather dismayed that as he approached, he seemed to be making no effort to slow down. I was stationary, I would have to let him pass and as the front of the lorry passed me, though worryingly closely, I thought all would be okay. That is until I saw the lorry's rear wheels fast approaching the front of my car and then hitting it. The lorry did stop, alas with me parked under it. I was shaken and thought at that moment I had diced with death.

The lorry reversed slightly to free my car and I was able to get out of the car. The lorry driver got out of his cab to see if I was okay, informing me he had seen me late and the only way he thought that he could avoid an accident was to drive through me.

Our cars had walkie talkies in them, me Alpha Bravo 7, so I was able to contact the office (Alpha Bravo 1) to say what had happened and the girls there informed the farmer what had happened. I was literally just over the fields from my destination. The office arranged for the car to be picked up while the farmer came and picked me up and took me back to the farm and gave me a cup of tea. I think I was in shock, how much closer would the lorry have had to be to have hit where I was sitting in the car and below head height. I was lucky.

I was picked up from the farm by one of the other vets and taken back home.

The next time I saw the car was to retrieve my equipment from it at the garage over the road. It was a mess, a write off in fact and again I realised how lucky I had been to walk out of it. My partners pulled out all the stops to get me a car so I would still be able to go on that holiday which was now even more needed.

St Mawes is a lovely place, and we had a wonderful break staying in the Ship Inn on the waterfront. I must go back there again sometime.

Strike 3! I was leaving a trail of destruction behind me in terms of cars, I seemed to be jinxed with them, and could now see why employers were so apprehensive about young vets and their practice cars. Though in fairness to me, twice it had been me who had been hit.

But despite the narrow country lanes, East Devon, the Culm Vale and the Honiton area was a beautiful area to drive around, to enjoy those wonderful summers days while going between farms and to breath in the countryside. A short trip of an hour up to my parents between Exford and Simonsbath to take in more of the panoramas and sleepiness of rural life, exploring the Exe and Barle valleys by horseback, visiting places you couldn't access by car.

Even some nights when going up there while crossing Winsford Hill I would stop on snow covered roads to aid a ewe lambing. She would be lying on the road pushing to expel her offspring and would just need a helping hand before I would continue on my way. With no water provided, the car would soon acquire that agricultural smell associated with our vehicles.

The other odour the car would soon acquire would be that off Parentrevite, a Vitamin B concoction made by the then drug company, Beechams. We used it as a pick-me up for ill cattle and sheep to improve appetite and liver function. It was a good drug, but it did have a very characteristic smell which was rather clingy. The other problem with it was that when it got warm it did have a habit of expanding rapidly. If you stuck a syringe and needle in it, it would almost self-fill, if the syringe came off then it would spray through the needle all over you or the car. The smell didn't go away in a hurry.

My green Marina was replaced by a Mustard coloured one and that had an uneventful career. But by now it had been decided to replace the cars on a regular basis and so after a couple of years I was given the choice of what car to have again. I fancied an Astra hatchback and was given the task of going to see what exchange deal I could get for the Marina. The salesman looked around the car, still in good condition, then inside. He was hit by the smell of Parentrevite. Next, he looked underneath the car, well caked with earth and muck from farm drives and country lanes.

He commented, "I can see it's a vet's car, and has already been undersealed".

I was a little embarrassed.

The rest of my motoring days in Devon and then in Gloucestershire passed uneventfully. The Astra was a lovely car to drive, and I was sorry to give it up when moving to the Forest of Dean. I had become the proud owner of a Cortina which never let me down. Perhaps in Gloucestershire the back roads are wider and less hazardous. Uneventful yes, mishaps only one. The car was a heavy car. One summers day we had a knock on the door asking if we would like our drive re-tarmacked. It was on a slope and did need doing. We agreed and paid over the cash. They arrived the next day and carried out their task. I was at work while they laboured on the drive and when I got home, I found we had a lovely looking drive up to the house. I had already been told not to use it for twenty-four hours.

I obeyed the instructions but on arriving back from work the following day I did park on our drive. When I set off for work the following morning an appreciable part of our new drive came with me! Cowboys, and they had stolen my pickaxe.

I arrived in Shropshire in '89 and with a partnership looming then the car perk would soon disappear. In partnership you usually own your own car, though it would be put through the business. I had a succession of Vauxhall Cavaliers and enjoyed driving them. But here in Telford it wasn't other cars hitting me that became the problem, more break-ins, four in total either at the office or when parked on my drive at night. The annoyance was that despite the drugs in the car, nothing of any note was ever stolen, it was just the hassle of getting windows replaced. One night I did while in bed suspect our security light had come on and I did get up to find someone on our drive. He hid beside our neighbour's house while I waited outside my front door in my dressing gown, armed with my five iron. In the end he obviously thought I wouldn't assault him, just pulled his hood over his face and walked straight past me and away. What could I do? At least for once the car wasn't damaged.

My pride and joy was a white Cavalier SRi. I loved that car. I had started doing French lessons at the local tech College in the evenings. One evening I finished my class and went out to drive home. That strange feeling when you are sure that the car should be parked at that spot, but it wasn't. You doubt yourself as to where you left the car but eventually have to admit to yourself that it has been stolen. A friend drove me home and I rang the local police.

"What sort of car is it?"

"A white Cavalier SRi."

"No chance you will see that again mate!"

"I am a vet, and the car is full of drugs."

Suddenly a different tone, "Okay, we will have a look as soon as possible."

They rang back within fifteen minutes to say they had found it. There was a place apparently where Cavaliers were taken when stolen and then broken up for parts by various gangs and the police knew exactly where it was. Without the mention of drugs in the car, they couldn't be bothered to look.

I got my car back the following morning, but alas it was in no state to drive. Another write off. Strike 4.

Unfortunate but now the boot was on the other foot. I was a partner, and it was me who had to deal with the succession of accidents that my employees had, and there were many. But I had been through it all myself as an assistant!

Misfortune would hit me once more. By now I had upgraded to a Vauxhall Omega and one day while driving through town on the way back from a call to the office, I stopped behind a car waiting to turn right into a car park. Sadly, the car behind me didn't.

Crunch and I shot forwards then sideways banging my head on the door frame. I had been hit by the Telford clown, Mr Magic. He admitted it was all his fault and it caused much amusement to colleagues when later they joked that I had had a clown up my backside. I did drive the car back to the office and then home later, badly shaken but when we inspected the car more closely and saw the damage to the fuel tank as well as the structural damage, again the car was a write off.

For me and the whiplash injury it caused, I have never really recovered. It took eighteen months before one day I woke up and realised I hadn't got a headache for the first time since the accident. I had various cognitive tests as my powers of concentration and memory had deteriorated considerably.

The hazards of a job where you can spend so much time in a car.

But nowadays things have changed. The perk of a car has become taxable. The new vet will either provide their own car along with a mileage allowance or they will be given a van to drive, without the same tax liabilities. You could take the option of leaving the car at the office every night, in which case it would not carry the same tax issues, but practically for a farm vet this is not possible. Night and weekend calls mean you need the car with you, and often one drives to a farm straight from home.

Changing times, and that great perk will probably never be seen again. My colleagues in my last practice all drive these large trucks which will get them through most road conditions, down farm tracks and across fields. Roomy but again, they probably lack a bit in comfort.

But some things don't change, they still seem to have a habit of hitting things. Vets driving reputations have not changed at all over the years.

8

SCRUMPY TIME

I have over the whole course of my career worked in some wonderful places, beautiful countryside and obviously very rural. I am excluding Telford in that as there are not many farm animals in the town perimeters but the surrounding areas extending into the Shropshire and Stretton Hills and into Wales are proper countryside. Although the landscape is changing as farming becomes more intensive, there are still many traditional farms and farmhouses. Even the big dairy farms of today are still based around an old farmhouse with its attached garden. And what a lot of these residents will then have will be an orchard.

In the West of England, Herefordshire would be the big apple growing area, extending into Worcestershire and the Vale of Evesham. Much cider would be produced in this area.

But it is not the only area in this neck of the woods that produces from the juices of apples. I hadn't been in Devon long to find that most farms would have an apple orchard and those especially around Honiton would produce not cider but Scrumpy.

My first introduction to Devon Scrumpy was when I was visiting my parents on Exmoor soon after I had started working in Cullompton. My elder brother was helping my parents out as mum had broken her arm and couldn't assist with the riding holidays they were now doing for a living. My brother, fed up with life in London, came down to help take the rides out and to do the cooking. Both, he was very adept at. In shopping in the local village, Exford, he had got to know some of the other locals, including the landlord of the pub (or more truthfully his brother who was looking after it for him), and one or two of the other local farmers on Exmoor. My brother would take me down to the pub for a couple of beers, but at closing time the doors would be locked, and it would very much be help yourself to what you wanted. The stand-in landlord was only too happy to give out his hospitality. Through these pub trips, we were invited to join a young couple looking after their parent's farm on a night out to a pub near Molland on the other edge of the Moor. We accepted their invitation and set off to meet them at the pub. They had some friends over from Southern Ireland who joined us. It was a cold winters night, and the order of the day was for mulled scrumpy served up by the pub. It didn't take a lot to realise this was potent stuff but our Irish colleagues, used to drinking Guinness, thought it nothing. We eventually left the pub and returned back to their farm for a coffee and in the Irish friend's case, a Whisky. By this stage he had become very talkative, and despite his bravado, it was plain to all that the effects of the Scrumpy were quickly having their effect on his mental state. Enough was enough, my brother and I returned back to my parents on a snow swept road. Our Irish colleague retired to bed where he was soon asleep, naked. But at some stage in the night, he decided he needed the toilet and in his stupor the first door he found were actually the French windows opening onto the outside. He opened them and out he stepped, but it was not a ground floor room. He fell, awkwardly, but in his desperation for the toilet he got up, relieved himself, only then to find he was locked out of the house. He luckily hadn't locked his car so slept naked in that for the rest of the night. Morning came, and by then the analgesic properties of the Scrumpy had worn off, lying naked in his car he found he had broken his ankle.

When we heard the story of the rest of the night it taught me to respect the strength of this locally brewed beverage.

The farms often had their own press and so when harvest had finished, planting done, then they would turn their attention to picking their crop of apples. Then pressing them would follow to produce the apple juice that would be used to make the Scrumpy. Pressed and left to ferment in barrels, the farmer would consider when it was ready to bottle and drink.

More than once I would visit one particular farm and just as I would be leaving, he would offer me some Scrumpy to take home with me. He would fill a five-litre clear plastic container with the brew, and I would set off. He would suggest that if I could get into the fridge as soon as possible then that would be a good idea. But no such fridge in the office was large enough to accommodate this container, it would sit in a corner in the office out of the way until it was time to go home or anyone else wanted to drink some of it. One soon found out the need for cool as you watched the brew carry on fermenting in the container which just expanded and expanded until it was positively bulging. At this stage, anyone passing by would have to release some of the gas and then tighten the top again before the whole process was repeated. Obviously when the day was done, I would take it home and try and get it in our fridge.

You soon learnt about its potency, and its effects on one's bowels. Again, I have always respected Scrumpy ever since.

The Scrumpy as a gift, despite its effects on oneself if drunk to excess in one go, I soon learnt was a gift of appreciation for the work I had done on that farm. I have found over the years that farmers are generally slow in coming forward in giving thanks for what you have done, after all they were paying the business for your services. Sometimes you would go out of your way to follow up cases, check on the farmer's well-being, just do a little bit more than the job expected. That was always, and still is appreciated.

In several of my jobs I only found out what was thought of me and how I was appreciated after I had left that employment. At times, when you had been slaving away at a calving or lambing in the middle of the night and it was the third time you had been called out of bed that night, then those two words, "*thank you*", were much appreciated. Maybe at times when not a word was said, you felt you were just taken for granted. And those cases that maybe didn't turn out just how you had hoped, then again you as the vet would feel it just as much as the farmer who may have incurred both the cost of your services and the loss of an animal. There was always a time of analysis and reflection after any case.

But through the year those little acts of generosity and appreciation continued, and it has always been pleasing to accept them, although stating it was "*not necessary*".

The scrumpy, a farmer who always gave me half a dozen of his free-range eggs whenever I visited, though more recently that half dozen had grown and on my last visit it was six dozen, I gave most of them to those hard-working girls in the office. Cakes, pies, fruit and vegetables would be other gifts. My latest attempt at wine making is from the donation of some rather scrumptious damsons given to me. The excess to make damson gin which is smooth and gorgeous.

Every year just before Christmas I would do Chris's Tuberculin test and PD his suckler cows to see if they were in calf again. And every year when I had finished, he would go to his truck and produce two 25kg bags of potatoes and a large bag of carrots. I would have a chat to him about the economics involved in growing this vegetable and done well it is a lucrative business.

Another time an unfortunate beef animal broke its leg slipping on the yard while we were Tuberculin testing, and later I would receive a couple of joints and steaks from the animal. This farmer was also fattening a few pigs and I received a large bag of pork sausages from him from one of the pigs. Other small holders would also want to give me a few sausages, but with the diversification in farming and the start of artisan traders selling their produce in local markets and fayres, then here I always felt I should give some sort of donation, this was their livelihood.

Gifts of bottles of wine, the dear lady, Barbara who would always give me a bottle of whisky for seeing the hedgehogs she had rescued. I would gladly have accepted nothing, I certainly didn't want to charge her for saving our natural fauna, but she would insist. Then the next time I visited, there would be another bottle, her graduating up to malts. Again, very much appreciated but unnecessary.

At Christmas, the bottles of wine would appear. Bob would give me his latest favourite from Majestic and luckily, we both preferred reds. Jill would give me mince pies with our coffee after we had finished her last Routine visit before the festival.

And in the autumn, more apples, especially cooking apples. That takes me back to cider. Gloucestershire grew its apples but in my time there I never was a great cider drinker. You could get rough cider in some of the pubs on the banks of the Severn and there would be the odd farmer in the Forest of Dean who would make his own, and after finishing a job for him you would share a glass with him. But on the whole, unless watching cricket in Gloucester with my friend Hugh, I left cider alone. That was bar an occasional visit to a pub in Redbrook on the banks of the Wye which had a whole range of ciders on offer from 4% in strength up to, well one wouldn't want to drink more than one pint of them as they exceeded ten percent.

But in Shropshire there were many farm orchards as well, and in our midst, one of our vets liked to brew his own cider. He had all the kit; a shredder and a water press to produce the juice which would then be put in large plastic decanters to ferment slowly over the winter months.

He introduced other members of staff into brewing their own cider and over the past four or five years it has become a tradition that on a couple of evenings in the autumn we would treat cider making as a Team Building exercise.

Every year we attend three agricultural/ country shows, Shropshire Show in May and two local shows Oswestry and Minsterley in August. They act as publicity for the practice but also offer hospitality to our existing clients, many who would be exhibiting their stock. For years we would buy bottles of wine, tins of beer, lager, cider, and of course soft drinks to offer to clients to quench their thirst, or in the case of the Young Farmers, an opportunity for a free drink. It occurred to us that instead of buying all this booze we should make our own. The cider making became the team building exercise to produce drink for our shows.

We were instructed as we did our rounds to collect or ask farmers for any apples they could spare, whether windfalls or not. Over the period of a few weeks the lambing room would slowly fill up with bags of apples. Then one evening, possibly two depending on the number of apples we had, those willing to give up a couple of hours would set to, starting the production cycle.

One, generally me, would sort and wash the apples, especially the windfalls and cut out any bits that were unsuitable, rotten or too damaged. The cleaned apples would be passed onto those manning the shredder where the apples would be poured in and come out the other end as small segments. These would be passed onto the next crew who would feed them into the water press, and slowly our apple juice would be produced to be put in their fermentation jars. Some would just go home with us just to drink as apple juice. Cookers, eaters and some crab apples, they all went in to produce the cider we wanted.

2019 was looking disappointing, what apples we had were very dirty and quite dry. Would we be able to produce a decent cider? But one day when I was on a farm, I espied a cooking apple tree in their garden with massive juicy apples under it blown off in the wind.

"Could I have some for our cider making?"

"Of course, help yourself."

Myself and the farmer set to and picked up four or five sacks of these juicy apples and they saved our cider that year.

What was always the great unknown was how strong it would be when ready, and also how dry. The fermenting containers would be stored in the roof space above the office, an area used as a storage area, and in winter generally very cool. One would sometimes wander upstairs to see this foul coloured juice fermenting merrily away and you wondered whether it would be drinkable. But when he thought it ready, our master brewer along with a couple of the other vets would bottle it all, some if he thought necessary, he would add a touch of Elderflower cordial to, it would just improve the taste.

Then a staff competition to come up with a name for our product. Grass staggers (hypomagnesaemia, a deficiency of Magnesium most often seen in spring when all the new grass is abundant) is a disease of cattle which in its early stages, produces staggering, an unsteady gate, hyperexcitability but then recumbency, fitting and can often be fatal. "Staggers" was the winning name and due to the high alcohol content of this brew seemed a more than appropriate name. As the writer amongst us, I was asked to come up with a label for it, warning of its potency, any clinical signs that may develop, and of course warning people not to drink and drive if consuming any quantity of it. Nor if they were experiencing any of these clinical signs. The following year the firm took over a Hoof Trimming business, a new clientele to entertain so an alternative brew was produced, appropriately named for our clients new and old, "Toe Curler". Produced again with the appropriate warning label, but generally not as strong as "Staggers", and with that touch of cordial added.

Both were a great success at our local Shows but of course we couldn't sell it, we just give it away to our clients. It became quite a topic of conversation and the first year we produced it we would have many clients arriving at our tent wanting to try it. Word of mouth, its reputation soon grew.

We would supply drink and also a bap of some sort, either from a Hog Roast or a beef roll, the beef coming from a local Longhorn producer. Cider and a roll, all local produce.

The first brew of "Staggers" was potent and sorted out the men from the boys in terms of drinking. That wasn't our aim! Several of our farmers 'wives weren't going to be left out in trying our nectar. Two I can remember in particular, Mrs Roberts who slowly sipped her way through a pint, trying to eat at the same time, but as I chatted to her, her eyes were getting more and more glazed. In the end we decided it was better she didn't finish her pint.

And dear Alison, one of our most lovely clients, always willing to learn to better her farm, and someone who is a lot of fun. She was going to try this "Staggers" and once she had started her pint, she was determined to finish it. Over the course of the next hour, she drank it, slowing markedly but she was determined and although with her words getting more and more slurred, she was going to finish. I would keep bumping into her, not literally, and each time a little more would have disappeared but she would repeat her will to finish it.

Triumph, finally she did and the smile on her face was something to see.

Like many others, the following year she was a bit more reticent about drinking it, this time limiting herself to a half, but it was not as strong as the previous year.

At the Shows in 2019 we would soon run out, the "Toe Curler", it was a triumph, though it had all gone by the time I got around to trying it. We did make limited quantities that year for the Shows of 2020, but Covid put an end to that and to having the Team Building exercise of producing the next lot. I guess somewhere, if Shows do occur, then we will still have the 2019 vintage in reserve.

Cider has been and I hope in the future remains very much part of rural and farming life. It is something I will miss.

9

EPIDEMICS & PANDEMICS

My retirement would come in the midst of a World pandemic, Covid 19. This has been a disease that has affected everyone in the country, in the World either directly from getting the disease or from the effects of lockdown on a nation and how that has affected day to day life, and to any individual what mental strain it may have caused. At the time of writing this chapter, I patiently wait for my call for vaccination whenever that may be. As it turned out I was the first member of staff to receive the vaccine, second dose then the booster.

But the food industry in any disaster must go on, there are millions of mouths to feed in this country and the farming industry is important in that chain, to produce food for you, the general public, to put on your table. We are obviously not self-sufficient in a lot of foodstuffs, perhaps we could be with some sort of food production policy then reducing our dependence on imports both from the Eurozone and the rest of the World. That is another story!

Both farmers work, and ours as keeping their animals healthy and productive must go on, but undeniably our work regimes have changed. COVID-19 had devastated the National economy as well as our day to day lives. But cattle, sheep, pigs, birds suffer too from rapidly spreading disease. Though we have not seen pandemics, in my time we have seen several epidemics in this country that have had severe implications on the financial and welfare state of the industry. Some of these diseases are endemic in parts of the world but not here in the United Kingdom. Here we would have a naïve population of stock with no immunity against incoming disease. These diseases in this country are classed as Notifiable Diseases and bring in special biosecurity and control measures if they manage to get into the country.

There is a trade of livestock, food products as well as migrations of other forms of animals, birds and insects. We are an island but not immune from exotic infections.

In my lifetime we have seen several outbreaks of these diseases across all our species but the most devastating have been Foot and Mouth Disease, Swine Vesicular Disease, Blue Tongue and Avian Influenza. While the human population deals with the effects of COVID-19 in the winter of 2020/1 and then throughout 2021, then we also have yet another outbreak of Avian Flu in the country, meaning domestic poultry are on a similar sort of lockdown to the human population. This would repeat itself again in the winter of 2021/2 with the migration of wild birds to these shores, carrying infection.

The management of these Notifiable Diseases comes under the control of the Animal and Plant Health Agency. We in general practice become OVs, official Veterinarians, having passed various courses with regular updates and accreditation, and can be called upon to help manage these outbreaks, working under the APHA umbrella.

My first experience of Foot and mouth Disease was in the outbreak in 1963. I was still at primary school then with my father having a dairy farm in Oxfordshire. The disease ravaged parts of the country with large numbers of cloven-hoofed animals having to be slaughtered in the outbreak. It is a viral disease, causing severe ulceration, blistering of the mouth, tongue and around the feet. Although it does not kill many animals, it is very infectious and with the effects on the animal and its long-term welfare, then we have a slaughter policy in the United Kingdom to control and eliminate it. Contain, control, and eliminate.

As a schoolboy, did it affect me. It did not quite reach us, stopping about twenty miles away but the worry it would be you next, and my parent's livelihood could be destroyed just like that was a very real threat. Dad was heavily involved with the National Farmers Union then and instigated biosecurity measures in our locality. The introduction of straw pads at the end of our farm drive, soaked in disinfectant to reduce the chance of disease being brought onto our farm on lorry wheels, by the milk tanker picking up our milk every day, as well as us as boys having to go to school and disinfect our footwear leaving the farm and returning in the evening. The smell of the disinfectant is something I will never forget.

We would watch the news on TV in the evening and see the pyres of cattle alight as slaughtered cattle were burnt to kill the virus they were infected with, again a sight one cannot forget. Some farms, especially where I spent my final years in practice in Shropshire were unfortunate to be infected twice. Re-stocking after their original outbreak, only then to find the disease returned and they had to endure the hardship a second time. Some of those memories will stay with me forever.

Infrequently over the years, there would be worrying news of isolated suspect cases of Foot and Mouth, if we have any suspicions, we are obliged to inform the authorities and remain on the farm until it has been confirmed or ruled out. But never anything as serious as 1963, until…

In 2001, in early spring there was a reported case of Foot and Mouth in pigs in an abattoir in Essex. It was confirmed and we all held our breath. Tracings took place that took us back through livestock markets in the North which showed the potential for a massive spread of the disease through many sheep that had gone through market and were now spread about through the country. We were on high disease alert; the threat was real, and the threat of a severe outbreak soon turned out to reality. The number of daily cases started as a trickle but were soon multiplying at an alarming rate. We were in the face of an epidemic. Sheep moved from one market to another, and it was found that Foot and Mouth was affecting stock in Cumbria and then spreading south. A Saturday in February and we had our first case in Shropshire, just north of Telford on a farm I used to go to. This was in piglets, causing sudden death. As in all cases a "Protection Zone" and a "Surveillance Zone" were set up three and ten kilometres in radius from the farm, disease controls were instigated.

OV's were needed and vets from General Practice were expected to answer the call. At the time, we were probably the largest practice in Shropshire and felt it our duty to volunteer. A couple of the other vets in the practice went first, but with the potential restrictions on a vet if he or she came in contact with the disease and then returning to practice and not being able to see our own clients a decision was made that I would go for the duration. This period would last for at least six weeks.

The winter of 2001 had been wet and forage was in short supply for stock. Not only did we have a disease sweeping the country, but also the welfare issues of starving animals, stuck where they were unable to move to other pastures because of restrictions placed on stock movement to risk the spread of disease.

I departed down to Worcester for my briefing, and it was brief, as I shared it with two French vets who had come over to assist but didn't speak English. Apologetically, the powers that be sent me up to their Shrewsbury Office hoping that I had picked up enough information from the mixed translations mainly in French but with a little English. I met the staff in the office there who, throughout my stay, were a tower of strength in getting things done and were always so helpful. I would meet up with Tess some years later when she came to work for us in my final employment. Kitted out with disposable suits, waterproofs, disinfectant and any possible sampling equipment I may need I started my stint.

By this time Shropshire had got up to five cases scattered around the county. For most of those working from Shrewsbury, our initial function was surveillance, making regular checks on premises surrounding Protection Zones to make sure any stock there was not infected. Those farms that had already had cases, there was a total cull and of contiguous farms. Days driving around the area, visiting a premise, fully disinfecting before entering, and again when leaving. Whether it was a premise with one sheep, one goat or a thousand, we had to routinely check them all.

I spent nearly three weeks assisting with this surveillance, staying "clean" as I had not seen any of the disease. But now the authorities were starting to trace these sheep that had come through these markets up North. Sheep can show very little signs, unlike cattle and pigs, but it became policy that these sheep and any contacts would have to be culled. If one of these sheep had been added to a flock of a hundred, then all of them would have to be destroyed.

One Friday, I was asked, along with another vet seconded to DEFRA, to supervise the slaughter of a flock of sheep in the west of the county which contained a couple of these tracer sheep. Over the course of the day nearly three thousand sheep were slaughtered on a sunny spring day, though some of those were because of the welfare situation of no food availability to them.

I went home more than a little dejected only to be served up lamb for my supper. I quickly lost my appetite.

The next day I was going to Twickenham to watch England play rugby, the Sunday I was scheduled to be working again.

I was now classed as "dirty", I had been with suspect contacts, and I would stay that way for the rest of my time with DEFRA. To be clean again I would have to be out of contact for a few days, though as the disease ravaged the country and with the ever-increasing number of vets needed, that period was shortened.

That Sunday I went into work and was sent out to meet up with the slaughter team to cull animals on contiguous farms to a positive case. The alarm to the farmer and his family I will never forget, he had received no warning but knew it would happen at some stage. Then the destruction of his large dairy herd, again something that I will not forget but wish I could.

At least I can say it was done in a humane way and at no stage could I say there was any distress to the cattle "waiting their turn". It was part of my job to ensure this would happen in the most welfare friendly way possible. Cows, calves, bulls, they all had to be destroyed before being loaded up onto lorries and taken to mass burial sites. This did not always happen straight away.

We finished there and were then sent to another cattle farm, and then on again to another which also had water buffalo. It was a soul-destroying day and I suppose started a time of darkness for me.

The slaughter crews were based in Gloucestershire and had to travel every day. That Sunday they would return to base but on the way had another cattle farm to go to on the way back, another vet would join them for that, I think I had experienced enough for one day.

And so, over the coming days and weeks my life would be spent supervising the slaughter of more and more cattle and sheep. I had trained to become a vet to save animal's lives and here I was slaughtering them every day. I guess over that time, vets involved in this would develop a very dark humour but it was almost certainly this that kept us going.

I would travel parts of Shropshire on dark overcast days, not seeing a living thing in sight, even the birds seemed to have disappeared. My mood deepened more. It was to me as if nature knew there was something wrong, spring was on hold.

But cases were slowing, that daily news bulletin I would tune into to see if we had reached a peak. How many new cases today? We were slowly but surely winning the battle, and with spring emerging the pressure on forage was easing as grass grew so the welfare slaughters were also diminishing.

My time was coming to an end with my secondment. At the end of the week, I would finish and then take a seven-day holiday, golfing in Devon with my friends, while I became "clean" again and could return to my practice and once again work with my farmers, curing animals, not killing them!

My last day arrived with some relief, I had a couple of things to do in the morning then I would be back in the Shrewsbury office in the afternoon to finish off my paperwork and say my goodbyes, especially to the girls in the office who had been so supportive.

But at around eleven I received a phone call asking me to go as a second opinion to a farm near the Welsh border, to a suspected case. It was a twenty-five-minute drive away, and on arriving I spoke to the original vet on the premises who took me to show me the cattle she suspected had Foot and Mouth. A quick look and I was on the phone to HQ in London.

To start with in Shropshire, I don't think we were that efficient with it taking some time to get carcases removed from premises once slaughtered, and then to get the disinfection and cleansing process done. This all had to be done before a premise could be declared clean. But now we had the army helping us. I was in contact with my office after Central Office had given the green light as an infected farm to instigate the cull and disposal of all stock on the farm. I needed to blood sample the eighty-odd sheep with the help of a couple of our support workers, and by the time I had finished, the slaughter crew had arrived. The slaughter of cattle and sheep was underway which I supervised along with explaining to the farmer and his wife everything that was happening and what was to follow over the next few days. The army soon arrived to, and I would have to compliment them on their speed and efficiency. What was a distressing situation for farmer and family, we had the whole operation over, carcases loaded onto trucks and removed from the premises by just after seven o'clock. Not a pleasant job but I felt we all had done it well. I started the long journey home across the county, I had finished.

But I had not! I had to go back into the office the following day to do all the paperwork. I was tired, and I was classed as dirty. In days to come I would be asked to join a committee in Worcester trying to pick out what we did well, what we did badly and if in future there would be another outbreak what we could do to be more prepared. Going along, we had learned a lot.

But for me, and I suspect many others involved in the outbreak, it wasn't the end of it. I could not return to my business while on Foot and Mouth duty, nor meet any of my farmers. But that did not stop my social life. My wife and I would be invited to parties, dinners or to the pub with local friends. My wife would be only to please to tell our friends, anyone we met, what I was doing. I was away working for the Government. She would try to involve me in conversations about the outbreak and about some of the things that they were giving bad news about it.

I didn't want to talk about it, my close friends could see that as I retreated into myself at these stories. They could see in my eyes, my expressions, how uncomfortable with the topic and would try and take me away from it. My humour had changed and had become very dark, it all had produced much mental strain on me. I guess in the end it made me look at my marriage as well and how little my wife understood me. A few months later we separated.

My golfing trip to Devon when I had finished my stint was enjoyable. But I was well aware that we were going to an area that would also be worried about Foot and Mouth, and I didn't want to be in conversation with locals that I had just finished and was still classed as "dirty". I asked my golfing companions not to talk about it after an initial chat, I just wanted to put it to the back of my mind. I had become very withdrawn and in fairness to them, they did their best to try and cheer me up but realised how much I had been affected by my experiences.

For me, I had my doubts if everything we had dealt with was really Foot and Mouth and that I had assisted in the needless slaughter of many farm animals.

It was the start of a downwards spiral for me.

Over my time in practice, we have had to deal with Tuberculosis (still ongoing), Brucellosis, Enzootic Bovine Leukosis, Swine Vesicular Disease, Equine Infectious Anaemia and BSE. I had seen the first case of this in Shropshire and many cases of it after that, and some of those cases were quite distressing. But nothing was in the scale of that 2001 that I had to assist with. Later came Blue Tongue and again the worry of a midge born disease that could easily spread throughout the country. And another Foot and Mouth scare which turned out to be very localised and didn't affect us in the Midlands.

But in the winter of 2016/7 Avian Influenza arrived in the Country, brought in by migrating birds. Bird and Swine influenza viruses can be pathogenic to man and can mutate rapidly. We had another health scare. In the Practice I now worked in; we had a contract with APHA that they could call in vets from practice to assist them in disease control. Our area included Lincolnshire, a county affected by this outbreak, mainly in turkey fattening units. The call came out for vets to go to Lincoln for disease control and surveillance. Two of our vets were volunteered, the first for three days and then the second for the next four days. I was that second person and so set off for Lincoln early on a Wednesday morning, freely admitting I didn't know a lot about Avian flu nor poultry in general.

I joined up with other vets from Midlands Practices, starting with a brief Health and Safety meeting, health check and then we all went into a briefing. We were told we would have a lecture on blood sampling so that we could undertake the surveillance work necessary (I was assured before we went that there would be no blood testing involved!). We seemed to sit around endlessly, a recurring theme, thinking we must have been sent here for some reason. At last, our lecture took place, and we were kitted out with PPE, especially respirators which had to fit exactly, and we were given our first tasks. Three of us would be sent up to the Louth area to inspect backyard poultry, one premises each, a total of about thirty birds between them. For that, each of us would have to dress up in full protective gear, two boiler suits, two pairs of gloves, wellies, the respirator and any personal equipment e.g. mobile phones would be wiped with a disinfectant and placed in plastic bags. It took a lot longer to dress and undress than it did to inspect the poultry. A man was even sent to spy on us to make sure we had dressed properly to ensure biosecurity was maintained. I had already spotted him lurking in a lay-by not far away, not that I was going to take any short cuts.

Job finished and it was back to HQ in Lincoln to debrief and then find my hotel. I found I was staying at the same place as one of the other vets sent to Lincoln, the lovely Vicki who was just starting her Veterinary career. She was great company in the evening when we would dine together whether in the hotel or in the city. It was good to talk to her about her, her present job and her aspirations for the future. By the end of the stay, we had decided she should move on for better career prospects, it rather sounded if she had been abandoned in Lincoln by her bosses. A lovely, lovely lady and she made the stay far better than it would have been otherwise (and I am pleased to say after making that job move, her career has really taken off).

The second day it was another trip to the Louth area to inspect one backyard flock of birds, about thirty and then sit around the office twiddling my fingers but trying to help the staff where I could in some of their office work.

Day three was worse, nothing to do except help sort out calls for the next day. I took myself off early to explore Lincoln Cathedral, quite eerie as evening drew in, especially in thick fog. The walk up Steepside was exhilarating, and I would love to visit the city again sometime.

Day four saw another infected premises and it was decided I would go down there to act as Welfare Officer for the cull of the turkey flock. There was a lot of preparation involved, including being given Tamiflu to protect against any chance of human infection from the virus.

We were to meet up at the farm the following morning. After dressing and a quick briefing, my first job was to inspect all the six houses to assess the state of the birds, and whether some should be euthanised as soon as possible. Most birds would be gassed humanely in chambers, a process that took only a few seconds.

This was the most horrific disease I had ever seen in terms of morbidity and mortality rates. The first house I entered was littered with carcases, with other birds severely ill, others slightly depressed, some normal. I would mark those that were in extremis to be dispatched straight away. But the disease was so rapid that by the time I had walked around the house once, by the time I had reached my starting point, other birds would have deteriorated so quickly that a speedy humane destruction was then necessary for them. I was relieved when the cull proper was able to begin so we could put these birds out of their misery.

Eighteen thousand birds took us into the next day, and the next. I won't spend any time on some of the inefficiencies I encountered in this process, it could have been done quicker without a lot more thought about how we undertook the task. All I can say is that those last birds to be destroyed were from the healthier houses and so didn't undergo any unnecessary suffering.

For me, I had to spend a day longer in Lincoln than intended, but I had checked out of my hotel and had to return back to my practice after that. It didn't have the same impact on me as the 2001 Foot and Mouth outbreak, you could see these birds were ill and rapidly dying so we were doing what was kindest for them. But like 2001 I had been involved in the culling of thousands of livestock. I had changed over those years and so it did not affect me so much, other than being more confident in myself, I wish perhaps that I had been more forceful in some of my suggestions to speed the process up. Some of us had field experience, I got the impression those in charge had not.

Thankfully, it was not too long after me leaving Lincoln that the Avian Flu epidemic of 2017 finished. I had a trip to Kenya to look forward to, to climb a mountain and go on Safari. I would be debriefed on my return to my proper job, but whether any of the suggestions we put forward were ever heeded, I do not know.

In my last months, weeks of practice, I waited to see if I would be called upon again in 2021. Avian influenza was in the country again and although there had been few outbreaks, they had been miles apart emphasising the threat that migrating birds bring in the spread of the disease. Our vets had been called upon to go to Hereford and Leicester so far, I awaited my call if that was necessary for the week I was on standby. The call never came much to my relief as spring brought about a reduction then elimination of new cases.

Over the years, even in my time, we have seen new diseases that have threatened the health and welfare of our farm species. No doubt in the course of time there will be others. Some, certainly in this country, we have been able to eradicate. Brucellosis and BSE to name two, but our job continues to try and eradicate others, to limit disease spread when epidemics occur and to ensure the future of our farming industry by maintaining the health of our national flocks and herds.

As I reach retirement, it is us humans too who are now threatened as Covid-19 decimates the country. I have dealt with epidemics, now a real pandemic. I don't have to write about how it has affected the lives of many, we all have our personal experiences. But just because we have experienced lockdowns, the country in different Tiers bringing about different restrictions in different parts of the country, lifting of restrictions and then tightening, it doesn't stop animals getting ill themselves.

How has it affected us as vets in farm animal work? We are classed as key workers and so work has gone on as normally as it can. Were we ahead of the game, the first lockdown started on March 23rd in 2020, happy birthday Rod! But we had already gone to remote working seven days previously. I cleared my desk and took home everything I thought I may need to limit having to go into the office. With social distancing and the other recommendations, then staff contact with each other was severely restricted. Vets were not allowed into the building, if one got infected or tested positive, we couldn't risk it spreading to other vets, nor having a number of staff in self-isolation. If we needed to pick up drugs, we would phone in and they would be placed on a table outside the building for us to collect from there. The office staff and pharmacy would have their own work area bubbles, the staff would be split into two teams so that in the first lockdown, only half the staff would go in, alternating. How wonderfully supportive they were to us remote workers.

For us out on the farms, then before each call we would have to check on the health status of everyone on the farm, and how we could do our jobs as best we could while observing social distancing. If work quietened off to begin with, it did soon pick up again as "turn-out" happened and we saw the usual problems with cows on spring grass and of course it was lambing time. Tuberculin testing presented challenges where a vet and farm staff would be working in close proximity of each other, especially with holding young calves. Problems arose, we found ways of getting round them. Clever use of straps to restrain cows that needed a Caesarean or stomach operation. Problems arose and we generally responded to them.

The farming community and us vets managed, working in harmony but safely. Biosecurity is a normal part of our way of life. Washing hands is a regular occurrence, we usually wear gloves anyway. It wasn't hard for us to follow the "rules", masks were up to our discretion. I, wearing glasses, especially in winter found they would usually steam up with a mask of any sort, we had to be practical.

As the months wore one were able to relax some of our restrictions. An area was made for us to be able to work in the building, isolated away from the office staff, so we could access company data and work on reports and health plans that we couldn't access at home. Shropshire had stayed as a low-level infection area. But around the Christmas period of 2020 we did see rising levels and the start of positive cases in our rural community. We had to restrict those farms, while isolating, to emergency calls only.

Ourselves, other than a couple of self-isolations, we so far had escaped any cases though personally, friends and neighbours had succumbed. We must have been doing something right!

I guess the hardest part had been the lack of contact between your work colleagues, some I hadn't even met yet. Clinical discussions would be done on Zoom, otherwise you may occasionally be in the car park at the same time as a colleague and you could chat briefly, otherwise you were on your own.

Some enjoyed remote working, others found it hard. For me, if we were busy and I was out on farm a lot then I was happy, but when we were quiet and there were days when there were no calls, then I found the isolation hard. But I had made the executive decision that I wasn't going to let it get me down. I had some great chats with the girls in the office, and at times I hoped I made their life a bit more enjoyable while they were stuck inside their bubbles at work. If we could all keep smiling, then we would get through it together.

I had one incident where one of the other vets had been on farm and the man working the cattle crush was found to be infected. The vet had to self-isolate as she was in close contact, and I had to go and finish her job three days later. The farm worker had been operating the crush, I would be examining the cattle in the same crush, my first job on farm would be to make sure that the crush was disinfected before we did anything else. Challenges, challenges.

I think what we can say throughout the pandemic is we had done our best to observe the rules and that at no stage had animal health or welfare suffered because of it. Avian Flu again in the winter of 2020/1 had added extra pressures especially when it has meant long distances from home. Now we are coping.

What it has shown us is that not only does animal disease and epidemic affect our routine, but so does human disease, especially with the challenges Covid-19 have thrown at us. When this is all over then we may be able to reflect and review how we worked through it. I would expect, as will be the same in many industries, we may stick to some of those practices we have started in working through it all. Working remotely may become more the norm but being able to access the office when necessary. Our delivery service for drugs on farm will continue. Nothing stays the same, I can see one of the effects of the pandemic is that in the future we will function more efficiently. Night calls and weekend duties will go on, cows do not know what day of the week it is: or do they! There will be change.

It won't affect me; I will be retired. What I had missed during the pandemic is just bumping into our farmers and chatting to them, whether about their business or just about life in general. And at the time of writing this, I worry that with no social gatherings, then I may not be able to say my goodbyes to people I have known and worked for over many years, in the way I may have hoped. We shall see. I have loved the farming community and cannot just walk away without a proper farewell.

10

THE CHANGING FARMING SCENE

I have been involved in farming all my life, from my childhood days on my parents' farm between Swindon and Oxford in The Vale of the White Horse, until my retirement from work in rural Shropshire. Probably the only time I have not been involved directly was my first three years at University in Bristol when we were in the city. It is therefore not surprising that I have a love of the countryside and everything to do with it. Despite having lived in Telford for the past thirty years I am still very much a country boy, happiest in the open spaces of rural England, breathing in clean air, enjoying the fauna and flora of what this country of ours has to offer. I think that is why I eventually chose this job above others that I contemplated, the chance to work with animals on farms, an environment that I knew from my childhood days.

Sadly, now my father suffers from dementia, but it is good to take him back to his early days in farming, he was the son of a garage owner in Warwickshire. Not only is it good to get him to stimulate his mind, but also interesting to reflect at the end of my career how much things have changed on the farm. Dad started off on a County Council Smallholding, buying his first half dozen cows from the farm auction of the previous tenant. Some real old bad-tempered Shorthorns and Ayrshires that in the mid-fifties were milked by hand in an old shippen.

This would be reminiscent of the cow byres portrayed in Herriot's Yorkshire Dales, small farms with walled fields and the farmer milking just a few cows. I have never been to that part of the country, on my bucket list of places to visit and I would love to walk the Dales. Whether much has changed up there, it wouldn't be for me to comment. But certainly, in those parts of the country I have worked, then there has been much change.

Dad expanded from his original few cows to milking a hundred and twenty before he sold the herd to move down to Exmoor. A milking parlour replaced the shippen, cubicles became the cow housing, slurry lagoons replace the muck heap, and fields got larger as he adopted a set stocking system. Though with the landscape of his farm, no hedges were dug up to make fields larger, only wooden fences removed (which were rotting anyway). The only real change to the landscape was the loss of trees, we had many old, huge elm trees on the farm, and they soon disappeared as they were ravaged by Dutch Elm Disease. The sight of huge flocks of Peewits was common as they nested on the ground amongst the cows. It was a miracle that nests weren't destroyed by cattle foraging, the cows just passed them by. If I were to return to that part of the country now, I would find that most of the land was now arable, all those small farms now gone and integrated into larger concerns. Dad may have been ahead of his time, very progressive in his ideas, but that sort of change has carried on over the years up to the present day.

My first experiences as a qualified vet would have been in Devon, where the small family farm was the norm. Milking parlours were more common and a necessity on expanding herds. We saw very much a mixture of different types of farms. Smallholdings, next door to each other so there would be a concentration of farms close to one another. Herds of fifty, sixty, seventy cows and probably a few sheep as well, plus hens running around the yard. The workforce tended to be family members, and, in all probability, sons would take over from dad when he hung his boots up. The traditional British breeds of cows were seen, Friesians, Ayrshires, and a few Jerseys. There was the start of the trend to use continental bulls, Charolais, Limousines, Blonde Aquitaine's as sires on these cows to produce big beef calves which would fatten well on grass, mature British beef. The traditional Hereford and Angus bulls were being used less and less.

Cows were part of the family and would all have names. Dad had his Greek God families, Andromeda, Persephone, Aphrodite; his wind family, Mistral, Tradewind, Sirocco; his nut family, Hazel, Walnut, Nutkin; his flower and berry families. A heifer calf would get a name which would carry on in that family…. but we never had a Buttercup. They were nurtured and tended for, a loss would be felt by everyone on the farm, the cow would always be someone's favourite. Cows grazed on lush grass fields full of flowers, foraged through hedgerows, not always to their good. It seemed an idealist way of life, but also a hard way of life. A trip to market was the closest thing to a day out, long hours were worked from dawn until dusk, milking often being done late at night when all the other jobs had been done. Then it was an early rise and start all over again.

As a vet, I would drive from one farm to the next, most likely next door and because of that one could do fifteen, sixteen, maybe more calls in a day. With the utmost certainty, whatever you had been called to see, there would always be a lame cow or two to see as well. Never mentioned in the call out, but when you got out of the car, you would always hear in that wonderful Devon dialect,

"While you'm here, just a couple of lame ones".

With that a long rope would be flung over the nearest beam, one end secured to the cow's leg, the other to haul the leg into the air so the vet could examine and pare the foot. Usually, a trodden-on stone or nail which had punctured the sole of the foot, with careful cutting we would find an abscess and release the pus from the lame foot. No pus, and the farmer would always be disappointed. What a joy it was to have a cow hopping around on one leg while you were examining the other, trying to do your job while supporting the affected limb on your knee, getting back ache leaning over and hoping you would not slip on the smooth but mucky floor. How many times did one get kicked doing this, and would just have to brush yourself down and get on with it? Over time you did find ways of securing the leg better, and then with the advent of cattle crushes life became far easier, and safer. Those were the smaller farms, now few and far between. A traditional way of producing milk from grass, or conserved grass, hay or silage, to feed the cows in the winter.

Long has it been my dream that these less intensive farms will survive into the future, despite the financial pressures of the modern dairy industry. One of my favourite farms I still attend, run by Jill and her father Clifford, still follow the plans of these more traditional farming methods. Jill started her career working in the financial sector, working herself up to being a bank manager in a busy town. But she got fed up with the rat race and came home to help her father and now runs the farm. Like most places, the cows have got bigger and give more milk than in the past, but this is still a very traditional type of dairy farm. The welfare standards are probably higher than on any other farm I go to, each cow is still an individual and easily recognised. And she has a name! Care and thought goes into all the running on the farm, and whether it is because it is still a small family farm, now of a hundred cows or it is because the staff are female, one always knows how much they care about their cattle and what a loss it is if one of them must go because of illness or accident. I will return to Jill later.

But even in the late seventies, early eighties things were starting to change. As a vet, it was a great learning curve doing so many calls on so many farms every day, giving one a good grounding in any and all conditions you may see in farm practice. Calvings and lambings were plentiful, there was even the odd farrowing of sows in difficulty in labour. We had Tuberculosis, Brucellosis and Warble Fly to contend with, diseases we were trying to eradicate though in those days we spent more time Brucellosis testing than Tuberculosis testing. How things have changed over forty years. Operations on cattle and sheep were common. All in all, it was a great experience for a young vet who was keen to learn in a busy and pleasant practice where there was plenty of support from one's colleagues.

Times move on and already farms were starting to get bigger and more specialised. The small family herd of forty or fifty cows were increasing with the more progressive farmers going up to well over a hundred cows. Milking units were changing as technology improved, the milking process was becoming more efficient and not so much of a manual task. Genetics were improving, slowly but surely the British Friesian was being replaced by Holstein cattle who produced far more milk. With that, the science of nutrition was changing too as the feeding requirements of these "milk producing machines" were far different from those of the Friesians and Jerseys producing milk from grass. The planting of maize was beginning and becoming more common, especially in the warm counties in the Southwest of England. A fast-growing crop in the right conditions that will produce a high quality and high energy forage for cattle, fed as maize silage in the winter months. With such a high-quality feed, farmers could also consider changing their milk production patterns, not being so reliant on spring grass to maximise milk yields. It is interesting now to look back on how far ahead of the ball game dad was when he was milking cows.

Those changes meant that our routines as vets were also changing. These bigger farms were increasing their efficiency and with that the economics of milk production were becoming more important. It was vital to get cows back in calf quickly to maintain an efficient production cycle. We still did our day-to-day fire brigade work, the births, the ill cows, the lame cows and the continual cycle of disease testing. But the role of fertility work was becoming more and more important in our daily lives. Now we would start visiting farms on a regular basis doing what we call Routine visits, going to the same farm every week, fortnight or four weeks depending how many cows they had. These visits would usually be a first call of the day for a vet, and it generally tended to be the same vet who attended one particular farm each visit. This allowed a familiarity between farmer and vet, so they knew what they were trying to achieve in terms of results. It allowed for cows to be checked on a regular basis to see if their reproductive tract had cleaned up after calving (there was no endometritis), to see cows that had not come bulling when it was time to serve them again, and give any hormone treatment if necessary, and then to pregnancy diagnose them some weeks later to see if they were in calf. This was the scene people love to joke about with us putting our arms up the cow's rectum and having a feel around inside, palpating the cow's uterus and ovaries through the rectal wall. We would be able to gently pick up the delicate foetal membranes in our fingers and feel them slipping away as we eased our touch, yes, she is in calf again. The farmer would also present any other cows he needed looking at, and of course there would be a lame cow or two as well. We would then discuss with the farmer or herdsman the results of the visit, and any actions or investigations that needed to be done if things were not going as well as hoped, blood tests, feed analysis etc.

Times were moving on rapidly with far more science coming into the job. Despite that, in the beautiful scenery of East Devon, work was enjoyable, relaxing and fun. Those farmers were lovely people to work for and all in all it was a great part of my life. Sadly, there were the occasional suicides amongst them, farmers who seemed so outwardly happy, but inside the pressures of farming, the losses and disappointment you get looking after livestock, it all becoming too much for them. Happiness, sadness, it was a great wrench to move on from his lovely area and its people.

Life was very different on the banks of the Severn when I moved to Gloucestershire. North of the river in Lydney we had a contrast of farms, those in the Forest of Dean and those on the grass growing lands reaching down to the river. Foresters in those days were a very insular lot and one never felt accepted by them as an outsider. Despite that, my children, as they were born in an area technically part of the Forest, did and do have Forester's rights, whatever they be.

The Forest was an area of woodland interspersed with villages, common land and some farmland. Not upland, but certainly higher than those farms on the banks of the river. The climate did tend to be a little harsher, often in winter it may snow there but not on the lowland pastures only a few miles away. But then they would be liable to flooding especially in high spring tides, with the "Bore" coming up the river before it narrows quickly before Gloucester. An area with a fascinating diversity of scenery and industry. The Forest historically had been an area of Opencast mining and so the villages tended to look a bit dirty and run down. What farms there were tended to be small with a few beef and sheep. The Forest has areas of common land where farmers have grazing rights in the summer with sheep wandering freely on commons and in the woodland, hefted sheep. I was once called out by the RSPCA to see a lame sheep near The Speech House, the site where the Verderer's courts would take place to settle any disputes that may arise between the locals, an old tradition. A Sunday afternoon and they would have no-one to help me. I didn't know quite what they expected me to do, take the sheep home with me or what, but I was obliged to go. There were hundreds of sheep lying about and grazing, which one was lame I will never know because having spent ages wandering around them all, I never found the poor animal.

Buildings tended to be old, handling facilities very basic and as a result vetting was a challenge. Farming tended to be very traditional and some of those old-fashioned remedies, "housewife's" tales, would still be tried before a vet was called. We were second choice and so faced an uphill struggle to succeed in treatments as too much pathology may have already taken place before we saw the animal. I guess at this time and with these frustrations, I did doubt whether this was the profession I wanted to stay in. Was I really doing any good if the farmer's attitude were that the vet was just an expense and would only be called out at the last resort?

The dairy farms on the banks of the river tended to be far bigger and more modern. There were big dairy units and beef units in far more up to date premises. This was a big milk producing area and we had herds up to three hundred cows in numbers plus the youngstock they would be rearing to be future milkers. Here, it was far more like the farming I had experienced in Devon, perhaps with larger herds but it did not cover such a large area so there were not so many of them. But here there was not the relaxed atmosphere of Devon. Changing times? Or were there just more pressures on farming as we moved into the eighties and towards the nineties? But here was a place that I could use the knowledge I had learnt in Devon and hopefully apply it to help these Gloucester farmers. Afterall, I would now be classed as an experienced vet. A mixture of Routine fertility work and fire brigade vetting, it was interesting but sometimes very frustrating.

Farmer DIY vetting often took place, with them trying to treat the cow or sheep before considering calling the vet out. If in doubt with their treatment, they would often say when they did call the vet, "we weren't sure what to treat it with, so we only gave half the dose".

I wonder why it did not work! We were left then to work a miracle and often could not.

We were entering a time when along with the Agricultural Training Board, and more farmers sons going to Agricultural College, the on-farm person was trying to be more equipped to do their own vetting. Courses on topics such as on lameness and foot trimming meant that we would not see the same number of lame cows as I did in Devon. With that, handling facilities were improving so farmers were happier to have a go themselves.

Changing times? Or just a progression in farming ideas, I am not sure. Through my lifetime associated with the industry, farming has tended to go through cycles, good times, and hard times. The good times, farmers made money and were happy to call out the vet when necessary, the hard times, then the opposite. We were an unnecessary expense and to be avoided. Every decision we made would be questioned, negative outcomes would be criticized. In those times, vetting was hard and pressurized, in the good times it was fun and relaxed although you were probably doing the same thing.

I crossed over the other side of the river. Again, a good grass growing area with a mixture of dairy farming along with as you ascended the Cotswold Edge, far more beef and large sheep flocks on big arable farms. A different and more intensive form of farming with high production and performance expected. The people were different again, easy to work with, appreciative of your efforts and willing to follow your advice. Was it different now because I was the main farm vet in a two-man practice? Or again, was it that I was more experienced or just that I had a more receptive audience? A combination of all three I think, with the added pressure that we were in the heartland of another couple of large farm practices. If we did not perform, then there was plenty of good competition that farmers could go to if dissatisfied with our service. Farmers did tend to be very loyal; it would take a lot to upset them but that did not mean that you could relax in your approach into looking after their stock.

Working here was very much like that in Devon, Routine visits, and a lot of fire brigade visits, other than nights and weekends, I did all the farm work. We were a small band and so in terms of progression, new techniques, equipment etc, then we did not move forward. I had no-one else to share experiences with, nor to learn the new ways.

Again, a lovely area to work in, but in terms of a future I had to move on. Shropshire, here I come!

Shropshire is a very diverse county as it harbours the River Severn further upstream on its journey to the sea. A county of plains, of river valleys, of hills as one looks towards the Welsh border and the Stretton Hills. A county that I knew was somewhere sort of west of Birmingham but that was about all I knew. It was an area of England there that I knew nothing about other than my two weeks lambing experience in Bishops Castle when I was a student. Now I was going to work there. That was at the start of 1989, and I have been there ever since. Though living in Telford, I would never call it home. It is a very rural county with historic towns such as Shrewsbury and

Ludlow, but also has one of the country's new towns in Telford. A dialect amongst the real locals that matches that of those lovely Devonian people, but a county full of immigrants such as me, who have moved there for jobs, especially in the new town.

Within this rural setting there are all sorts of different types of farms from backyard "the Good Life" types to small holdings with mixed stock to large dairy units, my largest now being four hundred plus. This was my Shropshire before the turn of the millennium and the start of a new venture in my career. Much to my surprise on my first visit to this large unit, I found the cowman was instantly recognisable to me as Doug, who used to work for dad when he was doing his sandwich course on farming at Agricultural College back in the early seventies. What a small world it can be at times!

Telford is a new town, built on farmland surrounding other former towns, Wellington and Madeley amongst others. Some of these farmers had been bought out on compulsory purchase orders and been given new farms in the surrounding area. With that they would often have new buildings and parlours, and bigger herds than they had before. Progress, but with those restraints of the farming cycle when times were good, and times were hard. But I guess I faced some of the same restrains as I faced in Gloucestershire, farming was not that progressive, it was standing still by in large, other than the only one or two or wanted to see a rich future in the industry.

In the bad times we were starting to see more famers giving up milking, and switching either to beef, rearing cattle to fatten, or as in so much of the country, going over to arable and growing corn. An easier life, less staff needed and only really the busy times were at planting and harvesting. Life would continue very much as it did before for the first fifteen years of my career in Shropshire, and the County has seen two thirds of my working life, then certainly over the last fifteen years then change there has been. Cycles of quick change and slow change, but those changes in farming practices and in our work have been far reaching.

As they say, "Things will never be the same again".

I moved to work in a practice just outside Shrewsbury in 2005. Again, I had become frustrated where I was, then in Much Wenlock. There seemed little ambition in the farming community as change was coming. It was very much an attitude of "what will happen will happen", the practice slowly but surely was devoting its energy more to horses, dogs and cats. I felt out on a limb and as I would later find out, after the Foot and Mouth epidemic of '01 and of going through a divorce, my mental state wasn't where it should be. I was asked to join a new exclusively farm practice that had been started up some fifteen months previously, beginning as a two-man band but rapidly increasing in numbers, being part-time I would be vet four and a half. Based in a small industrial unit just outside town, this was the type of practice I really wanted to work in, the first of its kind since I had left Devon.

Here was a different type of farming, especially the dairy farming. Whereas most of the farms around Telford were now arable, there were still a few of the small holdings that I went to that had a few cows, most had sold up and put the land down into corn. The surrounds of the town that I came to in 1989 was a very different scene to that of the present day.

But around Shrewsbury, and especially in the Rea Valley, we were in cow country. Yes, there is some arable and over time there have been more and more people going out of the dairy industry. But what dairy farms persisted were serious and we started seeing many herds of two fifty, three hundred cows. And some got bigger and bigger and bigger to the extent that we now have thousand cow, fifteen hundred cow herds that became more and more demanding of one's time. Despite fluctuating milk prices and in the farming cycle there have been lucrative years. But there have also been hard years when the cost of production has exceeded the sale price to the farmer, these real dairy men have stuck at it, bringing a new efficiency into their farming methods to maximise production while being careful with costs.

Here, the days of the small dairy have gone and will never be seen again. Being able to compete and produce milk on a large scale, the opportunities for a young person wanting to milk cows has gone, the money needed to buy suitable buildings and a large enough herd to be productive and profitable have gone. The industry is now there for those already in it unless outside money is invested, entrepreneurs looking for a new venture, as they come into farming. I used to go to one quaint old farm run by the Edwards brothers. They milked their thirty cows every day through an old-fashioned milking shed, no raised standings here for the cows, so milking was a back breaking job as you leant down to attach the units to the cow's teats. It was only a couple of years ago that they finally gave up milking. They were still milking cows into their eighties! Real old-fashioned farmers, the likes of which we will never see again.

The Jill's of this world will keep the traditions of the family farm going. Traditional dairy farming, producing milk off grass with more traditional dairy breeds, still using Friesian bloodlines rather than the modern Holsteins. But there will come a time when the costs of carrying on, replacing machinery, modernising the parlour and buildings, and staffing, will see an end to these types of farms as well. The tradition of son following on from father disappears, other careers look far more appealing and in time the likes of Jill and her family farm, small by comparison with the modern dairy farm, will disappear too.

Farmers do not milk cows anymore; they harvest milk. The more efficient they can be the more profitable and their chances of survival are better. That is not bad for the cow, the modern Holstein is made to produce milk and if you feed her properly, she will quite happily oblige. On a positive note, for cow and farmer, the advent of Farm Assurance, of Red Tractor logos, has meant that health and welfare standards must be met for any milk buyer to want to buy your product. Those same farm assurance standards have followed into the pig, the sheep and the beef industries ensuring that the food put on your (the consumers) table is produced to the highest standards of animal care. The likes of Tesco's, Waitrose and Sainsburys have a big say in the product they are buying and retailing in their supermarkets and how that product will be produced.

Farming is becoming far more of science. That has impacted both on the way the farmer thinks, and on the way us as farm vets now go about our day to day lives.

The twenty first century has seen a rapid acceleration in the science and technology applying to all sectors of the industry, though the beef industry has probably been affected least. Milking parlours have changed from the Abreast and Herring bone parlours of my father's days to multi-unit harvesting machines. Parlours where you would milk six or eight cows at a time are now catered for milking twenty cows at a time, some even more. The limiting factor would be the cowman and how many he could cope with. His jobs being teat preparation, attaching the milking cluster and then teat dipping after the machine has been removed. Even some of that is now automated, now allowing the cowman to assess udder and cow health while they are in the parlour. We have huge Rotary parlours that can take forty-eight cows on them, the cowmen standing at one point initiating the milking process before the next cow enters the "wheel" as the last one moves on. With two or three milkers, they can milk hundreds of cows in a short space of time. The cows face inwards, and when they have finished being milked, and reach the exit point, their tail bar lifts and they can reverse out to go back to feeding or resting. Even other parts of the routine are now automated. Cluster removal, when the cow has no more milk to give, is now triggered by technology. Teat spraying with disinfectant to protect the open milk canal from bacterial invasion post-milking is now, especially in these rotary parlours, an automated function with a spray of an Iodophor coming up from the floor onto the teats. Speedy milking that also makes the cowman's life easier. If it is easier for him, then this feeling of calm follows likewise for the cow experiencing less stress throughout the milking process. Milk output is monitored and goes into a computer so if there is any significant daily drop in yield which may indicate ill-health, then a warning will be given. Technology has advanced the milking process so much in modern days.

Then there are the Robots, where cows go into a unit themselves to be milked when they want to. Technology that cleans the teats then lines up the teat cups to the individual teats before attaching them and milking then commences. Again, the automated warnings if yield is down, synching into the herdsman's phone so he can check on the cow.

Cows will have monitors on them measuring feed intake, rumen function, other factors that will be fed into a computer and give warnings if a cow is below par.

Breeding, genetics, the use of sexed semen so that you only produce heifer calves from your best cows. The rest will be served with beef bulls which going forward rules out the need for that emotional topic of slaughtering male dairy bulls at birth as they have no value.

Monitoring growth rates in both beef cattle and dairy replacement is the norm now, as habits and production systems have changed, and the animal is encouraged to reach its potential at an earlier age.

The use of synchronised breeding techniques is now common. Lambing can be done in days instead of weeks, the same with cows to tighten a calving pattern to optimise production at peak grass growth. The use of flushing cows and ewes, super ovulating them to produce multiple eggs which that are removed and then implanted in other females so more high-quality progeny of high genetic merit can be produced. This is now common practice in high value flocks and herds.

Animal housing is advancing and with it, animal handling systems. Gone are the days I have described earlier of a rope over a high beam being used for lame cows. Now we have specialised crushes that restrain the animal securely and safely, some tip the cow on her side so the bottoms of the feet are clearly visible and easy to work with, restoring foot shape. Pedicures for cows are now a regular feature of the modern dairy farm, keeping feet healthy on the adage that if a cow can't walk, it can't feed and ruminate. Foot care in cattle is not the back breaking exercise it used to be, and other than the severe cases that may need surgery or veterinary intervention, then that role in cattle practice has largely been taken over by specialised foot trimmers. They will take their specialised equipment from farm to farm, seeing a lot of cows on each destination either for a quick file or more intense foot care, working to keep the feet healthy to prevent future lameness.

Our work on these farms has changed in these times. Yes, we still do the fire brigade work, but now even more time is spent on Routine visits, trying to maintain these cows for maximum production, health and fertility. We work alongside advisors on breeding, on feeding and on economics to try and produce a food stuff to the General Public efficiently and in a welfare friendly way. Farm Assurance standards are set to maintain and monitor that all requirements are met, and the health of animals is not compromised.

If I have not mentioned pigs very much, rest assured that in those years then technology in production has also continued to develop along with ever improving welfare standards. Much pig housing is now in electronically controlled environments, meaning they do not get cold nor too hot. Again, the genetic improvement in the national pig herd goes on, along with a pyramid of high health feeder herds supplying high quality gilts and boars to pig units.

One also must not forget the Organic movement, perhaps a return to more traditional farming methods where management takes the place of some of the technological advances. Yields do not tend to be so high in these systems of farming but to some members of the public, this is the way they want their food produced.

It has meant our job has changed a lot from my early days. Gone are the days of seeing a cow on one farm, going next door and seeing another and so on. A busy day then of fifteen to twenty calls is now replaced by visits seeing twenty, fifty, more cows on one visit. Six or seven calls in a day is a busy day, sometimes it may only be two or three taking all day. More time spent in front of a computer analysing data, reviewing laboratory data, longer drives between farms, an ever-changing picture.

I of course now talk of my Shropshire experiences. I do not know but would suspect in the more upland areas of the country, the Scottish and Welsh Hill and the Fells and Dales then farming may still be a bit more traditional, and still very much more family orientated. The farmer's sons stay at home to work and at some stage in the future take over the farm. In those more rural areas, there may still be a workforce to carry on farming traditions. In Shropshire that workforce is diminishing, and staffing becomes ever more reliant on foreign labour. Polish, Romanians, and Latvian workers are common. It is strange from my point of view that if you ask them anything or for a helping hand, they suddenly do not speak a word of English! British people do not seem to want a life on the land anymore, is it too hard and the hours too long. For me it has been an unforgettable experience, although as a vet, viewed slightly from the outside.

With time, everything changes. Farming has become an industry serving the nation to put food on its table. It has become more intensified, more scientific and that has spread into our role in the industry as well. But what it has not become is an industry of factory farming. There is still a compassion amongst the majority of livestock keepers for the animals they look after. I cannot deny there are a few bad eggs, but then if one looks at the injustices man does to his own kind, that is hardly surprising. Will change be so rapid as over the next few years only time will tell.

Life will never be the same again, especially for me. I am retiring!

11

LOST AND FOUND

Over the years there are somethings that do not change, and one of those things is our propensity to be able to lose things. Vets are no different, in fact we are probably the worst. Almost every practice, whether catering for large or small animals, will have a notice board in their reception area where they put up general information. Also notices from clients, whether selling a service, puppies, kittens looking for new homes, many things. But we will frequently, even in a farm practice, be asked to put notices up about lost pets. This is not a problem; we are only glad to help and will always be delighted if pet and owner can be re-united, especially if we are able to assist in this.

Rural crime is on the increase with both machinery and livestock frequently disappearing from farms, even with their increased security. It is not uncommon now to find large electronically operated gates as farm entrances to reduce the risk of illegal entry. Even more codes to remember so we can easily enter the farm ourselves! Crime is now a part of modern life, a sad reflection on our society and something we must put up with. It does not make life any easier. As I have alluded to earlier, the numerous times my car has been broken into, being a considerable inconvenience to the job we are trying to do.

But us farm vets do not tend to be the tidiest people ourselves, often creating situations of wasted time as we search for things we have put somewhere, but that where is the question. Those heady days of years ago and in that untrustworthy Viva, even if it was in the garage every three weeks, one thing I could say is that it was always tidy and organised. Us farm vets' cars are full of drugs, equipment, and protective clothing, with probably a good amount of paperwork sitting on the front passenger seat as well. In those early days of my career, one would have wooden boxes with hinged lids passed on from vet to vet, suitable for carrying the large bottles of Calcium and Magnesium, Glucose and Phosphorus for treating cows with Milk Fever, Staggers and Ketosis. All glass, these sectioned bottles saved us from the constant noise of bottles rattling against each other as we drove down bumpy country lanes and roads. Other smaller boxes containing drugs, others with the tools of our trade. In time we would each evolve our own systems of storage within the car. Four-door cars or estates were a bonus as the backseat more often than not was also an area of storage as well as the boot area.

I could proudly say with that Viva that even if you blindfolded me, I could have found anything I was looking for because it was tidy, and I knew where it all was. Have things changed that much, do I now travel with more drugs, more equipment? I do not know. Certainly, in those COVID-19 days I did have more in the car, we worked remotely and so carried more rather than endlessly making extra journeys to the office to pick up more. I have stuck to hatchbacks. With the advent of these plastic storage boxes one can buy in DIY stores I have found a system which works for me, especially as my last four cars have all been the same make, so it has been easy to transfer boxes from one car to the next as the car was replaced. Others in the practice, as they have used these big four-wheel drive trucks with long storage areas in the back, have built themselves sophisticated sets of long draws, allowing greater tidiness, so long as they can remember where they have stored everything. I have never fancied this size of vehicle.

It often amuses me when I see little John (by which I mean little John, not as in Robin Hood) leaning into the back of his truck. One slip and I wonder if he will fall in and be lost forever.

These days we do have to carry more and more equipment, it is a job to stay so tidy. The extra space we must find now for surgical packs and operating kits, ultrasound scanners, drugs, stomach pumps etc and for those experts that use exploratory laparotomy kits. These are bulky things that do not fit neatly into a car boot, it is harder and harder to have an organised car.

But we do not help ourselves. From my experience, we are a very messy profession. For all those small animal nurses who help and then clear up after surgery, we have had none in the farm practices I have worked in. Those wonderful girls in the office do clean and then autoclave our surgical kits for us, the vet usually just abandoning a dirty kit covered in blood and body fluids on a surface somewhere to miraculously be cleaned. We are improving, especially during Covid when we have had to clean the kits ourselves with remote working, then cold sterilise them as we have had no access to the office. But we are still messy individuals, and if we can leave anything about, we will. It is our duty to dispose of needles, scalpel blades ourselves, after all we are the ones who know what they have been used for. But often if we can leave things lying about, we will. I have had to write Health and Safety policies myself in the past, so I hope I am very good, and it is a genuine mistake on my behalf if I have left anything untoward for the girls to clear up. Others are not so good.

They are notorious at leaving faeces samples in the plastic arm length gloves that they were collected in, to be sent off to the lab. Our laboratories now send us curt notices if they receive samples like this, they want them in proper specimen pots so they can be handled safely by their staff. We are having to train farmers to bring samples in contained in appropriate containers as well, the girls should not have to handle these glove packets.

Vets seem notorious for leaving dirty plates, mugs, and coffee cups either on their desks or in the kitchen area. Incapable of putting them in the dish washer themselves, nor of wiping surfaces that they have spilt things on. A messy profession. A wonder what home is like?

We all carry a certain amount of basic equipment about with us such as hoof knives, a stomach pump, a scanner. Other equipment we share such as dehorning equipment, nose punches, microscopes and specialist tools for testing ram and bull fertility. Things that have a place in the office and should be returned and cleaned before the next person may need them. It is often a bugbear for us that one has a call and needs some of this equipment to take out with you. When you go to find it, it is not there. The last person to use it has not returned it and you then have a frantic search to find someone who owns up to having it in their possession, and then getting it to you. A frustration that a lot of time can be wasted waiting for that equipment to return!

But we are also notoriously good at leaving things on farm. The commonest things are boxes of arm length examination gloves and the lube we use with them. Also common are stethoscopes, hung over a gate when we have finished using them and continuing our examination, then forgotten until next time you need it, or the farmer rings the office to say it has been left there. I carry three with me in case this happens to me, as on the few occasions it has happened, I have always got a spare until I can retrieve the one that I have left.

One would frequently on your rounds get asked just to pop in somewhere to retrieve someone else's lost property as you were closest. And that missing equipment, it did not usually take too many guesses whose car it would be in. I will not name names! Thankfully, me being the guilty party was rare. We did in most cases manage to find what was lost.

I had to attend one farm a couple of winters ago, taken over recently by a new client. I had been to the farm many times historically, to its previous occupant. A series of livestock houses where the ventilation inside was far from ideal. When full of cattle, I knew that there would be pneumonia problems inside them. This particular winter, pneumonia had arisen again, and the new farmer asked me to attend the farm on a regular basis to make sure the cattle were healthy and to treat any that were not. After the initial outbreak when I was going virtually every day, we got some control of the disease so that I started going on just every third day to check on all the housed cattle. We had moved the ill ones into one pen in the bottom building, a well-ventilated shed with plenty of air flow, unlike the sheds lying side by side further up the yard. I was able to park my car on the concrete pad close by, making it easy to get any drugs that I may need.

Here one could not fault the conditions the cattle were kept in, in what was basically a hospital pen. Here, we may have four or five cattle that needed observation and further treatment if necessary. It was easy to pen any bullock that needed closer examination behind a gate and give a full examination. This would involve taking its temperature and auscultating its chest for normal sounds associated with pneumonia in cattle.

For some years now I had been wearing hearing aids. Like most men who say there is nothing wrong with their hearing, I had sooner than most taken myself to the doctors, then a referral to a specialist to find I had a hereditary condition, otosclerosis (my twin brother and father have also been diagnosed with it). I originally had been given those horrible huge hearing aids with the moulded plastic part made to fit your ear. I had found them very cumbersome, especially at work when I would frequently be using a stethoscope. One of the ladies in the audiology department at the local hospital, Elaine, had listened to my tales of woe with these aids and had fitted me with some new ones the NHS were trying out, far lighter and far more comfortable to fit in the ear. I found that I could wear these and use a stethoscope at the same time, but more commonly took my left one (my better hearing ear) out. Using just one side properly I found I got more than satisfactory hearing to be able to make a suitable diagnosis.

My process would be to take the temperature of the animal, then take the left hearing aid out and use the stethoscope to listen to the animal's lung function. The aid would be put in one of my pockets, on this day, into my waistcoat pocket.

I did all that I had to do to the cattle and returned to the car, first as always washing, and disinfecting my boots. Swapping them for my shoes I got back into the car and was ready to drive off. I reached down into my pocket to get and replace my hearing aid back into my ear.

Horror!

It was not there, it must have fallen out, more than probably into the well-strawed yard the cattle had been in. There was nothing I could do now, being winter, darkness came early, and was there any great likelihood I would find it in the dark and in all the straw. There was nothing I could do. I did have a spare at home though it was the old-fashioned moulded one.

My next visit to the farm was on the following Monday afternoon, and from the cattle's point of view, all had a clean bill of health. Les, the stockman and I did catch one just to check it over, but it was fine.

I did just ask him, "I know it is a long shot, but have you seen a hearing aid I dropped, lost here when I was here on Friday afternoon?"

"No, he had not," he replied.

We did turn over the straw quickly where we had examined cattle those three days previously, but it was like searching for a needle in a haystack. It would be immediately obvious, or it was a waste of time. We soon abandoned the search, and I made my way back to the car which was parked a little further down the yard than it had been on the Friday.

I was just stepping out of the pen when I thought I saw something small and grey lying on the concrete where I had parked on the previous visit. From a distance, it had to be my lost hearing aid. It must have fallen out of my pocket when I was getting back into the car. Rejoice, somehow, I had found it.

I wandered over to retrieve my possession just as a car drove into the yard, me and it were heading in the same direction. The car was gone, and I reached the point where I saw my aid. The car had run straight over the top of it, it was crushed, and I would be donating another fifty pounds to Audiology for a replacement.

At the end of the week, I was on the same farm again continuing the surveillance of disease amongst these cattle. Les was assisting me again and once again I had finished my clinical examinations and was returning to the car to leave the farm, it was getting late in the afternoon, and I had one more call to do about fifteen miles away.

As I went to get into the car, I reached into my pocket to get my car keys. Nothing there! I tried all the other pockets but to no avail. This was getting silly. Perhaps I had taken them out of my pocket and left them in the boot of the car when I had gone back to get an injection? Or they had slipped out of my pocket and behind the car seat? I religiously searched through the car, then the boot. Nothing!

It was time to start unloading first the contents inside the car enabling me to have a good look under the seats and on the car floor. Then the boot but again nothing, I would have to look inside my boxes. Again nothing, what could I do?

I was only about four miles from home, although my wife was at work someone would have a spare key to get in the house, get my other car key and run it up to me. Her son would help.

Les kindly said he would run me home where I could meet Paul and get the key, and my spare house key (my house key was with the car key). Time was running on, and I hoped that one of the other vets could do my last call for me so as not to delay the farmer to long as it got dark. There was no one else.

We went home, got the key and re-organising the drugs and equipment in my car as best as I could after the turmoil of searching for keys, I set off on my way to that last call.

I arrived and got out of the car to put my boots on. As my foot touched the bottom of the inside of the boot there was something strange rubbing on my ankle. I took my foot out again to investigate. It was winter and I had a pair of trousers on that had an inner lining. Feeling at the bottom of the trouser leg there was something hard, a SET OF KEYS. I put my hand in the pocket of that trouser leg, there was a small hole there, the keys had worked their way through and disappeared.

I felt very stupid, but also with a sense of relief that the keys which also included the office keys had been recovered.

It was some months later when on another farm I was calving a cow. The call was that she seemed ill and wouldn't get up but on arrival it was evident her problem was that she had started to calve, it was coming backwards and was tight. The cow had got up and then lay down again right across the door of the calving box she was in. The farmer and I managed to climb over her, shut the door again and after a little struggle managed to deliver a live bull calf. Most of our hard work had been done in the narrow space between her rear end and the box wall.

A good job done, the cow was now far more comfortable and was soon up, licking the calf which we had moved to the other end of the box, away from the door. Her maternal instincts were soon in action, she now seemed fine.

We admired cow and calf before collecting our calving ropes up. I felt something strange in my left ear, and naturally put my hand up to investigate. The earpiece of my hearing aid was still in my ear, but there was nothing behind, just the tube dangling loosely there. The working part including the battery had fallen off and into the straw bedding of the calving box.

Not again!

We would start a futile search for something grey in poor light amongst all this straw, it would be hopeless, but I couldn't go back to Audiology again and say I had lost another one. We looked for ten minutes, slowly turning the straw back so that if it were there it would fall gently to the floor underneath, and we would hopefully find it as we moved the straw away.

Nothing, we were about to give up when I had one last look about two feet behind where we had been looking.

"There's something there," I proclaimed.

I had found it once again, that was a close call and more than lucky. I would go back to Audiology, but not to part with another fifty quid, but just to get a better fitting tube. Kindly, this time Elaine gave me some spares as well.

But it would happen again, his time on another farm but again examining a group of calves with pneumonia. A bunch of twenty where one was ill and as we entered the pen those other nineteen thought it was feeding time and so were constantly nuzzling us saying "where is my milk?"

I treated the affected calf and we returned to my car. I had again put the hearing aid into my waistcoat pocket when using my stethoscope. I had returned to the car to get some drugs to treat the calf and then injected it.

I cleaned up and as usual went to retrieve my hearing aid to put back in my ear. It was not there.

Not again!

The lady who had been assisting me insisted we went back to look for it in the pen of calves despite me saying it would be hopeless. I was lucky, incredibly lucky last time, I would not be so lucky twice. But we did look, it was a big pen, we did have a rough idea where we had looked at the calf in it, but we were not going to find it I knew.

All I could do was thank her for her help but there was nothing more we could do. I went back to the car, did have a quick search of the boot just in case I had put it somewhere in there when I went back to get some drugs. If necessary, I would take some of the contents out in case it had dropped down somewhere. I was not hopeful.

I got back into the car, put my hand in my waistcoat pocket and got my car keys out. There caught up in the key ring was the tube of my hearing aid, the whole thing was still intact. I was lucky again.

I have learnt my lesson. I have discovered that the pockets in my waistcoat, which does keep me very warm in winter, are very shallow. It is easy to put something in the pocket and unintentionally pull it back out again as one withdraws one's hand. I now leave one hearing aid in the car if I know I am going to use my stethoscope or put it on a firm ledge if available above where we are working.

Other than once when leaning out of the driver's side door while reversing and my glasses falling off, not stopping in time, and running them over, I have managed to keep hold of my personal possessions intact and undamaged.

It used to be me picking up everybody else's lost and found, now it seems to be me the culprit!

12

DRUGS, REMEDIES and CONCOCTIONS

Vets have been treating animals for years and years. Over those years many remedies have been invented and used, just the same as in human medicine. How well they worked, I am not old enough to tell, but some will have persisted in veterinary medicine until the not-too-distant past.

I can remember when we decided we needed to clear out the old Dispensary when I first came to Shropshire, some of the "medicines" we threw away looked to say the least, a bit dubious. Winchesters full of some sort of flower petals, suspended in, I do not know what. Castor Oil, Turpentine and other liquids which would now have to be described as poisons such as Strychnine. An array of old fashioned "drugs" which had their place in their day, some being incorporated into medicines we used until very recently, and they did work. It used to be a common practice with very sick cows who wouldn't eat that you would offer them Ivy leaves and one couldn't deny that it did get a significant number on the mend. That is probably the basis of homeopathy, a little can have the opposite effect of a deadly poison.

Penicillin was discovered in 1928 by Alexander Fleming and I can remember my father using this drug in his herd, those little metal tubes that contained the antibiotic for treating mastitis in cows. When I entered the profession, we did have a slightly larger range of antibiotics to use, some new synthetic Penicillins, Streptomycin, Tetracyclines and Chloramphenicol on top of the old tried and trusted Sulphadimidines. The Pharmaceutical industry was evolving and starting to produce more and more innovative medicines for us to use in both small animal and farm practice.

We had forms of cortisone injections and tablets, vitamins, gut spasmolytics and some hormone treatments for the use in fertility especially in our dairy herds. The importance of trying to get the cow to produce a calf once every three hundred and sixty-five days, her calving index, was being realised to get her to maximum productivity and to maximise profit from her.

There were also a couple of "mixtures", "The Stomach Drench" was an example which did contain low levels of the likes of Strychnine amongst other ingredients, with defined doses of how much you should drench a cow in one go. And these drenches worked.

In my first job I was very limited in what I could use, usually being told what I was going to treat an animal with before I had left the office. If I strayed from that line of treatment then I would get my knuckles wrapped. When I moved to Devon, it was a different story. We had two large dispensaries full of different drugs, and now it was up to me what I wanted to use. There was also an array of drugs I had not used before but had heard of. Boxes full of little packets such as an oral antibiotic for cattle, Nitrofurazolidine, weighed out packets of Aspirin (Salicylic Acid) for cows which were our first non-steroidal anti-inflammatory drugs. Time evolves and if I had not come across this since then, it is now produced as a licenced product in Farm Animal Practice.

We had Local Anaesthetic, Procaine and Lignocaine which we used for operations on cows, either by local flank infiltration for Caesareans and laparotomies in cattle. We used "local" for cornual blocks to disbud and dehorn cattle and one or two now more sophisticated techniques such as paravertebral blocks for anaesthetising the flank of a cow. A technique where using long needles and sterility, these needles were inserted just in front of the transverse processes of the spine to block the nerves as they emerged from the spinal cord, using this block on four or five of the lumbar vertebrae. A technique which was made a lot easier if your needles are sharp; good restraint was needed.

And in those early days that was one thing we did not have, chemical restraint. We relied on manpower, ropes, and a prayer. Even now most cow and sheep operations are done on conscious animals, and especially in cattle, with them standing so restraint is essential to be able to carry out whatever op you are trying to do while making the animal free from pain. Local anaesthesia facilitates that, but it can often be a painful experience while injecting it into the operation site. Many times, we would be kicked just in trying to give local, to the point the cow would know what was coming and would be trying to kick you even before you had put the next needle in.

Barbiturates were being used in small animal practice by then, but we could not use them in cows and sheep, a recumbent ruminant will regurgitate her ruminal contents. They had to remain conscious to maintain their laryngeal reflex and be able to swallow, otherwise they could inhale their ruminal contents after regurgitation, causing an aspiration pneumonia. This is life threatening.

Chloral hydrate was used specially in equine medicine, and I would later use it in cattle. It worked very well as a short acting sedative which when used with local as well, would allow quick procedures to take place before the cow was quickly back up on her feet. I would often do Displaced abomasum operations using this, rolling the cow onto her back, giving local along the midline, by which time the gas filled fourth stomach would have floated up. It was then a simple technique to open the cow up, fix the stomach to the incision, and sow her up again. It would take minutes. But then Chloral Hydrate was banned for use in food-producing animals and that was that. It was such a lovely drug to use, mixing in four hundred ml. of water and then given slowly intra-venously. The cow would slowly lie down, dreaming of the fairies or lovely green pastures, and we would place on her back supported by a bale of straw either side while you operated. There was no worry about what her feet were doing, they just pointed upwards until you were done when we rolled her back on her side. She would usually be up in minutes.

We were moving away from the drugs of the "old school" vets as slowly more and more drugs were discovered and then licensed for use in Veterinary Medicine. Some were variations of what we already had, especially as the patents came off the original drug, and some were novel, we had never had an equivalent in the past.

It almost certainly would not be true now, but certainly if you had asked me back in the late seventies what was the best new drugs that had come out were, then my answer would have been easy. One was a prostaglandin I will mention in a minute, the other was a sedative for cows, Xylazine. It was licensed across all the species but would cause vomiting in dogs. Here we had a drug which could be given both intramuscularly and intravenously, depending what purpose you were wanting to us it for. For fractious cows and bulls, we could get them behind a gate and jab it into them, then waiting while it had its affect. Or we could give a far smaller dose intravenously for more easily handleable cattle, and they would soon lie down. Even smaller doses would just quieten them, they would remain standing but were generally then quite amenable to whatever you wanted to do to them. It was a good drug to use to operate on calves or to quieten them down to put a cast on a broken leg. What it did not do was to give a level of analgesia similar to Chloral hydrate, I only once tried doing a displaced abomasum using Xylazine with the cow on her back. Even while infiltrating the operation site with local anaesthetic, and certainly during the operation, you did have to worry about her feet which were constantly coming in your direction.

The invention of this drug made one feel far safer in one's work, and there were also the welfare aspects of the animal to consider. Certainly there would be times when, especially working with the emergency services, the use of sedatives made the job a lot easier. This was both in terms of safety to those assisting and in the welfare considerations of the animal we were trying to help. The most important aspect was patience while the drug worked, as it seemed to vary from animal to animal how long it took to get the desired effect you as the vet required.

Little has changed since then in terms of what we use, there are combinations with Ketamine, but a good drug has maintained its place in our repertoire. I did have to use it not so long ago in combination with Ketamine to do some dentistry on an ageing pet pig. The owners had no means of restraint, so sedation was essential. It took a lot of research to find a suitable combination of drugs to use but the literature gave a massive range of drug to use per kilogram body weight. It was guesswork. Firstly in the dosage rate, and secondly in the weight of the pig, owner and vet differing considerably in their estimations. Happily, Clem went to sleep, and I was able to make a good job of trimming his long and sharp tusks. The only question then would be how long it would take him to wake up again, he seemed to be enjoying his rest. He was soon back on his feet and looking for food and company. I wish I could remember what dose rate I had used, but I will probably never have to do it again, someone else can do the research next time.

The second drug was the prostaglandin, used in fertility work in cattle. This drug works on the corpus luteum on the ovary, causing it to "dissolve" which in turn starts a cycle of hormonal events leading to the cow coming bulling and ready to serve. It would make fertility control far easier in that the time of bulling was generally about seventy-two hours after injection. If you injected the cow on Tuesday, you would serve her on the Friday. Much to an AI man's annoyance, if you injected a cow on December 22nd, he would have to serve her on Christmas Day!

There were hormone treatments before this, but none of them had the reliability of this new drug, marketed as Estrumate. Even forty years on, and despite the fact that other pharmaceutical companies now market it under different names, Estrumate is still what it is known as, whatever brand one uses. It offered a degree of fertility management we did not have before, and is still widely used, though now in conjunction with other hormones. Whether by injection or by intra-vaginal device, all of which have enabled us to control and synchronise cow breeding more precisely. Along with ultrasound scanners where you have a visible picture of what the cow's ovary is doing, at what stage of her cycle she is at, breeding management has been able to become far more precise. It is these new regimes that we will use on our weekly or fortnightly fertility visits.

Over my years as a vet, drugs have come under far more control, especially under the Veterinary Medicine Directorate. Drugs must go through stringent licensing regimes before they become available to us. Over my time, many new drugs have come onto the market, coming under different categories as to who they can be sold to and whether they need a prescription or not. They need to be licensed, and some, because of the large expense of this process and the sales figures of these drugs don't make it worthwhile to relicense. These we lose. Good and effective drugs that have a place in our car but are not viable economically to carry on producing. Combination drugs, containing a mixture of antibiotics, have their licences withdrawn, drug resistance becoming a more and more important issue.

There have been important strides forward in terms of animal welfare, the advent of non-steroidal anti-inflammatory drugs which benefit the animal enormously in helping in toxaemias, in pain relief, in reducing elevated temperatures rapidly and getting the animal eating again quickly. If asked now what the most important new drug was, then on welfare grounds alone I would have to place this one above the two previously mentioned.

We have had a whole new range of antibiotics to use, important especially in our treatments of mastitis and of pneumonia across the farm species we deal with. More welfare friendly in the fact that they very often are long acting and are administered sub-cutaneous so are less painful to administer and the animal does not have the stress of being handled so often to inject it.

But we are also coming under increasing pressure as a profession from the likes of the World Health Organisation and bodies in this country as to what we can use and what we cannot. Antibiotic resistance is becoming more and more of an issue. We have been set standards to reduce antibiotic use to below certain limits in a given time frame. We are succeeding but I fully expect our reward for that will be even lower limits. The milk buyers and the food retailers are looking for these reductions and limiting which drugs we can use, especially in the different classes of antibiotics. Third and fourth generation Cephalosporins, Floxacillin's are now no-no's in our treatment regimes, highly effective medicines but now the emphasis is for reserving them for human medicine.

It almost seems that as I reach retirement, despite the number of new antibiotics that have reached the market, rapidly we are approaching the situation of having the same number I started with. Certainly on some farms some broader categories of antibiotic, as well as well as those named above, we can no longer use unless we have a clinical justification to do so having exhausted other possibilities. This will have implications to livestock farming in the future. The role of farmer and vet working hand in hand will become ever more important to control disease. Great strides have been made in the reduction of antibiotic usage, especially in the pig and poultry sectors where vast quantities of antibiotics were used in feed both as growth promoters and to dampen down endemic disease on some farms. This can only be a good thing both in terms of welfare and how the public, the consumers, see their food being produced. The reduction in use goes hand in hand with better husbandry practices, a win, win situation.

Other drugs have disappeared too, again for the better. When I started, the feeding of growth promoters to cattle was common practice. A cow that had finished her productive life as a milking cow would have an anabolic steroid implant injected in under the skin of her ear, a part of the carcase that would not be used for meat. She would then be turned out to grass to work out, build up her body mass before going to slaughter for meat. A practice now long gone, and something the modern consumer almost certainly would not tolerate.

Whether it is right that the likes of supermarket buyers and milk retailers should be dictating to us what we can and cannot treat our patients with is a question open to debate. We do have methods to by-pass these restrictions if we sample and find the permissible drugs do not work so we can justify using an alternative. But at the end of the day, the important consideration is more can we prevent disease rather than treating it. Farm assurance schemes are now common practice. Herd and Flock Health plans are to be a benefit and be embraced by all parts of the industry so there must be something to gain. That benefit is that the public will feel happy and safe in buying your product. To that extent if we can show better husbandry practices, and the public see "happy "cows and sheep, inquisitive piglets, and free-range hens, then they will be happy to buy farm produce.

The organic movement increases the pressure on ensuring good farming practice. We have several farms that have gone down the organic route, where antibiotics and anthelmintics can only be used as a last resort for the benefit of the welfare of the animal. Good husbandry is essential here, along with the reduced pressure put on each animal as its production figures are not as demanding as on more conventional systems. A number of treatments would mean that animal no longer being classed as organic. Other farms are on a strict "No Antibiotic" contracts. If the cow should receive any antibiotic, then her milk cannot be sold under this contract, she would have to be sold to a more conventional farm or go for meat. Sometimes it is unavoidable that a cow will need treating and she will have to leave the system, on welfare grounds it would be wrong not to treat her, those are the demands of the contract.

The organic movement has led to more and more organic farmers going down the Homeopathic route to treat sick animals. I would fully admit I don't know enough about homeopathy to comment, but in some cases, it does seem to work. I'm not sure that treating a whole herd with nosodes against certain diseases, especially the ones we can't cure by conventional methods, is the right way to go, time will tell.

The medications available to us are now tightly controlled. We have to be able to justify any treatments especially if we are going off licence because nothing else has worked on a farm. We must record those cases, apply appropriate food withdrawal times so there will be no residues in the product, more paperwork but in the end the important thing is that the product that reaches the consumer's table is safe.

Gone are those wonderful remedies, concoctions that we made up in the back room, when veterinary medicine was a little bit of an adventure. A wart remedy which was basically milk, heated to not quite boiling with a little Tryptophan Blue in it to disguise it. It was something that worked and was probably more effective than modern drugs and probably worked on the basis of injecting a denatured protein would stimulate a body response against any other foreign protein, i.e., the wart. We could not use it now. Other little potions that a vet would make up, but it was his secret what it contained. The like of these, now long gone.

Which I guess takes us to the most important "new drug" which goes hand in hand with improved husbandry. In a time when we are looking to come through this COVID-19 pandemic, what is it that is giving us hope now? Vaccines!

Over the years, more and more life threatening but common diseases are now controlled by vaccination. One cannot pretend that they are the total answer, vaccination programmes go hand in hand with improved husbandry, improved housing and stocking densities. We would now be at the stage where not many farm animals would not receive a vaccination at some stage of its life.

Prevention is better than cure!

For sheep against Clostridial disease where the usual first sign is death. For poultry, any number of vaccines now exist where whole poultry houses can be vaccinated by using vaccines in sprays which will be inhaled. In pigs any number of diseases are now controlled by vaccine, both to the sow and to the piglets whose immune system can cope with inoculation soon after birth. The effectiveness of these vaccines has contributed to the marked reduction of antibiotic use in these two species.

In cattle we have a full range of vaccines with even more being developed, and as time goes on, improvement of the vaccines that already exist. Novel vaccines such as the one against lungworm, causing Husk, a parasite that can invade the lungs especially of growing cattle, causing severe damage and often death. But here we have a vaccine that relies on meeting the parasite to work, boosting immunity.

There are any number of vaccines now available against respiratory disease and with the advancement of laboratory analysis, Elisa, and PCR tests, we can tailor a vaccination program to any individual farm to what bacteria and viruses they have on that farm. We can now initiate vaccination programs against infectious diseases that can sweep through a dairy or beef herd causing infertility, abortion, and respiratory disease. In time, these can be used as an aid to eradication of the disease in this country as is happening in some countries in Europe.

New innovations like vaccines against mastitis are now available, and although they will not prevent this disease of the cow's udder, it certainly lessens the severity of it so cure rates are better and mortality reduced.

A few years ago, in 2017 I was lucky enough to be invited over to one of a pharmaceutical company's production sites in Catalonia, northern Spain. It was a trip organised by the company's local representative and I was joined by six other vets from the Midlands region, none of whom I had met before. We had a designated meeting time at Birmingham Airport, and as the trip was for only two nights, I decided it was easier to get the train to Birmingham International then I could go straight to the Departure Lounge as I had been checked in online and only had hand luggage. I eventually met my colleagues, and we were treated to a good lunch in one of the restaurants there, before boarding our plane to fly to Barcelona. This gave us a chance to get to know each other, though still missing one who was flying from Stansted.

An uneventful flight took us across France and the Pyrenees before landing in Spain, flying out across the sea, before crossing back onto land and the huge airport that Barcelona is. Two had luggage to collect before we went in search of our bus which would take us to our destination. It was a struggle to find it and the last member of our group but eventually we did, and we were soon on the motorway out of this wonderful city and driving towards Girona, a trip which would take some ninety minutes.

We checked into our hotel before going in search of the tapas restaurant we had been booked into to eat. What a wonderful place, one wall just a vast wine rack, and by now, I had been elected the expert on Rioja. I do not know why but once elected I was determined we were going to try as much as possible. The tapas were exceptional, a variety of starters, main dishes and then desserts. I think we may have just exceeded our allowed quota. There were a few gaps in the wine rack when we left, my love of Riojas unspoilt.

The next day took us to a farm, north of the city of Girona, where we would have a discussion and practical session on mastitis in the dairy cow, and then an introduction into mastitis vaccines that the company was developing. A mixture of talks and farm walks, then a session in the milking parlour observing milking techniques and examining cows for teat damage post-milking amongst other things that can impact on udder health. What these cows had to cope with in terms of heat stress, despite the presence of fans in their housing! The temperature was excessive! I guess it was reaching not far off one hundred degrees Fahrenheit. An ample lunch was provided by the farmer, all produced from his own farm, excellent.

Then it was back into the city of Girona for a shower and an evening meal in a steak house near the centre. We had decided we would leave early to get there; we were to have had a brief city tour first but another group of vets on a similar trip had stolen our guide. After enjoying a beer in the pleasant sunshine outside the hotel, we decided we would do our own tour, finding a way to cross the river then walking through the old town until we found the castle and cathedral. The old town, streets bars, cafes, boutiques, restaurants all on narrow streets surrounded by tall buildings either side. Beautiful and enchanting as we walked on before reaching a tall archway, part of the town wall. The wall and the cathedral in front of us were amazing sights, it would have been nice if we had been earlier and been able to have a look inside this spectacular building, for now we would just see the rear of it.

We were thirsty and eventually found a bar in a garden at the back of the cathedral, overlooking a stage where a band was rehearsing its music. Girona hosts a big music festival in the summer months, catering for all tastes from opera to modern music. This was an incredibly relaxing place, watching the sun go down over a beautiful city while enjoying a cool beer.

It was time to move on and find our steakhouse, a quaint restaurant in a back street just off the central city square. Introductions all around between us and the staff before we had our orders taken. In Spain, my true wish was a paella, but it was not on the menu so I ordered veal on the basis it would be small and not very filling. Our table was next to a window where we could see all the steaks being cooked by flame on a grill. I pitied the person who was going to have that massive steak cooking away. Our meals arrived; it was mine. My veal looked twice the size of anything else anybody had ordered but I would have to admit it was very light and I did manage to finish it all. It was lovely meal with again more Rioja, the rest of the team were starting to like this stuff. It was time to leave and return to the hotel. But four of us decided we would like to go back to the square opposite the cathedral and have another drink. Wisely, or unwisely, our rep entrusted us with her credit card, saying she trusted me that we would us it sensibly and not to excess.

We found a nice bar where we could sit outside and enjoy a cocktail or two (and it was only two). Here, as had been a common occurrence on this type of thing, one learns a lot about how other practices work, about your fellow colleagues and how they have organised their work/life agenda. It has always been remarkably interesting and informative. I did get offered two jobs that night.

It was a lovely way to finish a long day in the warm night air of Catalonia. After much chat and light-hearted banter, we made our way back to our hotel only to find those that had not joined us in the square, enjoying a drink in the hotel.

The next day, we had to vacate our rooms then head off to what we had really come here for, to visit the headquarters of the pharmaceutical company who had organised the trip.

A trip through the heart of Catalonia and their flags, wanting independence, was very much evident. We reached the town of Almer and the site of the company, where we disembarked from the bus and entered HQ. We were introduced to the Managing Director and then taken for a series of talks, firstly about the company and what its plans were in vaccine development. This was then followed by talks about some of the diseases they produced vaccines against, and how to control them, this being more a discussion as we came face to face with these diseases on a daily basis. Again, an interesting comparison of different vets' views of how they dealt with different diseases.

It was then the chance to go into the building where the vaccines were produced, this would be fascinating.

Here, biosecurity was the name of the game. As we entered we had to dress in full protective clothing, although we would only be viewing from behind windows the vaccine production, we were not going to take in any potential pathogens in with us. The process involving growing egg cells, the medium that virus replication would take place on, they imported vast numbers of eggs, especially from Germany, secure in the knowledge they would be pathogen free. The process involved storage, virus inoculation and harvesting in biosecure rooms and the emergency procedures and mechanisms in place if there was accidental spillage or escape of these potential pathogens. We were told about the highly trained staff that worked on vaccine production, shown how the vaccine bottles were sterilised and then filled with vaccine and then stored. It was a fascinating insight to something we as vets use every day, but I would fully admit that I never knew the intricacies in vaccine production.

This is the future of disease prevention and control; it was so interesting seeing the process from Research and Development to production. An eye-opening experience.

It was time to think about returning to the UK, but first they had one last treat for us. Lunch in one of the best, I lie, the best restaurant I have been in ever. A restaurant that did have a Michelin star while the father was alive, but now taken over by his two daughters. We were treated to the most exquisite meal, food I would not think I would like but superb, octopus, pork cooked on the rare side, a new experience; and a lovely sweet. This was served with, for once, a white wine I had chosen from those on offer, a light local Catalonian wine called "A thousand", the number of days it took to produce.

A memorable meal hosted by the MD of the company with lots of good chat about his business, Catalonian independence and of course, football.

It was time to go to the airport, we were flying back from Girona on our return flight, unfortunately with Ryanair. We checked in with time to spare and waited patiently in the departure lounge. No sign of a plane. An hour passed and still no sign. Was I getting worried? Not at this stage but I did have in the back of my mind that having gone to Birmingham by train, what time did the last train leave back to Telford. More time passed and still no sign of a plane. We were now nearing the time we should have landed back in Birmingham.

A plane did finally arrive, and we boarded and took off. I knew it was going to be touch and go as to whether I could catch the last train. A couple of the other vets who had driven did offer to go out of their way and take me home but I was still hopeful I could catch my train. Luckily with no baggage recall, as soon as I was through immigration I could just run and get aboard the shuttle to Birmingham International and hope. I arrived on the platform just as the doors were closing, I squeezed on. I had made it by the skin of my teeth.

An unforgettable trip which made me want to go back to Girona again but as a tourist.

As my luck would have it, I was invited back on the same trip the following year and was only too pleased to accept, this time with a different group of vets. Again, a meet up and lunch at Birmingham where I met other vets from the Midlands and Wales regions, again all strangers to me bar one of my own work colleagues. Again, I had gone on the train. This time we flew direct to Girona and on landing were taken to the same hotel in the centre of the new town.

I had been before, I was nominated as the tour guide and had to try and find the same tapas restaurant from the previous year. My colleagues were doubting me until I pointed out the front door. I had guided them safely to our meal. Again, that vast wine rack of Rioja was waiting to be sampled, but it was a slightly different form of meal this year. One chose one's main course and then helped oneself to tapas dishes before it arrived. This was not the place to go if you were on a diet. Once again, it was a lovely meal and all I had to do was guide us back to the hotel. All was fine until I got into deep conversation with a couple of the other vets about my trips to Africa, Kenya, and I missed a road we were supposed to take. I realised my mistake and got us back by a slightly circuitous route. Time for bed!

The next day would see us visiting another farm to discuss milking and mastitis, but this time I had experience of their new vaccine. In fact, some of the data presented to us had come from one of the farms in my practice. It was possible for me to give practical advice to back up their more technical information. An interesting few hours was again spent on a Spanish farm, but again in blistering heat. Lunch was again provided, and again quite filling, meat produced from the farm we were on.

Our next activity was to visit a vineyard where we were shown the vines and then the production process before being taken into a cellar to sample their produce along with a selection of Spanish cold meats and cheeses. Again, I found this interesting having already visited vineyards in Southern Italy, Sardinia and more recently in Dorset, slight differences in each location. We had seen a lot of food and I don't think anybody could eat any more. It was still early evening, what could we do?

I wanted to go back into Girona again like the previous year to explore some more. Kathy, our rep, was also interested and suggested if anybody wanted to join us then we could meet up outside the hotel and I would be the guide again. All but one came with me, and we once again followed my footsteps of the previous year, making our way to the cathedral, the park behind it and then looking for somewhere to get a cool drink. We chose a bar with outside tables, a rather bizarre situation that although the tables were outside this one bar, they belonged to a bar down the street. We did at last manage to procure some refreshment before continuing our tour which took us to the front of the cathedral and its magnificent steps up to the main doors. Aficionados of "Game of Thrones" will know the cathedral steps as the start of Cersei Lannister's walk of shame, the city had been used a lot in the filming of the series. A fantastic building, incredible architecture as it stands looking down on the river.

Then, back over the river and through the square from where most returned back to the hotel. Four of us wanted to prolong the ambience of this beautiful city and stayed there longer to enjoy the night air, in fact until the hostelry closed, but again having one of those wonderful vet conversations that one has late at night over a beer or two.

The following day we returned to the factory and although I had seen it before, I found it just as fascinating. Over the previous twelve months they had developed a vaccine delivery system for piglets which didn't need needles, somehow inoculating the vaccine intradermally by pressure, far less stressful for the recipient, though expensive and only suitable therefore for the larger producer.

Lastly it was another tremendous lunch in a local restaurant, one of those massive paellas that you see cooked in Spain. I was happy, I had got my paella at last.

This time we did catch our plane leaving on time and headed back to Birmingham with time to spare.

But arriving back on the platform, we found our train had been cancelled, there was a body on the line. My work colleague plus one of the Welsh vets and myself were stranded. We did eventually manage to get as far as Wolverhampton, then came to a stop. What now, a taxi?

After a long chat with one of the Rail staff, I did ascertain a train would be coming soon. I eventually reached Telford at ten thirty at night, the others had a little further to go. I was going on holiday to Dorset early the next day as soon as my wife got home from work at about seven o'clock in the morning. I needed to mow the lawn, I finished this task just before midnight.

But despite the travel hiccups once again, it had been a great experience and highlighted the future of veterinary medicine. Those days of bucket chemistry, mixing potions have long gone, antimicrobials arrived and have been greatly beneficial. But the future is in prevention and control, vaccines, and good husbandry. Companies like this represent the way forward.

I am incredibly grateful to this company to take me not once, but twice to their location outside Girona, Northern Spain. An unforgettable city and surrounding area but the whole experience, the chance to see a pharmaceutical premise largely devoted to vaccine production was an education. The rest of their hospitality was exceptional as well and this is certainly a city and region I intend to visit again in my retirement, but next time with my wife, Jane.

But of course, they are not the only pharmaceutical company and this is an industry we must work hand in hand with. The direction of treatments may change to prevention and control, vaccination, and improved husbandry but that does not mean that we will not have the need for new and innovative medicines. This is especially so more in the fields I do not deal with, companion animal and equine medicine where they are trying to combat cancer, auto-immune diseases, hormonal disease, some similar to what the medics have to deal with. In some of these medicines there is a cross over between the two disciplines. Not long ago I was sent out to a farm, a small holder to test one cow for Tuberculosis, she had escaped on the previous visit when testing was attempted.. After much cajoling and trickery, I did manage to complete the task I had set out to do, then over a cuppa, he told me how he was involved in the development of medicines used in eye conditions in humans, one of which was adapted from a drug used to treat "Dry Eye" in canines. An interesting bloke and informative to discuss his work with him.

The industry is big business and has changed a lot in my time. The old names of Coopers, Burroughs Welcome, Glaxo etc long gone in the Veterinary field whether my merger, takeover or whatever. Especially over the past few years it has been hard work keeping up with who is who, and who they used to be. Companies like Pfizer, now famous for its COVID-19 vaccine, big players in past times as a Veterinary drug company but now working under the name of Zoetis, yes, it is a job to know who is who these days.

But we as vets have to be grateful for their continued investment in our field of work. Not only do they produce new drugs for us to use, but they also contribute more and more in support and in continuing education. Obviously, they have a vested interest in this in hoping we will use their drugs and so increase their profits, but that help and support is invaluable.

When I started it was unusual for me to meet many of the drug reps as they called round on practices, trying to promote their products. It was the partners who saw them, it was their business, and they would decide what drugs we would use. It would be them who would negotiate a suitable deal and discount on purchasing those drugs. In fact, I guess it would be true to say that the only ones we as humble assistants ever met were the ones the bosses didn't want to see. Those embarrassing moments when you had to see someone when you wished you were somewhere else as they had nothing of interest for you.

As one became more experienced, then you did see more of the reps, and certainly when I did become a partner then it was my chance to build a relationship up with some of the reps and their companies. Even after twenty-five years I still have close contact with a couple, one being a dear friend, another marrying one of my farm clients, so I see her regularly at routine visits and in the herd health planning for this particular farm. A trust over the years has developed.

Years back, it was a hard sell but now there is far more focus on education and from that, then why you should use their product. Along with that now goes a lot of technical support, the opportunity to do field trials with some medicines and all the backup that brings with it. We do now, as I come to the end of my career work far more hand in hand with these companies for each other's, and the farmer's mutual benefit.

One hears of all the jollies that the medical profession receives from their reps. Do we have that, or have we had that? Yes, but to a far lesser extent. Exotic trips, no, not us. Though I suppose I would have to put my two trips to Girona in that category. But I have never been flown halfway round the world to attend some cattle congress plus leisure time. I have hoped, but it has never happened!

We would be entertained royally at Veterinary Cattle Congresses. Here after lecture sessions all day, with the intention continuing education, we would adjourn in the evening for a meal and again those chats with other vets where you learnt just as much practical stuff on how other vets do things, as you did in some of the lectures. But this "learning process" would usually be over a beer of four, and it was usually those reps you had built that relationship with who supplied said beverage. Chats, beers, until one, two in the morning were not uncommon. Conferences could be long, hard and tiring work!

The other events we would attend would be where there was a new drug launch and we would be invited away for a night or two, depending on where the event would take place. Then we would have an afternoon on the veterinary topic, again followed by a formal meal, then chat through to the early hours for those with the stamina. The following day would be clay pigeon shooting, golf, cross-country driving in Range Rovers, whatever had been organise for us. My choice was usually golf, and I did get the opportunity to play on some lovely courses in England and Scotland on these trips.

Two would spring to mind, one in Lockerbie and the other in Bradford.

The Lockerbie trip was a long trip. Meeting up in Manchester the night before in a hotel with of course a meal and beer before flying up to Edinburgh the next morning. Breakfast was provided on the plane, served as soon as we had reached our ascent and soon cleared away because as soon as we had reached that height, it was almost time to start to descend again to land. We were taken to a hotel where we had our educational bit for the rest of the day, before drinks and a formal meal. My first experience of Haggis, and I enjoyed it. Scottish hospitality was wonderful.

The next day, I played golf at Lockerbie GC in the company of some very pleasant and amicable vets, and even on the golf course the education continued.

Bradford perhaps was memorable or forgettable for different reasons. Namely in that having set off from home early to drive up to Yorkshire and finding the hotel we were meeting in, it turned into an awfully long day after lectures, and an even longer night. I think we left the bar at four in the morning, the expensive room the drug company had provided me I think I used for about four hours! At that time, being on the first tee at eight thirty did not seem the greatest idea! I had chosen golf as my activity again. But I could not let my golf partners down, especially as the four I had been picked to play in contained the event organiser. I rushed a cooked breakfast, I wasn't going to miss out on that. I was packed, out of my room and with a severe headache and in my car deciding whether I should be wearing my wet weather golf shoes, or my Dryjoys. I reached the first tee to meet my partners for the day, not feeling perhaps as well as I could have done but after a not too spectacular first tee shot, I settled into the round.

I think it was on about the seventh hole when my tee shot had landed in a fairway bunker that I noticed my big mistake. Not only had I taken one Wetjoy and one Dryjoy to wear, but they were both left feet. I think my embarrassment soon cleared my head as I tried to hide my footwear from my playing partners, and none of them did notice until we had finished which is when I told them. However, it must have done something for my golf because this was the only time on one of these events that I won it, including driving the green on a par four.

I have not made that mistake since.

A couple of the Companies would often get a bundle of tickets for rugby internationals. I was never lucky enough to be the recipient of one of those. I did get offered tickets for Murrayfield and the Millennium Stadium a couple of times, but those invitations were very late, someone had obviously dropped out at the last minute. It was too short notice, and my heart is England so if they weren't playing, then there was little interest to drink all day and watch a game I would rather watch on the TV.

I did meet one embarrassed rep outside the gates at Twickenham once, me with a group of friends, he with a group of vets. He felt guilty one of his tickets and the company hospitality had not come my way, never mind, I would enjoy the game with my mates and would almost certainly finish the day more sober.

But, as I have said, the pharmaceutical industry now offer invaluable support and continuing education opportunities and it is through that partnership of working together that we continue to change and adapt our treatments to new challenges while always now considering the need for improving husbandry.

Over my time in Farm Practice, we have seen new drugs, new antibiotics, the Macrolides especially offering longer duration of action, different pharmokinetics, all in the advancement of science. Some, even though they have only been available a short time, on some retailer contracts we already cannot use them without justification as we work along World Health Organisation guidelines for antibiotic use. Science will advance, we will see new drugs though in what form they will take only time will tell. Not long ago I answered a questionnaire on phone from a Market Research Company about a drug a company were developing. I could guess what this product would be if research proceeds, it would be wrong for me to say what it is other than I can see a place for it if all comes to fruition.

We will continue to work hand in hand with these companies and may their support of us continue. A long with vaccine research, a lot has happened in my time in drug development. At this stage of my career, the end, I can only thank all those involved in the industry for their support, development and assistance when required.

Even in my time, we have come a long way. Changing times, and if one other thing has changed in my time, when I started, I hated Rioja. Now it is my favourite wine!

And I love Girona.

13

SURGERY

One of the most daunting things when you first qualify is not the first consultation, but the first operation you must do, especially if by yourself. In Small Animal Practice you would normally have a trained nurse helping you as the anaesthetist, and she (normally) would have seen loads of operations before and could help guide you through it if there was no other vet around. You would have seen a lot of operations as a student and helped with some as well. In farm and equine work that is far less likely. Certainly, the many students we would have had "seeing practice" with us as part of their extra mural studies would have seen ops out on farms whenever we could facilitate it. We would try to show them the fundamentals of large animal surgery, even if we could not let them undertake it as we were on a farm doing a job and being paid for our results. But hopefully now, the modern graduate on qualification will have witnessed several of most of the different types of operations we do on farm, and to be honest there are not that many different ops we actually perform.

Perhaps when I was a student, I was unlucky but when I qualified I had seen only a couple of caesareans on cows and that was about it. As mere students, we had been allowed to castrate calves under supervision but that was about all. I had when on the farm alone as a teenager, "stuck" a cow when she was blown but that was it, we never had a caesarean, stomach op or anything of that kind. That was a lifesaving procedure when one of dad's cow's rumen had become full of gas and if I had not acted quickly, she soon would have died. The Herriot tales of blown cows, being stuck while someone was smoking and there then being an enormous flame from the methane expelled from the rumen has never happened to me thank heavens but will remain an amusing tale from others on such incidents. For me, luckily dad had the right instrument, a trocar and cannula for me to punch through the cow's side into her stomach to release the gas and she lived to be milked many more times. Others in emergency have used any knife they could find, whether it be their pocketknife or a kitchen knife, in emergency, and this can be an emergency, you use what you can find.

It is a common occurrence on cows grazed on lush clover filled meadows, and to increase protein intake, this is what a lot of our organic farmers now graze. So even with modern technology and nutrition methods, this problem has not gone away and if it does occur, it will often be with multiple cow numbers. Not so long ago I had a farm where dozens of cows were blowing up, some of which just by moving them off the pasture and keeping them mobile, the situation resolved itself, the stomach deflated as the cow managed to release the gas. Others, we had to go down to the local pub, no not another drink, but to procure from them as much cooking oil as they could spare. It acted as a surfactant to help disperse the gas bubble in the stomach and then release the gas by eructation (burping). But on that night, there was still the necessity to "stick" over a dozen of the cows to save their lives, with obvious risks of peritonitis that could follow. We only lost four of them in the end, but it was a situation that required prompt and decisive action. My experience all those years ago has served me well as once you have done it a first time, it is easy the next and every subsequent time after that, a simple but brave emergency procedure.

That is probably the simplest surgery we perform; castration would be the commonest. I can remember my old tutor at university telling us that castration is something we should be able to do in our sleep, a thought I found rather frightening as the only male I ever go to bed with is myself. I have taken the precaution of never taking a scalpel blade to bed and am pleased to say after all these years I am still entire!

Across our main farm species in any given year there will be a lot of males born which if left alone would grow into bulls, boars, and rams. Male piglets used to be castrated. I would watch my parents doing it to the male piglets they had when they started farming, just a few and done at an early age. Now, with genetic improvement, pigs grow very quickly up to slaughter weight for pork and bacon, so castration is very rare. Boar taint used to be the problem with slow growing pigs, giving the meat an unpleasant taste, but for many years now they are served up as your Sunday roast before this occurs. Other than the occasional pet pig such as Kune Kunes, it is now a rare procedure that we carry out.

Ram lambs for as long as I can remember have had rubber rings applied to their private parts soon after birth, a relatively painless procedure which does not set them back and with little chance of infection. Soon after the application of the ring they will be skipping around the fields with their mates in one of those wonderful spring scenes. A procedure almost certainly carried out by the shepherd, so we have little involvement in castration of sheep other than, again, the occasional pet ram.

Cattle are a different matter, and if fifty percent of calves are likely to be male, then one does not want a large population of bulls around which are potentially extremely dangerous animals. One of my lasting childhood memories would be of my father being tossed in the air by the Ayrshire bull we had then. There are still many fatalities on the farm caused by bulls.

Friesian and Holstein bull calves cause some debate over their value, and in times of hardship on farms, they have become worthless. One would often hear of cases when a farmer has taken animals to market and when he had returned to his vehicle, a couple of small Holstein bull calves would have been deposited on him. They were selling for just a couple of quid, worthless, their ear tags would have cost more than that. In times gone by, a farmer would estimate the number of heifer calves he would need which would mean serving twice that number of cows with a dairy bull. The remainder would be served with a beef bull, producing a valuable calf whichever sex it was.

Times have changed and now a lot of Holstein bull calves will be reared as bull beef, fattening them quickly on cereal diets so they would be a saleable beef animal at not much over a year old. There has been no need to castrate these.

The other big change over recent years has been the introduction of sexed semen using Artificial Insemination. Ones best, highest genetic potential cows and heifers will be served with sexed semen, knowing that about ninety percent of those calves will be female and will be your future breeding and milking herd. The rest can be put in calf to beef bulls, and these will be the chaps who will need castrating. They will have a longer life, almost certainly spending some of it getting fat on grass, to produce the higher quality beef that the consumer requires, slow maturing beef. One cannot have all these bulls running around a field, it would be dangerous and would produce the wrong sort of carcase quality the butcher is looking for. We castrate these.

The other advantage of using sexed semen now is that it has eliminated the need for that controversial topic of slaughtering dairy bull calves at birth when they were worthless. It is now a Farm Assurance requirement by many of the milk purchasers that this calf slaughter is forbidden. Sexed semen has allowed this unnecessary event to cease, all calves can be reared and have some purpose whether to be future milking cows or to be beef. One can serve the number of cows one wants a heifer calf from with sexed semen, the rest can be served to a beef bull.

Castration continues and is a fairly routine event for us as farm vets. There are strict welfare rules concerning this procedure, being updated all the time, which can only be a good thing for the welfare of the calves. Farmers do use rubber rings in very young calves but after a certain age this is forbidden and castration requires a local anaesthetic, and now also some sort of systemic pain relief. A definite step in the right direction, and with this, bull calves are found to grow quicker with this use of pain relief.

As I said earlier, our tutor at university said we should be capable of performing the op in our sleep. It does seem to fall on the young ones in the practice who get given these jobs. When I started you may go on a farm and do half a dozen, a dozen, but now on some units we could do fifty to a hundred in one go. Our preference has always been to do them young; they are easier to handle so it is safer for all involved.

All those year ago in Devon I can remember one particular farmer who would call us out just once a year to disbud, dehorn and castrate all his calves. It can only be described as a rodeo, his facilities for handling cattle were poor so it was a job we did when we had Vet students seeing practice with us in their vacations. I found it a challenge and fun, even if it was the rodeo that I expected it to be and would not worry if it was my name that was selected for the job. To me, as we were supplying the labour for the farmer, the students, then I felt it was in my rights to let the students get on and do the work, a great experience for them under my direction. I would hold the calves, of varying sizes while the student lopped the horns off and castrated them.

We would spend an afternoon going through all the youngstock doing what was necessary to each one. The farm was a shambles and there would be wire, tin sticking out everywhere so at the end of the session we would be covered in scratches and small cuts, but it was fun. What next? A well-deserved pint. A lot of the calves had ringworm and it would only be a few days later that I found that where I had a scratch or cut on my arms from holding the cattle, I now had a ringworm lesion. Boy, did they itch, especially at night and in those days when I had a metal spring base to the bed then I would often put my arm under the mattress and rub it up and down on the springs for a scratch. Luckily a friend recommended something called Whitfield's Ointment to me which when applied soon alleviated the condition.

Handling conditions, I am pleased to say have improved greatly, which is just as well for the size of some of the bulls we must castrate. It is still a job I am quite happy to take students out to, and to act as their instructor as they perform the operation. There are more and more female students about now and it has often amused me how gently they try to be when doing his. A good friend's daughter was training to be a vet and had all the makings of being an excellent one (she has since followed the small animal route). I took her out to a couple of farms and let her get on with it. After administering the local anaesthetic, she would stroke the skin of the scrotum with the scalpel blade, not achieving much as she did it.

Instruction was needed. I showed her that a bold cut was needed, and the job would soon be easily done.

I said to her, "Think of the calf as the boyfriend you have just dumped and what you would like to do to him!"

With a quick cut, she had grasped it (who knows what was going on in her mind!) and in not many moments the bull was soon a steer.

As mentioned, some of the bulls we have to do are quite large, and as well as anaesthetic it is necessary to hold the bull's tail up as a form of restraint to stop him kicking. The poor vet is standing directly behind so is in the firing line. There is one wonderful theory that you, the vet, should make the farmer stand right beside the bull, not outside the cattle crush. The theory is that once the farmer has been kicked enough then he will consider doing his cattle at a far younger age when they are far more manageable. They soon learn!

But the most daunting of operations we must perform, especially when first qualified are those where we have to enter the cow's abdomen, namely rumenotomies, displaced abomasum's (fourth stomach) and Caesareans. Techniques have changed slightly over the years but not a lot, but when we first set out as vets it was still a big decision to make to operate. Farmers would see us as young and inexperienced, not really knowing what we were doing, and would be reluctant to let us "experiment" on their livestock.

Especially for a Caesarean. We would have to try and calve the cow for a long time, up to a couple of hours, before we could persuade the farmer that the calf was not going to come out of the back end. He would have suggested those barbaric techniques they used to use like trying to pull the calf out with the tractor (something we would find abhorrent to try), trying to cut the calf up inside the cow, an embryotomy, or calling out someone more experienced. By the time you started a Caesar, you were knackered, the cow was knackered, and the calf invariably had died because of the protracted birth. All made for a glum scenario where the farmer thought you had done a bad job, you as a young vet were disheartened, and the cow, almost certainly would not have a good outcome.

In my first job I was not required to do a Caesar, but my mate Andy in a neighbouring practice had, and under those circumstances. A last resort. There only tended to be one vet on call at night so you had to get on and do whatever was necessary, then however tired you were, work the next day.

Luckily when I moved to Devon we always tended to operate in pairs, so you always had another pair of hands to back you up on your decision and to have help when performing the operation. East Devon had a high cattle population, and especially with the use of large Continental beef breeds which frequently exceeded their predicted gestation length, then Caesars were quite common. But it was still a daunting decision even if it were helped by farmers being used to the operation. If they had good experiences of previous operations, they had no quibbles about another one.

The first time I had to inject the local when in Devon with the paravertebral technique, something I had never done before, this was more than a bit scary. Then that first incision with the scalpel through the skin and then through the muscle layers before entering the abdomen. Every blood vessel would be clamped off to stop the bleeding, over the years I would find this unnecessary as most of them stopped by themselves, it was a laborious and nerve jingling experience. This while expecting to get kicked and trying not to cut yourself. Then to put your arm inside to find the uterus and find a calf's leg through its wall to pull it up though the wound and incise the uterus open to grab the calf. Was the incision long enough? Was the skin wound big enough to get a large calf out? All these decisions you had to make while working "on the hoof". Then it was time to close the wound in the uterus, stitch it up while all the time it was trying to contract away from you. It always seemed the new boy's job to hold this muscular structure while it was closed up and it got really tiring on your fingers holding it outside the skin wound while your partner stitched, ensuring a good closure of the wound.

Lastly, stitching the abdominal muscles and then the skin ensuring that all the layers came together well without any gaping holes. I spent many of my first operations working with George Dart and over time we developed as a good team, being able to predict what the other required next to make the operation go smoothly and quickly.

The one who had attended the calving in the first place, when deciding it was going to be a C-section, would phone the other. Usually by the time he had arrived then number one would have clipped and prepared the operation site so that we could start straight after the second vet had arrived and got scrubbed up.

An efficient team developed, and we had many positive outcomes because we opted early to operate and because of the efficiency we developed together. If lacking confidence to begin with, after having got the calf out, you would get your first chance to suture yourself with George to advise. With practice one became more and more proficient.

As has been the case throughout my whole career, all you would have to watch out for if the ever-willing farmer wanting to help, who would try and put his mitts in the cow to help pull the calf out but had made no effort to scrub up or wash his hands at all.

Occasionally, especially during the day, you would work with one of the other vets. I will always remember helping Don, one of the partners with a C-section and having got the calf out and closed the uterine incision, he said he could manage the rest by himself. I think he must have stitched faster than a sewing machine because by the time I had washed and cleaned up, he had finished. After years of experience now, I wouldn't beat him in a race, but wouldn't be far behind him.

There has not been that much that has changed over the years. In Gloucestershire it was like taking a step back in that farmers were more reluctant to have an operation, perhaps they had had poor outcomes in the past, but once they had seen you do an op with a successful outcome, their fears were removed. The other difference was that invariably you had to do the op by yourself and had to adapt your techniques accordingly. A life saver was a drug that came out that relaxed the uterine muscles so that when you were suturing it back up, it was not contracting away from you so rapidly. A great help. Then, new suture materials other than catgut, which caused less reaction as the wound healed.

Especially with some of the pedigree breeders of beef cattle, and with the introduction of Belgian Blue cattle into the country, then Caesars often became the norm. The farmer would himself become a very useful pair of hands to assist. He would know what you wanted and when, so would become your assistant. And he knew he had to scrub up before putting is hands inside the cow. He would have a special crush that would restrain the cow easily to be able to perform the operation, rather than in a lot of cases just having to halter her to a post or gate. Caesars are usually performed with the cow standing which makes for a far easier procedure, if the cow is lying down, it can be a bit back breaking, leaning over the wound while operating and then suturing.

But if all goes well, then the results are always exhilarating with a live calf trying to get to its feet by the time you are putting the last stitch in, and then being able to suckle mum. If she has good maternal instincts, she will be ready to receive her new-born calf while taking little notice of what she has just been through. Resilient animals are cows.

Although there are mainly autumn and spring calving herds in both the beef and dairy industry, cows can and do calve at any time of year. Because of that, Caesars can occur throughout the year. Unlike cattle, sheep are seasonal breeders with their oestrous cycles very much initiated by the light, as it starts to fade, as days become shorter in late summer, then sheep begin their reproductive activity so usually by just before Christmas we will begin our lambing season and that will extend through to early June. Most farmers will have hoped their lambing season will have finished long before then, so they can go to bed without worrying about having to get up at frequent intervals to see if anything is lambing. It can be a long season!

During those few months, and especially from February through to April, we would expect to do many lambings and more than a few of those would turn out to be caesareans, whether because of an oversized single lamb or a tangle of lambs inside the ewe's uterus, or her cervix just never dilated fully to allow the lamb to pass through. There can be many reasons, but in essence when deciding surgery is necessary, then the main difference between a cow and a sheep is obviously size. A different form of restraint is needed as the operation will be done again through a flank incision but with the ewe lying on her side. There is nothing more than frustrating than trying to operate while your patient is trying to get up and run away. Sedatives do not tend to be that effective in sheep and you really want her to be up on her feet and ready to mother the lamb as soon as the last stitch has been tied and she has been cleaned up.

This is where if you are into bondage, you are on a winner. With either a couple of people holding her down by her legs, or this is where those wooden pallets come in handy making an excellent operating table and offering plenty of scope to be able to tie the sheep down, so she is fully restrained. The pallet is put on a couple of bales then it eases the strain on us poor vets backs as we lean over to carry out the procedure. After that, it is the same as a cow but in degrees of size and can easily be done in less than half an hour, hopefully then producing a healthy pair of twins for mum to rear. Most ewes are sensational mothers, and just hearing the lambs bleating will get her attention so she can become a little restless while finishing closing the wound.

It is very satisfying when, a lot of these operations will be done at base, the farmer coming to us whereas in a calving we go to the farm, loading the ewe and lambs back into the trailer happy with the farmer driving away happy as well.

These would be classed as obstetrical procedures. We do carry out other operations other than abdominal surgery but a lot of these could be classed as fairly minor; opening abscesses, removing lumps like warts and the odd rarity like cutting contracted tendons in calves to allow them to straighten their legs.

If one has a stomach for pus, then lancing abscesses can be quite fun. Though I can remember once when opening a massive swelling on a cow's side being trapped between the cattle crush and a wall as gallons of fetid liquid poured from the wound that I had just made, projecting against the wall two feet away at a steady stream. I did not want it all over me! I stood there for minutes as this horrid yellow fluid poured out. It was at last relenting and I was able to get where I wanted to and then be able to flush the abscess out with a hose and water, and then with dilute Hydrogen Peroxide which has a wonderful cleansing affect. A profusion of bubbles exudes from the wound as it cleans the abscess and has the effect of attracting inflammatory cells to the site. It is amazing that after how much pus comes from a wound like this, how quickly it clears up, again a testament to the resilience of a cow. I guess the cow has an ability to wall the infection off from the rest of her body and so does not suffer from the septicaemia that say a cat wound when it has a cat bite abscess and is usually ill with it.

Whether one is extracting pus from an abscess in a cow's foot or from a swelling as described above, there is always a great sense of satisfaction that in letting the pus escape. A hose pipe is a wonderful tool for then flushing it until clean, that you have achieved something beneficial to the well-being of the animal, and the satisfaction that the farmer sees from seeing the infection escape. I hope people do not think we have warped minds in this!

Abdominal surgery is not uncommon in the modern cow but not very common in youngstock and sheep. If it is carried out in the latter two mentioned, then it is far more likely as a diagnostic tool to confirm a diagnosis. We do not have the hospital facilities to give the post-operation care to farmstock, nor is it economically viable, nor that practical to be administering vast amounts of intravenous fluids etc to farm patients. Restraint and the volumes necessary are key issues, even before one considers the different anatomical features of the ruminant's gut compared with a dog, a cat or us even. Disappointingly, heroic intervention in what would be life threatening abdominal catastrophes usually end in disappointment and failure, making euthanasia the kinder option in the first place.

But that is not to say that we do not perform abdominal surgery in cattle, with a couple of ops quite common when I first started. A ruminant's abdomen makes up a large part of its body and this is filled with a large fermentation chamber, the rumen. Cows and sheep have four stomachs when fully developed, the reticulum, the rumen, the omasum and the abomasum. The reticulum is a small sack at the entrance of the stomachs, attached to the front of the largest of the stomachs, the rumen. This is the fermentation chamber of ruminants where micro-organisms set to work on breaking down the animal's diet, grass, silage, concentrates (corn, soya, all forms of starch or protein). There is a fine balance in feeding to keep this population micro-organisms stable, so a good digestive process takes place, the animal then regurgitates the food and chews it again before it is re-swallowed back into the rumen. A soup of digested food can then pass through the omasum into the abomasum which is a bit like our own stomach in how it functions, being vey acidic and adding digestive juices to the gut contents before they pass on further down into the small and large intestines. Digestion continues as it continues to pass on through the digestive tract, a spiral attached to the roof of the abdomen, circling down suspended by mesentery and the blood supply to the guts. Nutrients are absorbed from the guts into the blood stream and utilised in the body. What passes out the other end, well I think you all know or can guess. An extremely basic description of the anatomy with the rumen lying on the left-hand side of the abdomen, the reticulum at the front of the rumen lying against the diaphragm with the heart just the other side lying in its own sack, the pericardium.

In lambs and calves, the rumen is undeveloped, and mum's milk passes directly into the abomasum to start to be digested. As the youngster starts to eat fibre in the form of grass or hay, then this will go into the rumen and this structure then develops to occupy a large volume of the abdomen and take over the digestive process.

One of the commonest problems requiring surgery used to be if the cow had eaten a piece of metal, usually a piece of wire or a nail. Especially with the improved technology of grass foraging equipment to make silage, their high-speed chopping mechanisms can make mincemeat of any metal that may go through the blades and end up in silage. These pieces of metal can have very sharp points and when ingested will fall into the reticulum. The stomach is always contracting, and it is easily possible that these sharp pointed bits of metal can prick through the reticular wall, penetrating it forwards towards the diaphragm producing a localised peritonitis. If it penetrates further, it can puncture through this and then enter the pericardial sac. The stomach contains bugs, and these will be inoculated into the sac causing infection and the production of large amounts of pus. If this builds up enough, it interferes with the ability of the heart to contract and expand, essentially then causing a constrictive heart failure. This invariably is fatal.

A cow with a "wire" can have several symptoms, but commonly if you pinch their backs, they tighten their muscles downwards and as they do this, they will often give a short grunt. This is caused by as they get a slight discomfort from the wire pricking its surrounds and the effect of a localised peritonitis. The other common test is to place a metal bar under the cow's sternum with a person both sides and lift gently. It will illicit the same response, a grunt.

As long as there were no signs of heart involvement then this would be the time you would decide to operate, again with the cow standing and using local anaesthetic. Once the abdomen was opened, two strings would be attached to the muscular wall of the rumen, one high, one lower and these would be used to pull some of the rumen through the body wall so that it could be opened without the risk of spillage of its contents into the abdomen. This was the youngster's job. First though the surgeon would feel down the outside of the stomachs looking for adhesions and signs of a penetration. On finding this, the surgeon would then reach down into the rumen through his incision down into the reticulum, scouring its surface to find the offending object. Once found, it would be pulled back through into the stomach, imparting that grunt again. It would then be pulled out and presented to the farmer as a "fait accomplis". There would be a tarnished, rusty nail, length of wire to show off as a successful diagnosis and operation. The stomach and the abdominal wall would then be sutured closed, antibiotics administered, and a successful outcome would be achieved.

Did my surgery lecturer tell us "If you say it is a wire, make sure it is. So always having a piece of wire on your person somewhere just in case, so you have something to show the farmer". Have I done this? I'll be honest: no, I have not.

But it is amazing some of the metal object that have some out of cows. Once when in Devon, the amount of shredded metal we took out of one cow's stomach was amazing. Handfuls of filings, razor sharp which I guess came from the construction of the M5 next door and had then gone through the silage making equipment and then consumed.

Progress has been made in that this is now not a common operation. Firstly, in the method of feeding, silage tends to be mixed with other ingredients of the diet in a mixer wagon, a TMR, and these often have magnets on them where the feed leaves the trailer via a conveyor to be put in the feeding areas of the cattle. This reduces the risk. There was a time when some tyres ended up going through these mechanical choppers and they are full of thin wires which when shredded had a large potential for getting inside the cow in silage, and these thin pieces of wire were not fussy where they migrated to, causing lesions and peritonitis throughout the abdomen, getting into the liver among other places. A few years ago, there were outbreaks of this on farm but gladly it is a problem we see far less of now. It pays to be tidy and to pile used tyres, they were used to hold down the sheeting covering silage clamps, away safely so they do not end up in fields.

Now, magnets have become an important treatment in cows. I was always sceptical I would have to admit that a magnet sitting in a cow's reticulum would be powerful enough to retrieve a wire or nail sticking through the stomach wall and into, or through the diaphragm. But having used them for a few years now, I am surprised how effective they are and now surgery only tends to be a last resort. The magnets are encased in a plastic frame, and one would be surprised if one is doing a post-mortem on a cow how much metal you can find attached to these magnets. Cows are foragers but in grazing low to the ground, or in their feed troughs all sorts of foreign bodies can be picked up with the potential to do harm. Where we do see herd outbreaks of wires, then we do sometimes put a magnet in every cow. It becomes a wrestling match trying to put the gun, a tube containing the magnet with a plunger to push it down when at the back of the mouth, in the cow's mouth while holding her head, and making sure she has swallowed the magnet.

Thankfully, this is a condition we see far less of now, and any suspected wire can easily be treated with a magnet and with relatively little expense.

I would have to mention, though not common here, that in my travels in Kenya and speaking to Animal Technicians there, it is not uncommon where cows are grazing loose in the towns and will often be seen rooting through the rubbish at the sides of the roads. A cow getting ill can often be because of their foraging. They are looking for food, any food and so will eat plastic bags etc which once contained it. This slowly collects in their rumen until reaching the point where digestion ceases, rumination ceases and they become bloated on plastic, causing them to starve to death. A sad scenario of something that could easily be prevented with proper waste disposal. Between my visits of 2017 and 2018 I was pleased to find that Kenya and Tanzania are now way ahead of us in their use, or now, non-use of plastic bags in shops; they are forbidden. Despite the affect it has had on their economy in that a lot of people were employed in the production of these bags, it is a great step forward firstly for the environment, and secondly for the welfare of these street cattle.

Our commonest operation now would be an LDA, a left-sided displaced abomasum, the cow's fourth stomach. In its normal position it lies on the right side of the rumen and is where digestion as opposed to fermentation (or bacterial digestion) begins to take place. It is an acidic chamber which leads on to the small intestine. However, soon after calving, when the rumen is reduced in size to make way for a large, calf filled uterus, there are conditions happening in the body which make the abomasum fill up with gas. It can either move sideways below the rumen and then up the left flank where it becomes trapped causing an LDA or dilate and move upwards and twist on itself causing a right-sided displaced abomasum (RDA) and torsion. Colloquially, either way, it gets called a twisted gut. Other conditions such as Milk Fever, retained foetal membranes, reduced food intake can all be precipitating factors, causing the cow to become ketotic and displace. On listening to the cow's abdomen with a stethoscope, the gas filled stomach will produce a characteristic ping as when flicking the flank with your finger, like if you were doing the same to a tractor tyre.

I have been to the occasional one where you have gone to operate later in the day after diagnosis, only to find that the stomachs have sorted themselves out and intervention is not necessary. Equally a few times you will see the same cow a couple of days later and the stomach is displaced again. Swingers, not the type of human swinger, but here referring to the cow's stomach.

So invariably some sort of correction is needed. In past times we used just to roll the cow. The cow would be cast on the ground using Rolfe's method, one of those wonderful tricks you are told about at university but the first time you have to do it yourself you are the real McCoy, a qualified vet and thinking to yourself, "How do I do this?"

A rope is needed and then a non-tightening noose is put around the cow's neck. Remembering those scout knotting days, a Bowline making a small loop in the rope, then a rabbit comes out of the hole (the loop), around the tree (the rope), then back down the hole again, simple! So long as the noose is the right size. Then the rope goes back to the shoulder, around the underside of the cow, back through the rope again and then back along to in front of the cow's hips and this is repeated. If you have done the loops the right way, with a couple of hefty men to pull on the end of the rope, the cow gently lies down on her righthand side, so the gas filled stomach on the left side I uppermost. Then rolling her slowly over onto her back, the stomach should float up as it is full of gas so now lying midline on the ventral abdominal wall, now the highest point of her abdomen. Then letting her lower slowly onto her left side, the abomasum returns to its normal position in the abdomen. Allowing the gas to move on into the intestines, the cow can then be allowed to stand up and fingers crossed, she will recover normally, soon tucking into her grub again.

However, maybe as cows have got bigger and deeper, recurrence was frequent. In my early days, rolling the cow worked, now it does not. Surgery has become the norm.

In those distant days in Devon when I started, then two of us operated. This was the friendly op! The cow would be opened either side, one vet performing on both flanks. The vet on the left would start, opening into the abdomen to find the displaced and gas filled abomasum. While he was doing this, the vet on the right would start his surgery, making an incision on this side through to the viscera inside. One of the wonderful things about a cow's insides is that if you give it an outlet, the guts just want to get out and so are soon trying to pour out through your wound opening.

The vet on the left would attach a nylon suture to the abomasum with long ends and then wind these ends around a pair of forceps.

The friendly part, we would both reach under or around the rumen until we could touch, shake each other's hand. How gentlemanly is that? Then having become friends, the forceps would be placed in the hands of the vet on the right and as he gently pulled on the nylon towards the right flank, the left vet would push the abomasum on its way under the rumen until it had gone back into its proper position. The sutures would then be attached to the bottom of the wound and then both sides would be closed, trying to prevent those guts trying to do a runner from extruding from the wound.

A remarkably successful operation, the cow would soon be eating and cudding again on the way to an uneventful recovery. Were there any complications? Yes, occasionally. One cow Pete and I operated on, all the cow wanted to do was to kick us, to get from one side of her to the other, the only safe way was to climb over her back.

Jerseys tended to be very fatty inside, there would be a lot of hard yellow fat and if one were to rough and caused damage to this, it would go necrotic and cause localised peritonitis. Luckily, most Jerseys are small and docile and so long as you were gentle then this risk could be minimised.

Then there were the rough, tough farmers that nothing bothered them. It was always advisable to ask if any of the helpers, the farmhands, were squeamish, could they stand the sight of blood. Of course, they could!

Just as you reached the crucial part of the operation when you were trying to shake hands with your colleague you would look up to find some big lump looking very pale, then sinking to the floor. Worryingly under the cow.

You would have to stop what you were doing and try and catch him before he banged his head, or the cow decided to kick out at this falling mass.

One soon gets to recognise the helpers who position themselves such that they will do the job you require of them restraining the cow, but their eyes at no stage, until you have sewed her back up again, look at what you are doing or anywhere there may be blood. Some farmers are not as tough as they think.

A method that worked well, so long as we had two pairs of hands. But as my career progressed then that became a luxury. I moved from Devon and suddenly found no-one wanted to help, I would have to find a way of doing the operation by myself.

I have described the use of Chloral Hydrate and doing the op with the cow positioned on her back earlier, again something that was quite simple. But then Chloral Hydrate was banned so we were left having to do cows standing again, but just operating from one side, the right, and reaching under to pull the offending stomach back to its proper position with a long muscular arm. As cows got taller, for a little guy this got harder and harder.

Another technique evolved where you operated on the left-hand side, attaching a suture to the abomasum, or the surrounding omentum and then reaching down with a strong needle in hand attached to the suture to push it through the abdominal floor on the right-hand side just behind the back of the sternum. This would be repeated with the other long end of the suture so someone could pull on both ends now dangling below the cow while the vet would push the abomasum down and back under the rumen. Once in the right position, the sutures could be drawn tight to secure, pexy, the abomasum in that position. Adhesions form which fix it there permanently, problem solved, and even after twenty-four hours the cow seems on the road to recovery.

It took me a long time to try this method, eventually only experimenting when on one farm, having got the cow in restrained, Bill the cowman told me when I said that I would need to operate and would need her turned around, "this cow is stroppy and will kick a lot. It would be better if you could operate on this side."

In for a penny, in for a pound, I agreed and found it far simpler, now adopting this as my preferred method of dealing with this condition. Now, there being nine of us vets before my retirement, you can guess who the surgeon was by which side they have worked on and their method of suturing.

It amazed me when in 2010 Jane and I went on a Nile cruise. One of our stops was at the temple of Kom Ombo and here there were many well preserved pillars still standing. On some covered with hieroglyphics would be inscriptions of surgery and instruments that this ancient civilisation used some two thousand plus years ago. One could not help but notice that a lot of these have not changed a lot over all those years. There were even graphics of caesarean sections being performed.

Some technology has moved on and over the past ten years or so, a change has come in the advent of keyhole surgery in cows. As I retire, Roel and Sean, both excellent surgeons (and the others vets in the practice are learning the techniques) now use keyhole surgery a lot in cow abdominal surgery. Especially for these displacement operations where through tubes they can see inside the cows through very small wounds, tie a suture to the abomasum and then take that suture to the ventral wall of the abdomen as described before to pexy the abomasum there. It intrigues me the subtlety of being able to do this, but they have worked on and are now very astute at this keyhole surgery. It also saves the need for exploratory laparotomies, opening the abdomen to see what is going on inside as they can visualise everything through their endoscopes before deciding whether greater intervention is necessary.

There is minimal intervention, and because of this, then very often there is no need for antibiotic treatment either, a double plus in that the cow's milk can be sold straight away and of course with growing pressure on antibiotic usage, this helps reduce it.

In this respect, times they are a changing, and some of our surgical techniques are catching up with the medics even on farm. What will the future hold? Our techniques are always under review, we as vets discuss our successes and failures amongst ourselves. We try slight modifications in technique that one may have tried, or had to find a solution to a problem which has then become part of his or her now adopted routine. Being able to film, record has been a great help and to show the insides of the patient we are operating on.

In surgery, change is now rapid and bringing far better and rewarding outcomes, but with the proviso, always pick your patient wisely.

14

ANTIPODEANS AND EUROPEANS

All those years ago when I qualified there were about three hundred and fifty graduates leaving the Veterinary Schools each year. You were one of the lucky few to get one of those places with many prospective students disappointed each year as there were not enough places for them to fill. The intake to some extent was judged on how many vets it was thought there would be needed. There would be times when jobs were a plenty, other times when they were in short supply. When I left Bristol there were the jobs about, but far fewer if like me you wanted to go into a largely farm animal-based career. The profession in this country was largely made up of people qualifying from the Home Unions and from Dublin. Scottish and Irish vets, there were many.

But we are of course in the Commonwealth, and it became common, especially when agriculture was going through a bad time in Australia, that we would get Kiwi and Aussie vets coming over here looking for work. Similarly, there would be several British vets who would go over to New Zealand to their cattle practices to learn, gain experience in big cattle practices and to explore the Southern Hemisphere. I guess in those days the closest we would get to a Gap Year but working. Agriculture was and still is one of the key industries of New Zealand, there are many cattle and sheep over there, it was a great experience to work with them.

I would have to admit in all my years I never got to work with an Aussie vet. From what I have been told by those that had worked with them, their methods were a bit cavalier, but they were very popular with clients and other staff members. I did work with a couple of South Africans who did not seem to have the same popularity despite their ability, perhaps they come across as a little arrogant. Those were in my early years and then I saw hardly any Commonwealth vets until the last couple of years when James, a lad from Zimbabwe, joined us to gain farm experience before he headed home to his family farm and to develop a practice in his native country. It was a shame because this guy was good, learnt quickly and became extremely popular around Shropshire. Ever helpful and never afraid to ask if he was unsure of anything, he became a great asset. He had the height and build to cope with most tasks easily. He was also a very personable and interesting chap to talk to when we would meet up socially. I would wish him every success now he has returned home.

The job grew broader over the years, especially with having to meet European legislation and Directives. Vets were needed for Poultry and Red Meat Inspection, for Government work as well as those vets who left General Practice to go into research or to join Pharmaceutical Companies as veterinary advisors. Numbers entering Universities in this country were increasing, but the need for vets was increasing as well, especially as more and more females joined the profession. Some, both male and female did not stay in the profession, and things like maternity leave would mean the necessity for locum cover. British vets did not want to take on the meat inspection work, nor the monotonous hours of Tuberculosis testing as the disease was becoming more prevalent. Vets from other countries would have to be recruited.

Our first experience was of Spanish vets, and it soon became apparent there were many of them looking for careers in the UK. Their problem often was their grasp of the English language with farmers (and their fellow vets) finding it hard to understand them, though no doubt that feeling was mutual, especially when a broad Salopian accent was added to the equation.

Our first was a petite Spanish lady who soon became popular with everyone she worked with. Yes, small and slim but she would always muck in to give a helping hand when necessary as well as doing her TB testing, something the farmers always appreciated. She had a wonderful sense of humour which is always a great help and was soon accepted by the farming community. Any sense of foreboding about a women, small at that, and one whose English was not brilliant was soon forgotten when it was found how good she was at doing her job. She would pioneer the way for many

Spanish vets to join us and for the acceptance that women could do as equally as good a job as men.

She would stay with us for four years before leaving to pursue her interests in the epidemiology of disease outbreaks, I would meet up with her again when I worked on the Avian Flu outbreak in Lincolnshire later in my career.

She was soon followed by my three amigos, Pelayo, Pablo and Pedro, keen football fans like myself and who would sometimes use my tickets at Old Trafford. Again, they became popular with the farmers and the rest of our staff. They were a lot of fun to work with, and I still keep in touch. The beautiful Alba joined us, always with a smile on her face and always ringing in to find out directions as to where she was supposed to be, she was lost again!

After the three Amigos, next came Rosa. Rosa originates from a town in Southern Spain, Chiclana de la Frontera, a town boasting one of the best beaches in Spain called La Barrosa. Rosa's father had trained to be a vet, so it was in the blood a bit, although he did not finish his course and instead turned to be a Biologist. She was unsure of what she wanted to do although it would be something along the biology line and so did eventually decide on a Veterinary career. Her grandparents had owned a few dairy cows, a few pigs but nothing to describe this as a serious farming background, even her father had reared a few beef animals. But Rosa's part of Spain would not be counted as a big farming area, unlike in the north in Asturia and in Catalonia where I had visited where there were sizable dairy units.

She had come over to England as a teenager to learn some English so was already acquainted with Yorkshire. She finished her university course in Cordoba but in Spanish Veterinary Schools they don't seem to give the students the amount of practical experience that our students receive in this country. This was limited to two months General practice in her last year plus the poor University cow that had to endure every student's arm examining her insides, and as her rectum became pathologically thickened from these repeated intrusions, less and less value was obtained from her discomfort!

Rosa was qualified at a time when the Spanish economy was suffering with more and more public service cutbacks. If you were bold enough and had the finances you could set yourself up in your own practice, otherwise there were few jobs available and all poorly paid working for local Government as these financial restraints on the country grew deeper and deeper. She wanted to work with large animals and wanted to learn English better, so she decided to come to England where she obtained a job in the

Meat Inspection service in abattoirs, working in Lincolnshire and working with poultry.

I asked her, "Why did you want to become a Vet if this is what you ended up doing?"

Rosa replied, "A good question, I ask myself everyday why!"

She found her way down to Shropshire where she joined the practice I was in, now with a regular community of Spanish vets carrying out most of the Tuberculosis test that we had to do. Getting the tender with our parent body XLVets in the Midlands region, this would guarantee work for the foreseeable future until at least it was time to reapply. Rosa settled in Shrewsbury and became a popular and important member of the team, always willing to help and to learn. For five years she stayed with us and was given the opportunity to swap over to the clinical team. We reached the stage when it seemed more sensible to appoint and train within rather than scour the country for that rare commodity, an experienced farm animal vet looking to move to another practice when there were no immediate chances of partnership on offer. The plan was to give her and another of the TB team clinical training, a type of internship while still performing her TB duties, gaining technique and experience before swapping teams completely. Alas Covid and remote working made this very hard, she could work in a bubble with one other vet but that would be all. Her training rather ground to a halt, although as we got into the winter of 2020/1, she did have the chance to rekindle some of this training. Before Covid she had come out with me a few times on farms, mainly on Routine fertility visits where she could follow me down a line of cows and with her Ultrasound scanner, perform pregnancy diagnosis on the cows. It gave us the opportunity to discuss what she had found and to talk through some of the pressures and issues on the modern dairy farm. The farmer only too happy to let her join in the discussion as he knew her from her TB testing role.

She would, before remote working, accompany us on night duties sometimes, allowing her to gain experience of calvings, lambings and caesareans. This would give her the chance to see and understand our decision making, along with giving her the chance to feel inside the imminent birth, and even have ago at undertaking the task herself under our supervision. She could suture the wound, all part of a learning curve to get her up to speed as a clinical vet, something her university education had not done.

There was progress but this was abruptly ended by Covid. We could not risk the possibility of vets meeting up, possibly being infected, and passing the virus onto other members of staff, and then the risk of losing a proportion of staff to self-isolation in a period when our workload had not fallen off. Rosa's training stuttered and whereas she would normally have returned to Spain at some stage of a normal year to visit her family, this now could not happen without again a two-week self-isolation period on her return. It was time to decide on her future, if the clinical part was not working out as planned, then she longed for home. Rosa had been in England now for eight years, five of them in Shropshire. She had enjoyed it but missed Spain, it was time to return home.

Her future in Spain, the same sort of jobs are not available, would either mean working for the Government or for a Town Hall. Working in a role that our Food Standards Agency would be doing, checking on local markets, food producers etc. And after the effects of the Euro crisis ten years back, in Spain, the role of the vet would be considered the lowest of the lows amongst the jobs classed as professional (doctors, architects, solicitors). Her prospective salary would be extremely low compared with a British salary.

It was time to go home, she would be missed. We would miss her prowess at such things as archery on our Team Building evenings out, and she did enjoy a pint as well. But the pull of the home country became too strong. Her introduction to the out of hours rota was to be working Christmas 2021, who will do that now? I fancy it will be my replacement!

Rosa would have overlapped with a lovely Spanish lady, Cristina, for a couple of years at the practice. Cristina's home was further north, from the region of Aragon so famous in British history being the birthplace of Catherine, first wife of Henry VIII. Cristina was born and brought up in the city of Zaragoza which is where she also obtained her Veterinary Degree at the University there.

She started her professional career doing small animal work in the city, giving her experience in consultations and some surgery. Her wages were low compared with a vet in this country but at least she was working with dogs, which were so important in her wanting to join the profession in the first place. If she had one special interest it was in dog behaviour and dog training. She was working but still living at home but at least her "vocation" was sort of progressing in the direction she wished. Opportunities of progression were limited. Perhaps she was thinking she was getting in a rut, she was standing still and with that, like so many of our profession it was having an impact on her mental health. The dreaded depression was soon to follow, Cristina needed a change of direction and scenery and so moved to Barcelona to continue her studies but in the part of the job that really interested her, canine behaviour as previously mentioned. While overcoming her mental anguish she did post-graduate studies but sooner or later she would have to take herself back to the workplace.

She obtained her further qualifications, but it was time to move on. Although applying and getting an interview for a veterinary job in the Netherlands related to her wish to work with animal behaviour, it was in England that she arrived to pursue her career. She was also hoping to improve her grasp of the English language while working over here.

So, after spending some time in Cheshire working as a TB tester, like Rosa, she arrived in Shropshire to work in the practice I did. Here was a lady full now of self-confidence, outwardly anyway, always with a smile on her face and always wanting to talk, even if her grasp of English was far from perfect. But it was fun to chat and correct her, when necessary, a lovely lady only too willing to acquire the local tongue.

She became a popular figure in the practice both with the farmers and with other members of staff. The requirements for TB testers over time changed meaning that as a "lay" person you could be trained up to carry out what had always been a vet only job in the past could now be carried out by non-veterinarian as long as one had had the necessary training under veterinary supervision. By 2020 Tuberculosis was running rife in the county and we were struggling to recruit more Vet TB testers. Spanish testers were now few and far between and the Veterinary source had changed to them being Romanian. Cristina had helped train these when they first arrived, offering a supervisory hand to them as they started this new work. It was not only the veterinary side she had to cope with in training but also a few hair-raising moments with them driving in a new country. No one's car was safe, even if parked safely in our own works car park. Cristina got to the stage where she would say she would meet her new testers at the farm to save her having to drive with them, something far easier on her nerves.

But in time she then had to start training the non-veterinarian testers embarking on a new career. Some were easy, others hard work and with associated negative comments from our farming clientele, her job was not getting any easier. She persevered until they were able to fend for themselves and were allowed to test by themselves without supervision.

Where her career will take her in the future, only time will tell. It is thought that most of our European colleagues who come over to work as TB testers have a longevity of about two years in the job before they look for a change of direction. She will no doubt look for something more intellectually stimulating, whether it be in Britain or back home. Like I had done, she would love to go over to Africa and work in a similar capacity to what I did, teaching, helping these wonderfully friendly people to find a way out of poverty and to feed themselves better. She is in her spare time undertaking a teaching course. She tells me, like Rosa did, about what a poorly rewarded profession it is back home in Spain, but they are a strongly family orientated society. Especially with Covid, she has not been able to return to Zaragoza and see her family and her dog, both of whom she dearly misses.

She has become a wonderful friend, and like Rosa, Raquel and my amigos, Pablo and Pelayo, happy people to be around and people I would hope to keep in contact with over the years. It does seem a shame that such highly qualified professionals have such limited opportunities to work back home, especially in large animal medicine and practice.

The different standing of a member of the Veterinary profession in different European countries, but what I would say is what a pleasure it was to work with them, always happy and definitely without that arrogance that some Aussies and South Africans I have worked with seem to have.

Changing times and changing personnel as along the way, and especially over the past five years we have worked with more nationalities. Romanians, Germans (Eva worked with us again for a few years and has only just returned to her home country, but again someone who it was a pleasure to work with) and the beautiful Renata from Portugal. With Brexit, how easy it will be to recruit international vets to fill some of these job vacancies, only time will tell. There is only a limited time you can do some of the repetitive jobs that they do in this country, but for some they are now finding, filling vacancies in clinical practice, and good luck to them.

For me it has been a pleasure to work with them and I hope I will get the opportunity sometime in the future for them to show me something of their hometowns and the areas they have lived in. Some great friends.

15

MENTAL HEALTH

It is often said that both farming and being a vet, especially a farm vet is a vocation, a calling. Myself, a farmer's son, then my mind was made up from the age of fourteen that I was to be a vet, a farm vet that is. Not many days before my retirement I had just finished a lambing at Steve's, a struggle but we managed to remove an over large dead lamb from the distressed ewe, if nothing else then saving her life. Having cleaned up and going back to my car our conversation turned from our usual topic of rugby, Wasps, the Tigers and England to our chosen professions.

"Yes, a vocation, a calling," Steve said to me.

I relied, "I may have just been on my knees for you lambing your ewe, but that was the only calling I was getting, nothing else. But yes, it is probably likely that especially those of us who choose to work with farm animals then it is a vocation. Certainly, the financial rewards are not the same as those who choose to work with pets."

Many farmers would have been sons who took on their father's farm and in modern times, daughters now doing the same. For vets, in days gone by (Siegfried and Tristan in the Herriot books) then it was not uncommon for son to follow dad's footsteps into his practice and take it over. But more recently as entry to university has become more academically demanding, then more and more today's vet is someone who has chosen that profession from an early age, often from their love of animals. A calling!

Times have changed from when I first qualified, and obviously long before that. Then, on day 1, you were a qualified vet and were expected to go out and do a day's work unassisted, and possibly not with any back-up. Nowadays we do tend to break a new graduate in. Whether on an internship scheme where they continue their education in a practice, accompanying an experienced vet to learn the tricks of the trade, or having available back-up all the time and starting on the more basic jobs.

Yet despite the love of the countryside, working with animals and country folk, the opportunity to do surgery, to mend and cure, we as a profession have one of the highest suicide rates of any profession. This is also true of farmers, who also come high in the charts for workplace accidents.

In my early days when in Devon, there were several incidents where someone who you thought of as a happy, jolly farmer had taken his own life. You found out one day that they had either shot themselves or hung themselves in their barn. I was young then, having no idea about mental health issues, unlike today, but I could appreciate the pressures on farmers in what can be a cyclical industry with good times and bad. They cared about their animals especially on these small family farms and any loss of stock would not only be a loss of income. Buttercup or Daisy would also be considered as part of the family as well, a cow or sheep that they had brought into the world, had reared and then had become a source of income. There was an emotional attachment as well as any financial pressures on farmers resulting in pressures from the bank, especially if starting a young family of their own. That farm may have had to support several members of the family as a source of income. As we are well aware now, men especially are not good at discussing problems with others and ultimately when it all got too much for them, even if outwardly they were the life and soul of the party, they took their own lives, a release for them but not for the rest of their family.

This emotional attachment also applies in small animal practice, an attachment and responsibility to the pet you are treating or its owner. It can become very easy to suffer the same pressures and distress if a pet you have been treating dies, or the case does not progress as one hoped. These pressures can mount up, especially if one throws in the pressures of out of hours work, working alone on difficult or emergency cases. If there is no outlet, then mental illness will affect us as the vet as well as that distress for the client in losing their beloved pet. Even more so these days where a blame culture exists, if ever it happens, even if it is inevitable, then someone must be blamed. The poor vet! The pressures on a new graduate first going into practice are now considerable, especially in small animal practice and it is essential that they get support and assistance from more senior colleagues.

I have loved working as a farm vet, my chosen profession, my vocation! I have worked in several practices in the West Country and in the West Midlands. I have met some wonderful people, had some great experiences and have been lucky enough to work in some of the most beautiful countryside in England. But if I talk more about farm work for the moment, then over those forty plus years then I have seen, and indeed suffered myself from mental illness. From the small year I qualified with from Bristol in 1977 then I know of at least twenty percent of my peers who have suffered depression or worse. And they are only the ones I know of, that figure may be far higher.

From my early years in the profession, farmers would tell me of former senior members of the practice I was working in who had serious drink problems. Often if they were called out in the night, even on arrival on the farm they would smell like a brewery. When on completion of their job, if offered a wee dram, they would never refuse, and a refill would be most welcome. We were more respected members of society, farmers would discuss problems with us (some anyway), our role in society extended further than just treating animals. The doctor, the vicar and the vet, we were pillars in a local community with the added pressure which that brought with it. As the profession has changed, with the disappearance of the small village or town practice and us now covering far wider areas, then that role has gone. Yes, I will still get asked to sign passport and Firearm Certificate applications, but I no longer live anywhere near the centre of the practice and so other than work I am not involved in the local community. I have already described the status of our Spanish colleagues in their home country, poorly paid and thought of as the lowest of the lows amongst the professionals.

That has removed some of the pressures from us as vets and I think that the level of drinking has now diminished. Yes, if a few vets meet up in the evening at a conference, then a few pints will go down, but there does not appear to be the levels of near alcoholism now as there was in my early days in the profession.

What were the reasons? Several I think but all being as a result of the job we do?

Firstly, being on call does have an impact on one's life. I for one never relaxed when on call even after forty plus years. The phone, when on call, governs your life. When will it ring again, and many times will it ever stop ringing? When you have done six or seven calvings in a day and night, or as in one Sunday, fifteen lambings plus the driving between each one. Often missing out on any meals during the day, then it is shattering. The pressure mounts up on you. I cannot describe what a relief it was when I finished my last weekend on call ever. It was if a great weight had been lifted from my shoulders, nights and weekends were my own.

Even more so, if you have a young family, then the weekend or the evenings are when you get to spend some time with them. That often did not happen, especially when until recently, even if one had worked a night or weekend and had been out the whole time, or the whole night, you were still expected to work the next day, and the next!

People now talk about the work, life balance, but in years gone by your chosen vocation ruled your life and sadly family came second. When my first, my child was born, I had to pick my wife and him up from hospital, drop them off at home and then return to work. In my next job, I only did evening surgeries every other week so for one week I did have the opportunity to spend some time with my children when work finished which was nice. But in my next job, it was invariably bedtime for my youngest when I got home, and I would have to be the disciplinarian because she had been winding her mother up all day. Not the basis for a good relationship with your kids.

Home life was obviously greatly impacted on and unless you had a really understanding wife, then it created a lot of pressures.

We spend five years at university learning our trade, our vocation. We wanted to be veterinary surgeons and we left to explore the big, wide world, often in my day starting your first job straight after leaving with your degree. The next ambition when you were settled was partnership. To take a financial share in the business and reap the rewards that that should bring. You would almost certainly have a mortgage, but then would have to take out another loan, a business loan to buy a share of the partnership, including that mysterious factor, Goodwill! And Goodwill was not cheap. When I first went into partnership, interest rates were fifteen percent and the loan would be taken out at two, two and a half percent above base rate. Financial pressure on top of the pressures of the job on your life.

On becoming a partner, one would be involved in the running of the practice. Having to make business decisions, business plans plus all the involvement in staff management, now Human Resources. Then later in my career all the work that is involved with Health and Safety, COSHH regulations as we handle hazardous substances, Working Time Directives because of the hours we work, etc, etc. We were trained as vets, not as business managers, that we would have to pick up on the hoof as it were (and do a day's work as a vet). In essence we were trained as vets and not as businessmen but as partners/directors that is what we had to do with varying levels of success.

More pressures, especially when trying to ensure there was enough income to support the loans one had, and to live, enough to drive a man to drink! I think from the Herriot books in the Yorkshire Dales one would get the impression of farmers being poor payers and having to bargain with them to get your invoices paid. Not all farmers are like that and certainly over my years, the levels of bad debt have fallen amongst the farming community to us. But in those early days, when servicing loans to become a partner, you were always conscious of bad debt and reducing it as far as possible. It was your income, your livelihood. Chasing bad debt also creates pressures, especially emotional ones. There is always a hard luck story, we will pay you next month or, and one must not forget at times these farmers were also going through hard financial times (the suicides I have previously mentioned).

All in all, there were many pressures put on oneself and they were just those from a business and family point of view. I have already touched on the emotional pressures of cases you are dealing with, and even more so in modern practice with the threat of litigation. In my early days you relied on clinical judgement, now you must justify, support your decisions with laboratory work, radiographs and more. You are covering your back against any future comeback. Add on to that long hours, lone working, variable support and that chosen vocation for a new graduate can soon become a nightmare. Stress and depression follow and unless there is someone out there looking out for you, life takes you into darker and darker places.

Thankfully, it is largely discontinued now, but we did have a horse "knockdown agent" called Immobilon. You would inject the horse with the computed dose, wait for it to go to sleep, not very long, and then when you had finished whatever procedure you were carrying out then you would administer an antidote. The horse would soon be back on its feet. This was an extremely dangerous drug, very toxic to humans who if it was accidentally administered to, even spillage onto the skin was sufficient to cause serious affects, then they would soon be in a narcoleptic state. Humans require a different antidote to horses.

It was a nasty drug, and more than a few vets used it as an easy way out of this world.

For those of you who may have read other books I have written then you will know that I suffered from depression. I became a partner in a business in 1991, the interest rates I have already mentioned that I had to pay to buy in with. But for a few years it was a comfortable existence with the hope that things would only get better. But a couple of decisions were made that would change my course. Firstly, when one senior partner retired, we made the decision to write Goodwill out of the contract, something I had borrowed money to pay for. I, like the other young partner would be compensated for this by the practice buying us a pension which as contributions increased would give us a payback. The reason, we decided that Goodwill was becoming too expensive, if it even existed any more in mixed practice where with an ever-increasing number of small animal practices opening meant clients had a huge freedom of choice to go where they wanted. Goodwill maybe a deterrent to a future vet wanting to buy into the partnership, and when we retired, we would want to sell our share.

Secondly, one of my fellow partners decided he did not want to continue in farm work, he wanted to continue just as a small animal practice. The partnership was dissolved, we went our separate ways. For me there were financial implications, a cost, even when I became a partner in a neighbouring practice, taking a lot of my farm clients with me.

Was this the first strain on my mental health? This was soon followed by the 2001 Foot and Mouth outbreak when I went to work for the Government for several weeks trying to bring the disease under control. The United Kingdom has a slaughter policy for this Notifiable disease and after three weeks working on surveillance, I spent the rest of my time supervising the slaughter of thousands of sheep and cattle. This was not what I had trained for, especially when I questioned if a lot of the cases we were seeing were actually Foot and Mouth. It took me to dark places in my mind, and what made it even harder was having a wife who did not understand what I was going through and if we were out at a party or dinner would tell everyone what I was doing, celebrity status! I did not want to talk about it and a lot of my friends realised I did not.

My marriage did not last a lot longer, my world was falling apart. Another failed relationship followed, again a period of deep mental anguish for me which also affected my career. I crashed.

But it took me a long time to realise that my mental state was not due to lack of sleep. I was suffering from depression. My doctor told me, and I did not believe him at first but eventually had to accept this mental illness was affecting me and had been for a number of years.

The rest is history. I realised that the only person who was going to solve my problems was me. I compartmentalised things into those that mattered, that I needed to find a solution to, and those that did not, and they were not worth worrying about. I climbed a mountain, Kilimanjaro, a lifetime ambition and became a new person, more confident, more content and with new direction. I have not looked back.

But in this profession, I am not the only one, and sadly some have found no answers. Mental illness continues in both the farming and the veterinary professions.

Have things changed? They are changing and slowly for the better.

In farming circles there are now rural support groups. People or groups that if you are worried about someone, you can ring them and they will go and speak, see if they can help desperate farmers or farm workers, counsel them, offer advice or point them in some direction to someone that may be able to help them more. I have been to a couple of these group meetings where supporters have been trained in the signs to look out for in depression, mental illness, how to speak to a sufferer, the right and wrong questions to ask. A variety of different people in associated industries have become these supporters, other farmers, vets, land agents, farm consultants, all there to look for signs of distress in their colleagues and to offer some support to those in mental anguish. With the stresses of modern life, mental illness, it is not a disease and has come to the forefront of many of our lives. There should not be a stigma attached to it and that is something that is important to get over to a colleague suffering from it. I kept mine to myself for a very long time, years, but found a solution. We out there must ensure that others suffering from depression or other forms of mental illness, are not alone and there are many out there only too willing to offer to help.

But what of vets? Are things changing in my profession? Having suffered myself, I am only too conscious of my fellow working colleagues, whether they seem quiet, reserved, uncommunicative, tired, not themselves.

The work/life balance has become more and more important. There have been positive changes whether just from a business point of view or if changes have been made to improve the lives of the employers and employees through working practices.

It would be hard for me to comment on small animal practice now as I have not been involved in it for years. Certainly, now though the out of hours work has been diminished as a lot of practices now use bespoke "Out of Hours" services, companies that specialise in this. So when your opening hours finish, then this service takes over until your doors open again the following day. This service makes positions in these practices far more attractive to employees. You work your day and that is it. A far cry from my early days when I did do mixed practice. Your working week is less hours, and your weekend is your own to pursue whatever you want, or just to spend time with your family.

But farm practice is different and as yet I know of no out of hours service on offer other than that offered by individual practices to their own clients. That is something that I do not see changing at any time in the future. Farmers expect to be able to contact their own vet at all times, day, night or at weekends. This maybe just for advice or they require a call out. When I worked in Devon it would be a quiet night if one had less than three calls, cows calve, sheep lamb at any time of day or night and very often milking begins early in the morning and can finish late at night. These are times of stock observation, and these are production animals so require prompt attention. In such a large practice we always had a back-up, a second call to help out if we were inundated with calls or needed a hand with a Caesarean.

But on the plus side it was unusual to have to drive more than fifteen or twenty miles to a call.

Until I arrived working in Shrewsbury in my last employment, out of hours in Shropshire work was working remotely, there were less calls. But you were on your own with no back up and that was mixing large and small animal work together.

But as I finished, my last sixteen years in a wholly farm practice we went back to a first and second call system so there was always a back-up. Some emergencies can take a long time, the next emergency may not have that amount of time to wait. The other big difference now is the great increase in mileage we can cover between calls. If you get the wrong two calls next to each other then you may have to drive fifty miles plus between them, conscious that another call may come in that would take you back in the direction you first came from. This can be stressful, especially if the traffic is busy.

Has anything changed? Yes, it has in that we probably do less out of hours work now because over the years we have trained farmers and their stockmen to do more themselves. They have become more skilled in their roles on the farm and so can cope with far more without our assistance. Those same staff very often are a greater help to us when we are carrying out emergency procedures, again we have trained them to assist us. All this reduces the strain on the vet considerably.

Communication has improved with the advent of mobile phones and better networks so one is able to keep in contact with the farmer as to your estimated time of arrival, and anything he can do to help the animal before your arrival.

We used to work the following day, even after a busy night, our next day off being the following weekend. But after a lot of persuasion, we managed to change our rota so that if one had worked the weekend then you would have the Monday off and the following Friday, allowing one to have a three-day weekend to relax and recover. If you were on second call for a weekend, then you would have the Wednesday off. And if you had a very busy night in the week, with calls between midnight and six in the morning, then one could take a couple of hours off the following afternoon to recuperate.

Again, the work/life balance greatly improved just by giving this little more time to recover, and the change was much appreciated. Different practices have tried to find different solutions to this out of hours work and how to improve one's quality of life. Our system worked for us.

The other big change has been the introduction of Practice Managers in many practices, people with more business training. It has allowed vets to be vets rather than juggling with being a vet and a businessman. Some of these managers have come from industry, some have worked their way up through the practice they work in, some are vets who have transferred over to the business side. Of course, Partners, Directors in the business still have the overall say in what decisions need to be made, but the day-to-day running is taken out of their hands.

When I was a partner in a firm, I tried to go down this route of having a Practice Manager, but my fellow Partners were unwilling to let go of the reins. So we fell between two sticks, us not being very good at running a business, but not letting someone who had the know-how take over instead.

It has been fascinating watching the field of Veterinary Practice management develop. Groups like XLVets which we belonged to provided business models, appropriate training of Directors and managers at all levels through the workplace. With refinement, the workplace became more and more efficient and with that, a less stressful place to work. But I hope there was never a "them" and "us" culture, everyone got on with everyone else.

Well-being came more and more to the forefront. A team building committee was started to organise events for all members of staff who wanted to join in. Archery, ten-pin bowling, axe throwing (not at each other), wine tasting or just a meal out together. It would bring directors, vets, TB testers and the support staff all together out of the working environment. We could learn by chatting informally away from work what made each other tick. With that then hopefully we would be able to recognise if any member of staff, or manager even seemed down, needed a chat or some help. Each other's well-being became more important to us, we could look out for each other. I hope that I have played an important role in instigating all this, certainly when I was suffering all those years ago, I was very much alone.

I think we have made great strides in improving this side of the job in farm practice. Mental health and well-being have become important in all industries now . We have advanced, and I hope in the future that the suicide rate in my profession will be on the decline.

16

MOTHER HEN

There is a saying "Behind every great man there is a great woman".

It would be very arrogant of us vets to think we are all great. Of course there are many very able women in the profession now doing a job equal to us men, and just as well. Farm animal vetting has for a long time been dominated by the male members of the profession, for numerous years in the past there even being a reluctance by Practices to employ female vets, firstly because they did not think the ladies were physically strong enough, and secondly there being a thought that farmers would not accept them either. The intake of females at universities now greatly exceeds the number of men entering the profession. As I have stated, there are now many more than competent female vets in farm practice, and becoming partners/directors in the businesses they work in. A major step forward in sex equality.

But "behind a great man". I have already talked about the long hours, night duties and weekends on call causing a lot of stress on a vet's life and the impact this can have on one's work/life balance, especially in those years at the start of my career. Your wife would be your spouse, your support as well as probably taking the phones in the evening when you were on call, passing on messages to you and taking the brunt of farmer's anxiety, impatience while waiting for the vet to arrive on farm. Over time, these duties were passed on from firstly Partner's wives, then to the wife of whoever was on call and then onto to bespoke out of hours answering services who would then page or phone the vet on call. Over the last few years of my career, and going forward then with the advent of better, more advanced Smart Phones, then the calls have gone direct to the vet. On busy duties the partner of the vet would have no idea if and when they would see the vet, when he or she may expect to be home, have a meal etc. A hard life to lead!

As well as that, they would also be disturbed in the night when the phone went, sometimes if the vet were very tired, even having to wake him or her up to answer it and then get them out of bed. Then, on return, this cold body would crawl back in under the sheets looking for warmth.

"Behind every great man!" Though I would have to say that those I have slept with (that sounds bad doesn't it) must sleep soundly. Very often I would go out and be back in again, possibly more than once in a night and in the morning my partner would be totally oblivious to the fact that I had been out at all, getting up and saying, "That was a quiet night wasn't it!"

The noble efforts of those who have supported us through our professional careers, though one or two (or more) marriages may have fallen on the wayside along the way.

But there is another band of people, and they have predominately been female, who have also supported us in our day to day lives. They are the girls who have worked in the office. We are a business, have telephones to answer during the day when the vets are out doing their calls, those calls to book and invoice, organise the daybook, book future routine calls, the list is long and over the course of my time as a vet, has become longer.

When I first started all those years ago, in my first practice I worked in it was the boss's wife who took the calls during the day and passed them on, though she too was a vet and ran the small animal part of the practice. With the help of a secretary that came in a couple of mornings a week and the boss doing the invoices, they worked through it all. Perhaps that reflected that it was only a small practice in a small market town. Also, perhaps in my early days in my first practice I did not have the confidence to develop a good working relationship with those that were there to help us, sort out our routine each day. The mysteries of business remained.

But I was then to move into a far larger practice, ninety percent large animal and with eight vets working there, they would take some organising. I guess it was there that I met my first "mother hen". In that practice in Devon, we had five ladies working with us. A receptionist for the small animal side and for dispensing drugs under a vet's directive, a nurse who in those days was very often a girl straight out from school who longed to work at a vets and a lady (Pat) who did the drug ordering and like my parents, also lived on Exmoor. It was easy to develop a friendship with her. That left the two who ran the office, the hub of the practice and who organised us vets. Pauline was "mother hen", a larger-than-life jovial women, married to the foreman of the garage over the road, the one that saw my Vauxhall Viva so often .Then there was Joyce, the daughter of one of our farmers and who had worked at the practice since she had left school.

Us vets had an office in one room, us each having a space and a tray on two large tables. The ladies had the office next door where they had their phones, switch boards and everything they needed to book calls, handle the chitties we would write out after a call, and to do the invoices. They would also look after laboratory reports, organise Min of Ag work, TB and Brucellosis tests, organise routine fertility visits, running the daybook as a whole.

If a call was rung in, they would enter it into the day diary which was in our office, each vet being allotted a column and whoever was allocated that call then a tick would be put in their column. When the call was done then that tick would be changed into a cross. Any messages for a vet or phone call that was needed for them to make, was added onto the list with a tick in the appropriate column. For such a large practice with so many vets and so many calls the system worked very efficiently and it was exceedingly rare that any error were made (compare that to computers today!).

Pauline especially, and Joyce, had one other very important function and that was to look after us vets, and sometimes we really needed it. Mother hen!

Joyce was a quiet girl, sheltered from the outside world a lot by an overbearing mother, and so apart from Young Farmers Club meetings had not really experienced life. When not at work, she would be expected to help out on the farm. But despite that, it was her ambition that some farmer would walk through the door and sweep her off her feet to a life happy ever after. She was always very pleasant to work with, always keen to help us vets when she could and knowing the farming community was a good bridge between us young vets and them, the farmers. It is a long time since

I have seen or heard from her, but I hope life turned out for her with all that she wanted from it.

Pauline on the other hand, was the complete opposite. She had had her family and was now working full time, trained initially as a secretary but now running our office. A large lady, but always elegant, she ran a very efficient ship. Of all the ladies over the years I have worked with, she would be the only one who could do shorthand. She had the respect of all those that worked with her, both the assistant vets and the Partners of the firm. One of those ladies who wore her glasses on the end of her nose when not reading closely, you always knew if you had displeased her with that stern look over the top of her glasses.

But she was a softy at heart and was always there to look out for us young vets. Times have changed, in those days we did not do gap years, we went straight from school to university and then into meaningful employment. We didn't have a great experience of life; we were single men straight out of college.

Pauline would be there to give advice, help whenever we needed. After my two car crashes in this practice, the first one in my first few days, my second just before I was due to take my first proper holiday since I had worked for the practice, who was there to offer a comforting shoulder? Pauline. This was especially so with the second crash where I was severely shaken, my ego battered more than a bit. I was supposed to be going away in a couple of days and my car was deemed no more. How would I get myself and my fiancée to St. Mawes? It was Pauline of course who sorted it all out for me, arranging another car through her husband at the garage and then ensuring there was a car for me when I returned to work. This was the time when the lorry thought it could drive through the crash, leaving my Morris Marina under his rear wheel arch. The car was a mess, touch and go whether a write off or not. But with a little surgery with a hammer, Pauline's husband ensured that it was so that on my return, I had another brand-new car.

It was a sad day when I left, Pauline (and Joyce) had looked after me, seen me through my early days when I was very unsure of myself. She had given me confidence, advice when needed specially with cooking (when I first started there I lived in a flat above the office), and also when we were arranging our wedding in Devon, not where my wife to be originated from. I left at Christmas time, and that year the Partners had decided there was to be no Christmas party as pennies were tight in the business. My work colleagues wanted to give me a leaving party, but we felt uncomfortable with it as the Christmas party was not going to take place, were we going behind their backs. I said I could only feel comfortable with it going ahead if we informed the partners, invited them as well. Who would talk to them? Pauline was keen on a party and would have a word with Oliver the Senior Partner. Good move, he was up for a party and agreed to it all. Rather than us paying individually, he would ensure that the practice would pay for it all. Christmas party or Rod's leaving party, it happened, and everyone came. The most popular tune of the night, "Oliver's Army" by Elvis Costello, we danced the night away! Thank you, Pauline, a real "Mother Hen".

I spent five years in that job, somewhere where I really enjoyed working but it was time to move on. I was looking for prospects for a partnership and although I loved it there, with the recent appointment of three young partners, then my time looked some way off. Pauline had looked after me well but did not get to see the arrival of my first child some ten weeks after I left, something she would have loved. It was a great experience, a great learning curve and my first encounter of how a business functions. A very efficient ship run by Pauline and Joyce while keeping the place a happy environment to work in.

Ellen and another Pauline were my office staff in my next job in the Forest of Dean. I actually met them at my job interview, probably spending more time with them than I did with those interviewing me, who were late back from calls. Ellen was the older of the two, living in a nearby village and in overall charge of the day to day running of the practice. Pauline had joined the practice after leaving school and had had made her role very much her own. They ran a similar style of office to that of the one in Devon, but it was a smaller practice, but with a larger small animal department. We probably worked a bit more remotely but us farm vets, they looked after in a similar fashion. Always friendly and always helpful.

Of course, when my firstborn arrived and I had to pick him up from hospital, then I was instructed by Ellen that my first port of call would be the office on the way home so that she could see the baby. Very maternal, she wanted to see all the latest offspring and cuddle them. No paternity leave in those days, it was dropping my wife and the baby back at home and then return to work.

There was a slight difference in our invoicing system but otherwise we functioned in a similar way to as in Devon, but with Ellen as our new "mother hen" to organise us and take care of us. Again, we had the experience of someone who had run an office in a different business coming into the veterinary profession to then run an office in the way she had been trained, teaching Pauline along the way.

Slightly different systems but both efficient in their own ways and with the size factor to consider. They also had to organise appointments and an accounting for small animal practice, and a filing system for case records and payments to run parallel with each other.

Ellen and Pauline were lovely people, again a pleasure to work with, and again it was sad to part company with them when I realised it was time to move on again. I missed them both and did keep in contact with them both for some time afterwards if I was that side of the river (the Severn).

I had worked in two practices where the office staff were both efficient and a pleasure to work with, looking after the needs of their vets and always there to offer help and advice when necessary.

That would be a complete contrast to my next practice where there were only two vets, me doing the majority of the farm work, my boss doing the small animal stuff. We had one girl who did all the reception work plus assisting operations on the dogs and cats, cleaning and anything else that needed doing. Her only training was what she picked up as she went along. There was no real system for anything, and this very much was the case of a single partner business with me as his assistant, him doing virtually all of the bureaucratic functions necessary in the business.

Efficient? No, in what seemed a very hit and miss billing system we got along but having gone to the practice to obtain a potential partnership, there was no way that I could, would ever consider joining a business run this way.

And no "mother hen" to look after us or the business, to run everything smoothly.

It was time to move on again, but this time it really was with the chance of prospects of partnership in no more than fifteen months from joining the practice. I moved to the first of my practices in Shropshire, again mixed and both departments initially run out of the same office.

This time it was Frances who ran the office, with the help of trained nurses to help the small animal side, plus a lady, Sadie, who came in at evening surgery to act as receptionist. There was a marked contrast in styles as to how these two worked. Frances, very pleasant and efficient in everything she did, the other far older and very set in her ways, not helped by her being partially deaf (I would later know that feeling myself!).

Frances was the wife of a local farm worker and knew a lot of the local agricultural community, as well as having dogs of her own. She therefore had a good knowledge of both sides of our mixed practice. But her reward was, unlike Pauline in Cullompton who had a few youngsters under her wing, that she had to look after three old men, one middle aged bloke and me. Apart from me, the new boy, she had to manage these men who were all very set in their ways and this she did amicably, pleasantly and usually with a smile on her face. Despite her frustrations, she managed us very efficiently, always having time to listen and help with everyone's problems while answering the phone, doing the billing and directing calls to the nearest vet out on the road. On top of that, she would have to act as the go between as dear Sadie could not understand the workings of the now highly trained veterinary nurses. Her sticking to her old-fashioned ways and with her deafness, sticking to what she wanted to tell clients as opposed to what they should be told. Frances, the mother hen, was the calming influence between the two factions. She would have to appease any farmer who had been put on hold when ringing in with a call in the evening because Sadie would think dealing with someone's pussy was more important than a farming emergency. Sadie was a lovely lady, but perhaps had been left behind with the times. The veterinary world was moving on!

We also had a branch surgery in a neighbouring village, Shifnal, which opened first thing in the morning and for an evening surgery for an hour. One of those old-fashioned branches where everyone knew everyone else, there were no appointments, you just turned up, an altogether it was quite a social occasion. We had a receptionist there, Jane, who when the branch closed in the morning, she would then come over to help Frances at the main office until lunchtime. Jane was one of those all-time drop-dead gorgeous blondes and one could see why clients and farmers were only too keen to drop in for a chat, or keen to prolong their stay at the branch surgery. One of those people with a fantastic personality who could charm anybody even without her looks, she developed the position to be her own. When she started working for us, she knew nothing about veterinary work, but she was genuinely interested. She was always willing to learn and ask questions, and to help where she could. This would be a career that she would pursue and still all these years on, even branching into practice management she still works in the veterinary field, ending up working for the same practice that she started with.

Jane, very popular with clients and with vets, as well as becoming a great help to Frances, also developed herself into a bit of a mother hen. She was so easy to talk to which meant all other members of staff (and clients) would be quite happy to bend her ear with all their problems.

Two wonderful members of staff to work with, and of course Frances would be the first member of staff that I worked with firstly as a veterinary assistant, and then as one of her bosses when I took up partnership in the firm. But she was such a wonderful person that I don't think it ever changed our relationship at all.

But for us all, technology was catching us up, we were going to become computerised! Now it was just a computer downstairs in the main office, and one in the upstairs office where Frances would be beavering away. But we were old and of an age where computers did not exist in schools when we were there. We had those massive calculator machines where you keyed in numbers and turned a handle before a result came up. Even logarithms were still in vogue, and we may have moved onto these small LED calculators in our latter years, something handheld, but with computers we were out of our depth. It had to be true that the person who knew most about them was the thirteen-year-old son of one of the other vets, to the rest of us they were a complete mystery. Perhaps that was the time when a computer evening class may have been more beneficial than French evening classes. For Frances, for Jane and for myself as well as the older vets, they were a mystery and so the full benefit of a computer was never utilised for quite some time. When Frances and I were left to do the monthly VAT returns, not that often, then we would usually revert to pen and paper just like in the good old days.

We very much relied on our mother hens to help us through the day to day running of a thriving mixed practice. Like with the VAT returns, between us we would muddle through without modern technology even if it did have a small presence in the building. A greatly under used resource, mainly because none of us knew an apple from a Mac or Intel, and certainly no real idea how to use them.

I think the catch phrase used to be when someone who thought they knew what they were doing, "I will just show you what to do", and then when they were struggling to get the damn thing to give the result required, they would always fall back on "oh well, just play around with it until you have sorted in out", and would then abandon you and the computer together, getting absolutely nowhere. Frustration would lead to some swearing and then reaching for the off button, which strangely enough still happens frequently some twenty-five years on! The mouse would be left, and I would go in search of a cat in the surgery which was more responsive and required attention that I could deal with.

But despite the advent of computers, Frances and Jane would leave a lasting impression as the last of the real "mother hens". Ladies who looked after us while coping with running an office and all the duties it entailed in a veterinary practice, while always managing to smile to client and fellow worker alike.

Times they were a changing, as the song goes. It was time to move on and to an altogether different and changing environment. Practice was changing fast, higher standards were being demanded of small animal practice, facilities needed to be better, better diagnostic equipment was becoming essential, technology was advancing rapidly. In the previous few years, we had renovated the surgery building, extending at the back to give a better operating theatre, better facilities for our cat and dog in-patients and better radiographic facilities. We were increasingly governed by more legislation as were many workplaces. I went on holiday one summer only to return and find in my absence that I had been appointed Health and Safety Officer and was put in charge of all COSHH requirements in the building and on farm. This entailed a lot of work, both in CPD to get to grips with what was required, and some of it was very subjective, and to then write the necessary policies to implement in the workplace.

When I joined the team, it could best be described as an ageing workforce, but as they retired a new generation of young vets was coming through who demanded better facilities. At one stage I had a dream about the possibility of building a purpose-built premises on some unused land next to a new retail park, close to the major road networks in town so handy for both the large and small animal parts of the practice. It would have required commitment from all sides in the practice and I probably felt that did not exist. It never happened and I often wonder if it had whether we would have become the leading practice in the area. Perhaps I did not have the small animal commitment to follow it through? The opportunity went, instead a large pub was built on the site and seems to have thrived ever since.

As I have said, time to move on as the practice was pursuing a solely small animal route and I wanted to stay a farm vet with a wish to move back down to the Southwest in time. Instead, I moved to a neighbouring practice, taking many of my farm clients with me with the intention I would bed them in with their new practice then I would move on. This was very much a mixed practice with a specialist equine department, working in a converted barn kitted out to facilitate small animal work with an accompanying stable block for any equine in-mates. There was one room in the centre of the building where x rays were taken, sometimes precariously as you were going from one end of the building to the other on small animal duties while some stroppy horse careered about in this room while the equine vets were trying to take their radiographs.

As well as us five vets, we had a support staff of four led by our new mother hen, Pat, a lady who at first sight seemed a bit of an ogre, ruling the rest of the staff with her stern manner and there was seldom a smile. The office was a small room, crowded, that functioned as the hub of the practice plus reception. Computers had arrived, or again should I say they had arrived but as before us oldies struggled with the advent of new technology.

My role initially was to take over the running of the farm side of the practice, combining their new clients that I had taken with me along with their existing clients. I would also have a smaller role in the small animal department, doing most of my work there in a fast-developing branch surgery in Telford. So, though not a partner, I did have to work closely with Pat in getting the expanding part of the farm side running efficiently. I would have to admit that despite her harshness to the rest of the staff, I always found her very pleasant, it was just that she had high standards and expected others to reach her standards as well. She was always there for me when a problem needed solving, even when our relationship changed from being a fellow employee to being one of her bosses. No, I did not move away after the few months as I had intended but became a partner in the business.

We took on many major projects as the practice expanded and she was always there to give her input when necessary. Again, I seemed to get lumbered with Health and Safety and with COSHH, but she helped me through it where she could. Human resources (as it is now called), staff management was also given to me with the sorting out of contracts etc. for new and existing staff to plod through with her help. If there was a problem, then staff usually went to her first and then to me. We had to act as a team.

The business was expanding, and our cramped office was now inadequate. We had a large loft space running the length of the building, and with a lot of planning we decided to convert this into the new office. The hub of the practice, with more room not only for the office staff but also as the number of vets employed in the practice was increasing, space for them to have their own desks and working space as well. This was Pat's new domain with her new title of office manager. If you were working in the office, then she had her eye on you. In fairness, she was becoming a more relaxed person as she developed new interests outside work and you could have a good laugh with her. Especially when it was the time of year to organise and run the staff Christmas party with associated mini panto when all staff were fair game to have the micky taken out of them. Their embarrassments, misdeeds of the previous twelve months would resurface for everyone's amusement.

Pat took on an assistant to help her, Mary, one of the loveliest ladies you could ever meet, efficient, always smiling and ever helpful. They, between them, made a formidable team. At the same time, technology came in a big way as the practice went completely computerised, with a management and accounting system, all appointments being entered on a computerised day diary. This definitely now was a new era and Mary was probably the most competent of all the staff to use it, along with a new telephone system just installed in the building.

One Friday afternoon the computer firm arrived to set the whole system up and throughout the three branch surgeries, on the Monday morning we would be live! All way over my head! An exciting evening following the technicians around as they set up each branch surgery and connected up the many monitors that needed to be installed for each reception and consulting room, plus the servers, routers etc that were needed. As evening drew in, I had to take them to Broseley but forgot that their van would not get across the old Coalport bridge as there was a height restriction on it. An about turn and redirect them along the banks of the Severn and over the new bridge. Having left them at the Broseley branch, my job was done for the evening. I could only now wait until the Monday morning, a new era would be upon us, now being completely computerised.

We now had younger members of staff who knew the workings of this new technology so very much the small animal nurses and reception staff were used to this sort of thing. It was us upstairs where the problems would arise, but of course we had Mary to help us, and where she could, she was very patient with us. There were still, even in this office, those who pretended to know far more than they did. I would go back to especially one of my fellow partners in the firm going through something with me and then getting frustrated when he could not get it to work, saying "play around and you will manage to sort it out".

Where had I heard that before! And of course, I did not sort it out, often the whole thing would crash, my computer skills were getting no better.

We were fast approaching the twenty first century and practice was changing so quickly now. Yes, our day to day lives as vets were as in the previous century even if small animal techniques were advancing fast as well. Cattle and sheep worked was not advancing at the same pace, and even if it were, you still needed farmers who wanted to advance at the same rate when they found it easier just to do the same as they always had.

But office life was changing fast what with computers, electronic drug ordering systems, in-house biochemistry equipment, instant invoicing etc. The staff were getting more specialised in their particular roles, and for us as directors/partners in the business the bureaucratic demands were ever increasing as well. I had not managed to get rid of my Health and Safety brief, COSHH, Human Resources and Employment law. Pat would help where she could but even for her it was becoming too much of a burden. Even if she were now officially office manager, staff would bypass her if they did not get what they wanted, going to one of the partners and then to another until they had exhausted all possibilities or had got one of us to unwittingly agree with them without knowing others had been asked first and turned them down. It did not improve the entente accordial!

The days of us trying to run a business and be full-time vets was coming to an end, the days of a mother hen also. We were having to become more business-like and that meant we would have to look at a different form of management system. I had advocated the appointment of a proper practice manager for some time (some practices had already gone down that route, appointing from within, very often a senior nurse who then got some management training) and with Pat's future now looking to be elsewhere, the time had come at last for us to now act on that. A practice manager was appointed, and someone from a business and accounting background rather than a veterinary one. We were moving into the twenty first century big time! The first appointment was a very strong-minded lady, certainly not a mother hen. If I was not in favour of her particular appointment to begin with, over her first few weeks I could see what a positive affect she was having on the whole running of the place, plus any staff issues would be directed firstly through her. She was a success but disappointingly for reasons I will not mention, did not stay as long as I had hoped. She was replaced by an ex-accountant who certainly ran the business well but under more partner control without perhaps wielding the same authority over the rest of the staff.

If it was sad that after my initial years as a vet where there had always been a father(mother) figure to turn to when one just needed a little help with life, at least as a business, practice was now taking big strides forward.

Perhaps by now, I needed a new challenge. It was also time for me to move on, now to a hundred percent farm practice. I was approached by two vets locally who had just set up their own farm practice, breaking away from an existing practice in Shrewsbury. A brave move, they had been going about a year when they approached me and I was excited to join their new adventure, now working out of a small unit on an industrial park. Back to the small office, a reception, drug store and one room that functioned as for anything else that it may be required for. Alistair and Tim had been joined by two of the vet nurses from their previous practice, Sadie and Sally both having farming backgrounds so were more than offay with what would be required of them in their new role. One other lady was recruited as more of an office manager. When I joined, I became the fifth vet, so as a practice it was fast expanding especially as every vet that had joined them had brought with them some of their existing customers from their previous local practice. I did the same.

So, we were a rapidly expanding practice in a very cramped office space. You had to get on with all your colleagues, when all office based, we were literally on top of each other. But this was almost like a throwback to my early years in practice. The office staff had a computer, we didn't and our room as much as it was, functioned as an office, library, rest room, refectory, you name it, we did it in that one room, bar any sheep caesareans that might arrive on our doorstep.

At this stage, when I had joined the practice, I was contemplating retirement though I could not really afford to retire. A new interest was needed, a new direction and when I was approached to join it was initially on a part time basis, working two days a week. It was late summer, and it provided a nice mix of relaxing some days, walking, gardening, whatever took my fancy, and at last which I had craved for the whole of my career, working in a completely farm animal practice.

But the practice was growing quickly, and it was soon obvious that it needed more vets, so my two days became three, then four and then full-time going back on to doing night duties and weekends as well.

I guess at the time, though nothing to do with this new job, the beginnings of my depression had started. The work I was now doing was enjoyable, at least it gave my brain some respite from the issues that were starting to drag me down. The expanding practice offered a new challenge to exercise my brain, but the now increasingly cramped office space did create its own issues.

Luckily at about his time an opportunity came up over the road in another larger industrial unit. An old dairy, we could take on some of that building, sharing the premises with an agricultural merchants, along with another couple of businesses. Having got the builders in, we were able to move into a spacious new premises offering a large reception, a lambing room, an office for us vets and also an office for the partners. A novelty, we all had our own desk, and even our own chairs plus as technology was now fast moving in practice, we had our own computer each as well. This was getting more like big business. The girls all had their own station at reception and their own computer, and we were getting to the stage of needing an office manager to oversee the smooth running of the operation. An appointment within, of which I will say no more. Throughout my career I think I can honestly say being an easy-going person, that I had always got on with everyone, but for the first time here was someone (and it may not have helped with my depression) that seemed to rub me up the wrong way.

The practice continued to expand, more vets were taken on and then a further addition would be vets taken on just to carry out Tuberculosis testing. TB was becoming an ever-increasing problem in Shropshire, especially our part of the county. To service us all, a practice manager was taken on, Jayne. She was a lovely woman and I guess the last of my mother hens. Easy to get along with, approachable, ever helpful, even in my dark days of depression she encouraged me greatly and I would guess it was her to encouraged me to get off my backside and write. You all have her to blame for this! I was greatly disappointed when she left but importantly, I guess, she had set up the mechanism whereby we would all start to try and look after each other. Well-being though in its infant days, was beginning in the workplace. She would try and find and then encourage each individual to develop their own strengths for the benefit of the practice. She was also a wonderful party animal, so when we met up as a team out of work hours, there were never any barriers too breakdown.

More vets came, then with TB tendering and winning the contract with XLVets, a consortium of practices throughout the regions working together to try and develop excellence in practice, more vets were needed to carry out TB testing as well. With that, the office was expanding as well, again more staff were needed and if I would mention one especially it was Sam who not only was a great receptionist but also knew her computers inside out. A great source of knowledge in expanding the IT side of the practice. I had hoped she would teach me more about the workings of computers and their uses, but sadly for me but good for her, work opportunities took her abroad. She now does my website.

The days of "Mother Hens" were over, the likes of Pauline will in probability never be seen again. Veterinary practice is now run as a proper business with proper protocols, more specialised staff on top of us veterinary professionals. I have worked with so many brilliant people, many of whom are still good friends, others are friends on social media outlets. Office managers, practice managers, receptionists, veterinary technicians, those that have specialised in the pharmacy side of the practice. I have lost count of how many wonderful girls I have worked with in my time in the profession. Some have a more than special place in my thoughts, not just because of the help they have given me in my career but also to because it has been great to see them develop their personality and skills in this profession. People like Charlotte who started as a shy and unconfident member of the reception staff, who left to pursue an Art degree, returning in university vacations to help out, but now with growing confidence has taken over the role of head of pharmacy. It has been a pleasure to see her career blossom, and yes, not working with her in the future is something I will miss.

The office, the job has become more computer based with specialised programs developed for veterinary practice, they continue to be developed. They have certainly changed the role of those ladies that I have worked with in the office. They do still have to answer the phones during the day and have a little more knowledge of what us vets do than in the past, but they are now more and more data inputters for the computers which are now the lynchpin of practice. When I finished, I may still have been very old fashioned in relying on paper rather than accessing stuff on smart phones, but in retirement I definitely was the exception.

Is it now that the new "Mother Hen" is in fact a computer system?

"I am not a robot!"

But there is one more person I should mention, a real character. Of course, we have to offer an out of hours service for those emergencies that may occur during the night or at the weekend. Cows and sheep, pigs too, do not have a work timetable and their needs could be an any hour whether through sickness or for a difficult calving or lambing. Someone has to answer the phones during these "antisocial hours" and in my forty plus years of practice, there have been several ways this has been dealt with. Initially it as partner's wives who took the phones, specialised out of hours services who would take calls and then ring or bleep the vet on call. This was always thought of as a very impersonal system by farmers who liked to speak to a familiar voice who knew where they farmed.

The opposite of this was one lady who for a while took the phones at night for us. Ivy was a local farmers wife, well known throughout the community by those that lived in the local town, but especially by the farming community. Equipped with her wonderful Shropshire accent, the phones would be put through to her when the office closed after evening surgery. If a call came in, the farmer would be speaking to someone they knew. Ivy would take the message and then either ring or bleep the duty vet. When they had finished the emergency, they would call her to say they had finished and would be on their way home unless she had another call to pass on.

If it were that simple!

The one thing Ivy could do was talk. Don't get me wrong, she was a lovely person but at night if there was one thing you wanted to do, it was to get on your way to the call and get it done, especially so if it were a real emergency. But with Ivy, when you had either rung her because the bleeper had told you to, or she had rung you direct what you did not want was a twenty-minute conversation on what she had done on her farm that day, what she was cooking for supper or whatever the local gossip was. But in all that, she was also interested in you and your welfare. There were plusses and minuses, but on the whole, it was nice to know someone was keeping an eye on you on busy nights and weekends, just checking you were okay, and if her conversations did delay you a little, at least it gave a bit of light relief from the rigours of work.

I guess another "Mother Hen" God bless her. I do hear from her still from time to time though it has been many years since I worked with her.

17

ADVANCING TECHNOLOGY

The world is changing fast. The speed of development of science and technology gains a pace, even more so in the later years of my career. If the day-to-day work of a farm vet has not changed a great deal, then certainly the science behind what we do and the technology that we now use has advanced in leaps and bounds.

In terms of the animals we treat, there has been much development in breeding and genetic selection. That would be no more so than in the dairy sector where when designing a breeding program one can look closely at the traits that one particular herd may require compared with his next-door neighbour who may be looking for something different. When I started, and when my father was a dairy farmer, then the chief trait we would be looking for was milk yield and milk quality. Now as our breeds have improved and especially with the Holstein, which is bred to produce large quantities of milk, we can now look at no end of different traits such as lameness, mastitis, even some traits that you would not think there was a genetic component, more a management component such as the incidence of displaced abomasums (which I have mentioned previously) and use selection processes to reduce the incidence of this.

With improved breeds, better selection of genetics combined with management, an individual animal is far more likely to reach her full potential in these modern times. But some of these changes and developments are the farmers choice, and our role is purely advisory with some of the new innovations we have at our hands, the new tools of our trade, to help us give them that appropriate advice. If they act on it, that is their choice but obviously with the combined right management, then there are considerable economic advantages in following the opportunities now offered. If one combines that with the innovation of sexed semen so one can maximise the genetic potential of your herd. Having a near hundred percent certainty that using this on your better, high potential cows then you will breed another female from her as a future replacement, and also with methods of super ovulating a high genetic merit cow, one increases the chances of having better and better cows in the herd. This technique is also used in both pedigree beef herds and sheep flocks to produce more high genetic merit bulls and tups, increasing the genetic potential of the breed and also producing males that will have a greater retail value because of their breeding.

Technology has produced ways of separating sperm in semen, allowing one to use those that will produce females and over the years this has become a far more reliable technique though the odd male will still get through. Techniques have developed so that you can harvest eggs from super ovulated sheep and cattle and then with better microscopes be able to grade those fertilised eggs in their quality so that the best eggs can be implanted into the best cows and ewes. Storage facilities have improved so that these embryos can be stored for days, months, years by freezing them and then when needed thawing them so that they are not damaged. Breeding programs have been developed to synchronise groups of female stock to all come into season at the same time so the implantation of embryos in them can all be carried out at the same time. The world moves on!

But what of our day to day lives? I suppose the biggest joke for everyone when they know you are a farm vet is their memory of James Herriot and him sticking his arm up a cow's backside. You would be introduced to somebody and upon going to shake their hand, they would jokingly remove theirs briefly, commenting that they did not know where yours had just been before with a smile on their face re-offering their hand and then shaking. How many times has that happened to me over the years? Too many to remember but it has been a joke that has perpetuated through my career.

A rectal examination of a cow is one of the best diagnostic tools we have as large animal vets, allowing us to palpate the complex twists and turns of the guts and reproductive organs of a bovine. Obviously the longer the arms you have, then the further in you can feel for any abnormality that may be present. It allows us to feel such things as a twist in the gut, an obstruction somewhere as well as being a method of feeling the cow's uterus to determine whether she is in calf or not. For the AI man (the artificial inseminator, not the changing term of Artificial Intelligence) it is a way for him to guide his syringe and catheter containing the semen he is going to insert into the cow's cervix by feeling that structure through the wall of the rectum while he uses his other hand to inseminate into the reproductive tract.

Ever since I qualified, we have always worn gowns to keep my arms as clean as possible, easy to wash off with a hose when we have finished our work on the farm and also waterproof. These gowns were always quite cumbersome though they did lessen the blow frequently if you were kicked by the cow. We now use an array of lighter more practical clothing, waterproof trousers and tops, or dungaree type outfits that are more comfortable to where and easier to get around in. I can remember my initial calving gown that had rubberised and elasticated ends to their sleeves. After a long job, it would seriously be impinging on the blood supply to your arm making you feel a lot more tired than you actually were. How many times did a pair of scissors come out to cut the elastic a little and restore circulation to an aching arm?

We have also had protective arm gloves made out of thin plastic, so our arms usually were protected from the contents of a cow's rectum. However, when I was a student, I did go on farm with one vet from a different generation who didn't use gloves and he thought that us as prospective vets should do the same as him. I had to do a pregnancy diagnosis session with a bare arm which obviously got dirtier and dirtier as the morning progressed. If I used to bite my nails, that was one day that I definitely didn't. Of course, from a health and safety point of view these days, it is important that we do where these gloves (which do occasionally split) as such diseases as Salmonellosis and Campylobacter can be carried by cattle and then could be transmitted to us.

What we do have now is a vast array of different coloured gloves replacing those initial faecal coloured ones I started with. Greens, blues, pinks and the most violent yellows, now with a mild elasticated top so they don't slip down your arm when in the cow's proverbial backside. We are good at leaving items on farms, some we will never see again but I could guarantee that if I had mistakenly left these yellow gloves, they would always be returned to me. Need I say more about their colour!

But with the advancement of science, do we still need to stick our arms up the rear end of a cow? The answer to this is still yes, both from the point of view of helping to making a diagnosis, but also in the most common procedures we carry out involved in fertility work. For years at the start of my career the method of pregnancy diagnosis was by feeling the cow's uterus through her rectal wall and depending how far in calf she would be. Either feeling the foetal membranes slip gently away between your fingers in early pregnancy, or later on, feeling either the cotyledons attaching the placenta to the uterine wall, or feeling the calf itself. A skill that took much practice but when you became skilled at it you could tell if a cow was pregnant at five weeks plus into her pregnancy. One could also feel her ovaries if she had not been seen bulling to see if there was a follicle there, or a corpus luteum present and then formulate a treatment for her depending what stage of her cycle she was in.

But one of the main developments that has occurred has been the use of Ultrasound for us to do the same techniques, we have swapped touch for sight. Ultrasound, as in humans for monitoring pregnancies, has been used for years for diagnosing pregnancy in sheep and pigs. In pigs it has been a straightforward are they in pig or not? With the long convoluted uterine horns of sows and with litter sizes of one to twenty plus, it is difficult to estimate the number of piglets in a sow. Yes or no, and check them a bit later in pregnancy to make sure they are still in pig as there are diseases that cause absorption, foetal death or abortion. With the widespread use of AI in pig herds or the visual sight of a boar serving a sow, it is easy to know how far the pig is pregnant, it makes management easy. With that adage we were taught at university of their gestation period being three months, three weeks, three days it makes management of the breeding sow very easy.

In sheep, in rams carry a colour on their undersides that they mark the ewe with when they are served, raddles, the colour being changed every three weeks so you have a rough idea when they will be due to lamb. In ewes, ultrasound is used not just to determine pregnancy but also to give an accurate number of lambs each ewe is carrying, and skilled operators will be near on a hundred percent accurate. This allows ewes to be fed during the latter part of pregnancy far more precisely as to their litter size and with the right management, such diseases as pregnancy toxaemia (twin lamb disease) can be prevented in the ideal. But it can certainly be managed better especially if this is combined with body condition scoring and with metabolic profiles to determine if problems are developing. For the modern farmer, this makes management so much easier and alleviated a lot of problems. The flock can be managed as singles, those carrying twins and those carrying triplets.

But as in human obstetrics these examinations of pigs and sheep are carried out externally, they are certainly non-invasive techniques giving accurate results that help management greatly.

In cattle we relied on using our arms for a long time, but technology was advancing until at last we had ultrasound scanners that we could use in this species. But the big difference was that with cattle and in early pregnancy, the uterus is small and is positioned high in the abdomen. There would be no chance of using an ultrasound scanner externally on a cow, plus the risks of getting kicked would be high as well. When these machines were invented for us cattle vets, our scanning probe would be on the end of a long tube carrying the necessary optics to a screen, but that probe would still have to be used per rectum. We had not got away from putting our arms up cow's backsides.

The problem though with the early models we used were their size,. Luckily for the cow, not the probe, she just had to put up with the size of the vet's arm, but the visual display, the screen that you observed what the scanner was showing you. Of course, we now have flat screen TVs, but if you can remember the old twelve-inch TVs, cumbersome things with a lot of depth to allow room for the ray tube, that was what these machines were like. The first one I used was large and it was heavy. We had acquired it mainly for use in equine work, and it was very good for scanning tendons etc when diagnosing causes of lameness. But here the horse would be standing in one place for this examination and any x rays that may be needed, it was not a problem if the scanner was static and close by. The horse would come to the scanner.

In cattle work, as well as accuracy, speed is the essence and with such a large and heavy scanner, one was having to bring the cow to the scanner rather than vice versa. With this particular scanner it was far too time consuming and when the farmer was paying by the hour, he wanted the old-fashioned arm in and out and on to the next one.

Thankfully over time, as they were developed more, they became smaller and lighter. This was especially with the development of goggles so rather than the display being on tv as it were, it was now on a small screen in front of your eyes. If there was a slight disadvantage it was that with the screen you could show the farmer what you were seeing, with the goggles only you had that picture.

But now with these light machines, and with the necessary training, we could view the cow's uterus and her ovaries. We had a far clearer picture of what was happening inside her as we could see. We could see the size of developing ovarian follicles so we could estimate when the cow should be bulling next, we could view different types of ovarian cysts and so treat them appropriately. But most important of all, we could see a calf, we could see the umbilical cord, its heart beating, and we could see all this at a far earlier date than we could have diagnosed pregnancy by the old-fashioned method of feel I have described earlier. With the grid on the screen, we could measure the length of the calf and from that give an accurate idea of how old the foetus is. For those skilled enough with scanning, one could even sex the calf at a very young age as well as diagnosing twinning. This was a serious advance in the service we offered at our routine fertility visits, and it was quick. This offered serious advances in how the farmer could manage his cows.

Can they develop more? I could not answer that, but certainly now they are robust and lightweight and make our job considerably easier. There would be one time when my scanner also was more than a help when I was asked to PD a particularly wild and aggressive cow to find if she was in calf or not. Generally, if you have your hand in their rectum they are not inclined to kick, but this cow I did not trust and although I had control of her tail and managed to get my arm and the scanning probe inside her, she was not having any of it and lashed out behind her with one hind foot. She was quick, but luckily for me, what she connected with was the scanner as I saw this foot flash towards and by me. It would have hurt, especially in the region she had aimed but the scanner took the force of it all, strong enough for it to break the strap that attached me to the scanner.

Luckily no lasting damage, and take two. With care we repeated the process having repaired the scanner and managed to complete the task I had started. We were prepared for what might be coming. She was in calf. I would not have wanted to calve her at a later date, she was a real danger to mankind.

The advent of ultrasound in cattle practice has been a real advance, and for some they do use it more extensively for example looking at lung pathology, liver pathology etc. It is a wonderful piece of kit and has advanced veterinary science considerably. The good news though, for anyone who wants to shake my hand, although I am a very right-handed person, I have always used my left for performing rectal examinations on cattle!

But there have been many other advances to help us with diagnosis as well, and many of them now available to use on farm. Some diagnostic tests are tried and trusted and have not changed for years. The faecal egg count for example. We carry out this test to see whether animals carry a parasitic worm burden in their guts which will be adversely affecting their performance, and more importantly in this modern age when we think differently, very important in determining whether you need to worm the animals or not. Like with some antibiotics, there is an increasing resistance problem with many of the anthelmintics we have used to kill these worms. So the more sparingly they can be used, then the longer it will take for resistance to build up and the longer we will be able to use these drugs when necessary. A simple technique of looking for worm eggs under a microscope in a specialised McMaster slide, suspending any eggs in a saline solution and then being able to count the number of worm eggs present, also typing them while you count them. A similar technique for liver fluke in cattle and sheep is also used, unchanged throughout the years.

What has changed is the development of tests we can do on farm as opposed to sending samples away to a laboratory and awaiting results. We, in these Covid times, have got used to the testing of large numbers of people, ourselves just to be sure we could go to our workplace. The use of the Lateral Flow Test has become part of our lives, and for those showing symptoms or travelling abroad, they have become familiar with the PCR tests. Some of these types of tests have become commonplace in farm animal practice where we can carry a kit in the car, and when we use it, we can get an almost instant result to give us a diagnosis. Scours in young calves are commonplace, even in the best husbandry conditions. There are many causes, the commonest being Rotavirus, Coronavirus, Cryptosporidiosis and E. coli scours. With adding a small sample of the calf's faeces to a test kit, within ten minutes we will get an answer as to the most likely cause and so can start the appropriate treatment immediately rather than having to wait up to forty-eight hours to get a result from the laboratory. Reducing this time delay for the health of the calf is very important.

E. coli can be a cause of mastitis in cattle and in its most acute form can have a high mortality rate as the bug quickly produces toxins that are absorbed into the cow's blood stream and make her seriously ill. If not treated quickly you will lose the cow. Mastitis in cattle can be cause by what are called Gram positive and Gram-negative bacteria, and the sensitivity of bacteria to antibiotics does depend on what type of they are. E. coli are Gram negative, Staphylococci and Streptococci, two other common bacteria involved in causing infection in the udder (mastitis) are Gram positive.

Whereas most Gram-positive infections need antibiotic treatment, science has now shown us that in less serious forms of E. coli infection where it causes inflammation but doesn't acutely affect the health of the cow, then very often the cows own immune system will self-cure the infection. Antibiotics in these cases are not needed. Again, in the past, we would send a milk sample off to the lab to find what the bug was and to get an antibiotic sensitivity to it so we could treat it with the right drug. But this took forty-eight to seventy-two hours so was often giving you the result of what to treat the next case with. Over the past couple of years, we have seen the development of cow-side tests, where with the farmer having a small incubator, a sample can be taken, and he will have a result in twenty-four hours whether it is gram positive or negative. Why is this a help? If it is Gram negative and the cow will self-cure, then she does not need antibiotics and we are becoming increasingly more conscious of the amount of antibiotic used on farm with the worries of drug resistance in human medicine. If it is a Gram-positive result, then she the cow will receive antibiotics. The only treatment necessary while awaiting results is to administer a jab of an anti-inflammatory drug to relieve any pain and make the cow feel more comfortable, better in herself.

Cows can suffer from ketosis, and increase in ketones in their blood stream, especially just after calving and this can cause a variety of symptoms. In its most serious form causing nervous system signs, cows will circle, they will have a wish to suck anything continuously, even you if you are standing too close or it can make them manic. In days gone by our diagnostic method was a bit of bucket chemistry, taking some milk from the cow and adding a reagent to it (Rothereux's) and seeing if the milk changed colour to a nice purple if there were ketones present. Now we just take a little blood, add a drop to a stick and place it in a meter which instantly gives a figure for the amount of ketones in the blood. Simple, quick and affective, making our lives so much easier in determining the correct treatment.

As science evolves, we have more and more of these tests available to help us diagnose disease in the animals under our care, so we restore them to full health again, and full production. Important steps in production animals and especially for their own welfare.

But if I have already mentioned them previously, I have to go back to what an influence the development of computers has had in our profession, like in so many industries. If my computer skills have not developed a lot over the past twenty years, it is undeniable how much they have moved the business forward. Not just in the day to day running of a business but also for the information computers give and the data analysis that can be obtained with the press of a button.

From the business point of view, it has made life for those wonderful ladies in the office much easier, as long as us vets are efficient and book our work quickly. Somewhere in the work manual it says about booking it the same day as you carry out that work, but what it says in theory and in practice are two completely different things. I hope I was good and not too far behind in booking what I had done, certainly no more than twenty-four hours behind. I would always be up to date on the last day of the month for invoicing and for stock control purposes. Others I'm afraid, and it was always the same people, would be far behind and the ladies would then have to keep harassing them to complete their booking to get the invoices out quickly. Hopefully if we worked efficiently this would be on the first working day of the next month.

For them, invoicing, having a readily available day diary at every point in the office so whoever was answering the phone, and there could be four or five phones going at the same time. There would never be any confusion about where each individual vet was, and if an emergency came in, who would be the most appropriate vet to send, who could be there quickest. Computers also offered an important method of stock control, rather than manually having to check how much of each drug was on the shelf, how much had been used and how much was needed to re-order to get stock levels to where they should be, this could all be done electronically. The first form of this was a handheld device which read bar codes on each drug, and when you had completed your stock take, connecting this device into a computer would give you your levels and automatically what needed to be re-ordered. Now, as a drug is booked out, this is done by the computer, life is easy. Then re-ordering becomes just as simple. What is more, if we vets book our work quickly and accurately, then the computer will know exactly how much is in each car as we have to book our drugs in and out of the car. If a small quantity of drug is needed, rather than opening a new bottle (and if the bottle is breached it should be used or disposed of within twenty-eight days), the drug can be dispensed from an open bottle from one of the vet's cars. The money that has been wasted by vet practices in the past just by poor stock control and not booking out drugs has been phenomenal. But these new systems, and they will no doubt improve more, and with that hopefully vet costs can be under some sort of control. The future will hopefully also allow for the practice to set drug limits on each farm as to how much can be dispensed, and if then highlighting if these limits look like being exceeded. Enquiries can be made as to whether there is a disease problem that needs further investigation.

One hopes it will be another step forward into reducing the amount of antibiotic use in farm practice, ensuring that the consumer has more confidence in the products they are buying, and also reducing the risks of drug resistance.

But it has also offered a lot to us as vets, with several specific vet programs now written and becoming more tailor made to the requirements of each individual practice. Practice manuals can be put on them for easy access, Health and Safety policies (now usually written by bespoke companies but with a little adjustment for each practice) along with learning guides and self-assessment tests to make sure you are up to date.

We used to have to write up our Herd Tuberculosis tests by hand, a long-winded process with the Avian reaction entered in red pen, the bovine reaction in blue. For the size of some of the herds we now test which could be fifteen hundred to two thousand animals the relief of finishing the test, often with a very early morning start would soon be dampened by the thought of hours writing the test up.

Now, through a system called SAM, it can all be done electronically and can be done in a short time. The Government Gateway has greatly speeded this process up meaning we can get on and do more tests quicker.

But of course, computers also offer a great deal of knowledge and can act as our library for researching difficult cases. Everything is there at the press of a button, rather than hoping you have the right book in the office to look something up. Information can be passed on readily to your clients, whether in passing papers on or writing a report from what you have found out with an action list showing a way forward. More and more client history can be stored on the V-drive (still beyond me what that actually is) and in your cloud, again another mystery to me how things can be stored up in the ether, floating around above us. Readily available, all the vets have access to what is happening on any one farm so there can be continuity in treatments and disease control from past history.

So much information is available if there is data to put in, and of course farmers are just as up to date as we vets are and are keen to be updated with what is happening on their farms. It allows them to work more efficiently as well as us, and to monitor production goals and where they are in reaching these.

All this along with the use of smart phones linked to the practice computer system, to CCTV cameras monitoring the premises out of hours, vet practices are targets like everywhere else for break-ins, trackers so that the office staff know where we are. An insurance in lone working that if you did have an accident in your travels, and we cover a lot more miles than we did in the past, then our whereabouts could be pinpointed, and assistance could be on its way.

With the use of Whatsapp, we have been able to send photos of cases throughout the team. So if advice has been needed on a case, then the attending vet has a ready mechanism to ask others who may have seen similar cases in the past.

Computers and associated technology have greatly changed the face of veterinary practice, both in increasing business efficiency but also in making our lives as vets better with such access to data and information. The perfect way of obtaining assistance in difficult cases and a way of improving communication between the rest of the team and of to your clients. Newsletters, communiques can now be delivered at a press of a button rather than laboriously putting a flyer in to so many envelopes, then addressing them and posting them. Communication in an instant.

And during our times of remote working during the Covid pandemic, this technology has offered a means of us being able to keep in touch with our colleagues when we have not been able to meet in person. We have been able to check on each other's well-being, have been able to continue clinical meetings, professional development (a mandatory requirement of the Royal College on us), Zoom meetings. It has kept us sane in a period when we may have felt very isolated.

And what the future brings with ever new technology, who knows! But that will not worry me. I often thought I needed to reach retirement before this world of technology got too advanced for me and left me behind. My wife often says to me in retirement, "Why don't you do some consultancy?"

It now also requires that knowledge of technology to deliver what you are consulting on.

But if I were to offer one sentence of caution. I not very long ago sat in on a clinical meeting with the rest of the team. The question was asked as to how we would investigate a herd problem on a dairy farm. We spent twenty minutes coming up with ways of finding a solution, looking at production figures and other data that the computer may give you. Analysing milk records, certain disease statistics, taking blood tests and analysing the data obtained from them. Information, information,

information all obtained from a computer and from technology. Evidence based science is the new buzz phrase.

We were asked if there was anything else that may help. At this stage I had said nothing. But to me, and now was my time to speak, there was one thing we had not looked at, and to me the most important thing. We as students were taught to use clinical judgement, use your experience, and if evidence-based medicine may have taken over, clinical judgement still has a crucial place.

I said, "Why don't we look at the cow?" The cows to me will tell us far more than any computer, and that is why we are trained vets.

Technology isn't everything, your eyes and other senses are, and will communicate far more to you and the farmer. He has to understand to!

18

DRURY LANE

Not everything has changed for me over those forty something years. If there is one thing that I have been passionate about, then it has to be my love of farming and the countryside. Our landscape is dictated by agricultural land, moorland, forest, mountain and heathland but the guardians of a lot of that land whether it be arable, or livestock farming is the farming community. Our rural landscape may be changing as farming gets more intensive and it is sad that a lot of "nature" has been removed with the grubbing of hedgerows to make larger fields whether for grazing or for arable where machinery gets bigger and bigger to bring in our harvest, the nation's food supply. Disease has also played a part, an example being the loss of the elm tree, so prominent on my father's farm in my youth but succumbing to Dutch Elm Disease. Others of our natural species are also now threatened such as the Ash with Ash Dieback and of course there is the diminishing habitat of such birds as the Plover, so common in my youth, and the Curlew.

That may sound as if farming doesn't care about the environment, but farmers do and are very often the guardians of our countryside. I think this would be especially true of the small family farm, so common in my days in Devon in the eighties but who are now being forced out of the industry by rising costs, obtaining milk contracts as the costs of collection rise, and the intensification of farming. But these small farms do so much to support the environment and the farmers do really care about their surroundings. Okay, the farmyard may often look a bit scruffy, with adapted old buildings converted into the milking parlour, calf housing and lambing sheds. But these farms will still have their hedgerows, old permanent pastures where the flowers grow, and bird and insect life still thrive in old-fashioned meadows.

The small twenty to thirty cow dairy herds may not exist anymore. Certainly in the parts of the country I have worked in, the farmers are getting older and their children have looked for careers outside of farming where they may get an easier living for greater reward. They won't have the chronic back and hip problems of their fathers from milking cows in an old fashioned shippen, stooping down to place the milking units on the cow's teats, nor will they have had to stack hundreds of straw and hay bales in the barn for storage. This is now all mechanised, bigger bales and far bigger machinery to handle it all.

For all the general public who see farmers as rich people who drive around town in big cars, some getting huge subsidies from the Government for their part in the food production cycle, there are equally a huge number of hard-working men and women working all hours of the day to scrape a living and produce a proportion of the country's food.

These were the types of farm I worked on in Devon all those years ago, where my round was often going to a farm, then to next door, and then again. The days of Buttercup and Daisy, all the cows having names not just the numbers of today.

Throughout my career these are the farms I have enjoyed going to. The small family farm where every animal on the place was important and any loss would be deeply felt both financially and emotionally. As farming has changed then it has always been my wish that a few of these could survive and that I would do everything I could to help those that I was involved with continue in farming and their way of life. These were the farms where you dealt with the farmer, his wife and not the herdsman or farm manager. To me there was always a different sort of relationship between vet and farmer. You had to become known and trusted, show you knew what they were about and trying to achieve and from then on you would become part of the team, the family, helping making decisions which could have a big impact on their livelihood.

The size of these farms may be bigger now than when I started, but the small farm is not economic. The thirty-cow herd I was referring to may now be eighty to a hundred cows, possibly with a little beef and a few sheep as well, but as I retire, I am pleased that some still survive and are still making a reasonable living from the land.

One such example would be Drury Lane, not the theatre in London but a small family farm in the hills above Ministerley, some nine or ten miles outside Shrewsbury. Drury Lane is a solely dairy unit milking a hundred cows and with dairy replacements that would add another forty young stock to the farm. A farm where you can stand in the yard and enjoy magnificent views over to the Stiperstones perched high on the hills the other side of the valley, but in winter while admiring the snow-covered hills beyond, you can get caught in a blizzard and have your b..ls frozen off. A lovely setting but on the wrong day after climbing the snow or ice-covered road to get there, all uphill off the main road you knew what winter was about.

But this for me was always a place where it was a pleasure to work at. The farm was owned by Clifford and his daughter Jill. Clifford was very much a good old-fashioned farmer and could talk the back end off a donkey with his tales of how things used to be, the important people he had met in his life and his knowledge of most of the old country folk. A very interesting man, he was very much part of a traditional farming community. Jill, on leaving school had gone into banking and through her hard work had become a manager at a bank in Surrey. But with life not going quite the way she wanted, she decided to change career and come back to the family farm along with her husband Dan who stayed in the finance industry. She joined her father on the farm, running it between them. As Clifford got older, she took over the reins more and more until she was effectively running it herself. A fresh mind with fresh ideas, Jill was always ready to learn and then implement what new ideas she found, first running them past dad.

She was and still is ably assisted by Julie, who used to farm the other side of Shrewsbury but now lives close by and milks the cows most days plus assisting in the calf rearing. This is a lady very much devoted to her animals and how they are kept. And a lady who can swear when she wants to, usually when an issue of animal welfare has come up that she has heard about.

Over the years, ever since my joining the practice I have carried out the routine work on this farm and have developed a great relationship with all involved. I would visit the farm on a fortnightly basis, nine forty-five sharp and would examine cows as post-calving checks, non-bullers and then pregnancy diagnosis on those that have been served long enough but had not repeated coming bulling. I would also look at anything else they wanted me to see, an ill cow or calf, whatever. Then over a cup of coffee we would review results, future policies, basically discussing anything that could improve the health and welfare, improve milk production, feeding, anything that we thought relevant to the farm.

This has been a farm for me that it has been a joy to work at, always met with a smile as Jill would announce "we have a mixed bag for you today". Over the years I hope we have achieved all that we have set out to do, with minimum stress to both us humans and to the livestock on the farm. There have been glitches like having Tuberculosis reactors on the farm, but that has been common throughout Shropshire over the years. This has created headaches as not being able to sell young stock because of movement restrictions has caused overstocking with its inherent problems. For a small farm like this, this disease which won't go away does cause great financial and emotional hardship both in terms of apparently healthy cattle being slaughtered as reactors and the extra burden of looking after too many stock in a limited capacity of housing. Thankfully at the time of writing, the farm is free from the disease again but however good their biosecurity, at the moment it is not if they get the disease again, but when!

But there have been many good times and fun times as well. Once I was presented with a cow with a swelling under her neck, just behind the angle of her jaw. It looked like a tumour and generally in these cases one would leave well alone or cull the cow. But here cows are part of the family so it was decided that I would try and remove the growth. This was going to be rather ambitious surgery as not only would I be operating on a conscious cow, but I would also be doing my surgery in a rather delicate area with some rather vital blood vessels in close proximity to my operating site, namely the Carotid artery and the Jugular vein.

The cow was lightly sedated and stood quietly in the cattle crush. We put a halter on her to fix her head to one side before the area was cleaned up and clipped before local anaesthetic was administered into the surrounding tissues. We were ready to start, though a sight like this was not for Jill's stomach, Clifford was my assistant. A bold incision with a scalpel, though care with the depth I went, those blood vessels were my major worry, and I was soon using blunt dissection to separate this mass from its surrounding tissues. Operating in warm sunshine outside, what could be more relaxing! What a worry that any wrong movement or struggle from the cow could mean a wrong cut and disaster. But with patience and perseverance, the mass was extracted, and the skin wound sutured closed.

I removed the sutures at my next routine visit, it had healed well, the cow had had an uneventful recovery and would survive in the herd for a good time to follow.

Jill, as I said, does not have the strongest of stomachs and if there were anything that involved pus or especially if a cow had a retained afterbirth and a subsequent endometritis, she would only be too quick to leave the scene. In these cases, there is a foul smell and often a foul pussy discharge. Even over the years she has not got used to this.

Another time we examined a cow who had a displaced abomasum, a condition I have described in a previous chapter and the treatment recommended is to operate, again described earlier. We hoped that our husbandry was right so that on this farm this was an unusual occurrence. On some farms there could be an incidence of five percent plus, especially those herds where a high proportion of maize was fed in their diet. Here at Drury Lane by regular monitoring of cow condition, if we got one a year it was unusual.

But we had a case and put the cow into a loose box, secured her and I proceeded to operate to return the abomasum to its rightful position in the cow's abdomen. The wound was sutured closed so afterwards the only visible signs were a wound on her left flank and a neat bow by her umbilicus where the abomasum had been secured to the body wall to form adhesions so it wouldn't displace again. An uneventful recovery ensued so that a fortnight later I went to check her over and remove the sutures. The flank done, I looked beneath her to remove my bow only to find there was nothing there. Strange, but on thinking about it at coffee time, Julie remembered that the cow had got out of the box and the only way she could have done that was to jump through the window.

On further thought, Julie remembered she had done that the same day of the operation, whatever was on the window ledge must have made a clean job of cutting straight through my bow! Thankfully the abomasum was still where it should be.

A few yards in front of the cattle crush Jill had a hen house. Though unable to get out these hens were happy to view the outside world through a wire mesh door, though shut in by a wooden door at night. While I was examining the cows, they would all be clucking happily away observing the vet at work. I was more than impressed when one day when I was there that I could hear music softly playing away in the background. Jill had installed Classic FM into the chicken house to improve their cultural outlook on life.

As I have previously said, the welfare of the animals was always the key issue, there would be no shouting or waving of sticks, cows were gently cajoled to where they were meant to be.

It was somewhat of a surprise one day to hear Julie shout "Get a move on you f-----g cow". We, Jill and I looked at her shocked and rather embarrassingly she explained she meant she was talking about her fellow helper whose mind was often off with the fairies rather than concentrating on the job in hand.

There are still a few farms like this, but this one has always had a special place in my heart as being such a great place to work. Your work was always appreciated and advice heeded, the perfect vet/farmer relationship in my mind was created. But also, their awareness on the countryside, on nature and their enjoyment of it was also important. As part of the farm, but not attached to where the livestock are, they also have an area of woodland on a hillside which will stay unspoilt as it is. A place where Jill can go for the peace and quiet it offers, a place that in spring will be covered with a carpet of bluebells, a place of beauty.

They are dairy farmers, but that woodland is their legacy to their part of rural England.

I could describe many farms over my career but this one is the one that sticks in my mind, and Jill and Dan have become firm friends, a friendship which will go beyond my veterinary days. It was a pleasure to have them at my wedding to Jane and also to enjoy their company at my private and small retirement dinner. But importantly for me with the changing scene of agriculture, may this type of farm survive into the future.

Drury Lane, the farm is not perfect and does need investment in it to improve some of the buildings and yards. Will that take place? I don't know. Is there anyone to follow in succession? Their son is studying Geology at university, and that is the problem of these small farms, who is going to carry it on.

But for me a lasting friendship, and looking back in gratitude, Jill was always there for me when I was suffering from depression and at other low points in my life.

Dan and Jill invited me round for a light lunch some six months after my official retirement, to catch up as Jane and I had just been abroad and to have a quick glance at her cattle at winter housing time. It was always a pleasure to go and give any advice that may have been beneficial to the running of the farm, and to feel my opinion was still very much appreciated after such a long relationship with the farm.

It gave me the opportunity, as I had often wondered what had driven her to give up a high-powered banking job to return home, to ask her what had made her decide on a change of career. There were no hesitations in her giving her reasons.

She was working in Surrey and had remarried to Dan who also worked in banking. She had been talking to a colleague who told her how his son had just reached eighteen years old and was off to university, and he had to admit he didn't know who his son was. The pressures of work! Jill and Dan had a two-year-old son, and she didn't want this to happen to her, only seeing the lad first thing in the morning and at bedtime when she returned from work. Family was very important to her, and that impacted on her other reason.

Clifford had started the farm from nothing, it was his legacy, something he had worked for his whole life and for that, as well as his work with Rural Stress he was a much-respected member of the local community. He now had three daughters including Jill, one a retired policewoman, the other a teacher. There were five grandchildren including Jill's son whose career looked to be in Geology, a granddaughter making great strides in becoming an opera singer, and one who had just started her veterinary course at Surrey University. There are great grandchildren as well. Jill viewed her role in the family as being the guardian of her father's legacy so that if one day, one of the others wanted a career in farming, then the farm was there for them. It may or may not happen, but the opportunity is there!

In her eyes, part of that legacy is also to be guardian of the land that she farms. The pastures at the top of the hill are productive new leys, but those at the bottom near surrounding woods are old fashioned permanent pastures, meadowland. She talks with pride of how the number of orchids growing in these meadowlands is increasing each year, of the other wildflowers, the birdlife and insects making this natural habitat their home. The hedgerows are flourishing and producing those wild fruits that I can use to make my homemade wine. She adores being so close to nature and helping its survival in this rural setting.

She showed me a photograph she regularly looks at, reminding her of why she wants to be involved in this guardianship. The cows walking up from these meadows, these old pasturelands with flowers in the background, flourishing flowing with the breeze. This epitomises to her how she can combine nature and farming together, she admits she will never make a fortune and can only survive because her husband is a banker. But her, Dan's reward, they only have to walk across their fields to see it.

It has been rewarding for me to work with someone with that attitude, and as vets in the future we have a role to play in ensuring livestock farming and nature can progress hand in hand, and it is important we do so. It won't happen on every farm, but it can and will on some.

Jill's attitude is to be praised and I hope there will be someone who will carry on her legacy to Drury Lane.

19

WATER, WATER

If my tale started in a river in Devon, then water has always played an important part in our daily lives as farm vets. This is mainly so we can get ourselves clean after being on a farm both for reasons of personal hygiene and to prevent the spread of disease from farm to farm. We would have it instilled into us especially if on disease outbreaks when working for Animal Health, the Governments official wing of veterinary control of Notifiable Diseases such as Foot and Mouth that on arrival at the farm we would bath ourselves in disinfectant, and for that we needed to dilute it to the right concentration in water.

Closer to home, certainly in the first series of *"All Creatures Great and Small"*, Herriot would be greeted by the farmer or his wife at the car with a bucket of clean warm water, a bar of soap and a clean towel. In my early days in Devon the same greeting would be present as you arrived to do your call, warm water and a bar of carbolic or something with a sweeter smell.

In the early days if one was doing a calving or a lambing and lubrication was needed to help with the birth, then plenty of soap and water would be applied to your arms and in and around the birth canal. This would supply extra lubrication to help ease the calf or lamb out. This would be especially important if the waters had broken some time ago, and the birth canal was becoming very dry.

This was the norm and what you as the visiting vet expected. Okay, sometimes the water was so steaming hot you could not put your hands into it, but water was provided. You would complete your job and be able to wash off in clean water ready for your next visit.

Times have changed! In my latter days as a farm vet, how often would this bucket of water be provided? One now has to ask, and if you are lucky, you will get one. Very often it just being cold water. This may be the change from the family farm to the big intensive farm where you don't deal with the farmer but with the cowman, but it is a greater challenge to keep up with the level of hygiene and cleanliness expected of us. The dairy hose is quite commonly all that is now on offer, if you are lucky there will still be some hot water, but it is not infrequent that especially after a difficult calving or caesarean all that is available is a cold-water tap. There is nothing like swilling yourself off on a cold frosty winter's night with water of a similar temperature and then with no towel provided getting into your car and turning the heater on at full blast to dry off and re-invent the circulation allegedly in your arms.

Lubricant gels have replaced soap and water as an obstetrical aid, but a bucket of water is also a great aid. A farm worker will wander off in search of your requirements and return with a battered bucket that certainly has seen better days and looks as if it has been recovered from under a tractor wheel. Hopefully it will not have a leak in it, if it has you hope you can finish your task while there is still some water left in the bucket.

One doesn't want to generalise, but what used to be, nowadays, no longer exists. The other trial would be when you have had to attend an animal down the field, often getting very dirty in the process. If water was provided, then did you have enough to clean yourself up sufficiently to get back to the buildings and do the job properly? If you were calving a cow then there would be your equipment to clean as well before all the excretions of the job dried and were more difficult to remove a little later, even more of a challenge at night when you couldn't see what you were doing with restricted light.

Another problem I found was that farmers never told you if you were clean or not, or more precisely whether you were still dirty. How many times when calving a cow would she strain and you standing right behind her trying to ease the calf out would get covered with foetal fluids being expelled through her vulva, and that was preferable to a cascade of faeces as she strained. The joys of being a farm vet!

One would clean oneself up as best you could, but especially in the dark you would miss bits both on equipment and on yourself. Arriving back home in the middle of the night one would go upstairs to get ready to get back into bed and snuggle your cold body up against that of your wife's. Going into the bathroom, seeing yourself in decent light at last, that's when you found out how well your wash had gone. Blood and foetal fluids still staining your skin on those more inaccessible parts to the naked eye, the backs of the arms and especially the elbows and under your fingernails. And that would be hoping there was also no malodours from the obstetrical procedures you had performed. Out came the scrubbing brush and much soap or shower gel to at last reach some semblance of being clean.

One last look in the mirror.

"No!"

Why didn't someone tell me my face was covered as well? More cleaning and at last bed.

It would be in the morning that you found out when you had leaned into the boot to get something from the car, drugs, whatever that you would find that you had spread the joys of your work over the car as well. More cleaning plus disinfecting calving ropes, calving jacks and generally tidying up a now rather dishevelled boot.

One would often reflect at this stage that it was lucky one hadn't met the boys in blue on the way home, car and your face covered in blood, they would have been wondering what illegal activities had occupied your evening.

As we reached our clinical years at university, years four and five, we were offered the opportunity to purchase through the course a parturition gown and some waders, what would in modern parlance be called PPE. The gown would cover all of your body from neck to mid-calf region, with ties at the back and elasticated arms covered by a rubber barrier, reaching down to just below the shoulder. Waterproof, these gowns offered full protection from the different substances we would encounter, easy to clean afterwards ready for their next use. They would often soften the blow when a kick from a cow was directed your way. The waders, knee length and with steel toe caps, completed our outfits though for more mundane day to day calls when I first qualified, a brown coat was more frequently used, carrying three or four in the car that could then be chucked in the washing machine when necessary.

For my scrawny arms when I first qualified, the parturition gown was fine but with my muscular development when working for a while, these elasticated arms began to feel like a tourniquet. As mentioned earlier, the need, not uncommonly, when in the middle of a calving to cut the elastic a little allowing blood to return to your quickly turning cyanotic arms was imperative. Along with the waders, I was never going to run a quick hundred metres wearing this outfit if chasing cows or sheep to where we needed to handle them. The other drawback of these gowns was when you were kneeling behind a cow, carefully trying to manoeuvre a calf out through her birth canal with the aid of the calving jack and the gown would get caught up in the ratchet mechanism of the jack just at a crucial stage. More than once, I would have to cut the gown free from the jack to be able to continue reaching the conclusion of a successful birth. The gown now was not as waterproof as it could be, read on!

The waders were also quite impeding, being quite rigid. The steel toe caps were supposed to be a safety feature, now common in Health and Safety directives. For us, the hazard was cows stepping on your toes, those fragile little pinkies nestling in the end of your boots. But I soon found out that what was far more painful was the cow's foot slipping off the toe cap onto the bridge of your foot, excruciatingly painful! That original pair was the only pair of steel toe caps I bought, softer nice green waders were far more comfortable, easier to store in the car, and okay, my toes may have suffered a little but that was far less painful to my feet.

But what did become common, especially with my Devon farmers was that they would be extremely keen to help you clean off, offering to wash you down with hoses of different strength, some a gentle flow, others you got the full blast as a forceful stream of water hit you and your parturition gown. The gown went but that was not going to stop their fun. Waders were fair game and if they could just get some of that water just to go over the top of the boots and into them, they were contented and would leave you with a smile on their faces.

Parturition gowns were replaced with parlour suits as my preference, far lighter and more comfortable, and less restricting on the arms. Waterproof trousers that would fit inside waders, or when at last not so many years ago I reverted to ordinary boots, they would fit over them, keeping your legs clean. I suddenly found that with the chance of giving you wet feet gone, farmers were less inclined to offer to wash you off, though the power now generated by some of these hoses was substantial. These hoses were used to flush down big parlours and so powerful that if you let go of them, they behaved like uncoiling snakes, and you needed to gain control of them quickly before you and anyone else around got seriously wet, drenched in fact. But used carefully, they would certainly wash you off effectively.

Water, water everywhere and that was certainly true of the winter of 2020/1. We are getting used to the changes in the season which everyone will blame on climate change and lately we have had some exceptionally mild but wet winters. I may have driven to work in the latter part of my career, heading down the M54 towards Shrewsbury and viewed snow on the Shropshire Hills and the Welsh Hills further in the distance but on the lower ground all we saw was rain, rain and eventually flooding. The River Severn as it winds its way through Shropshire meets several places where it narrows considerably, at Shrewsbury, at Bridgnorth, at Bewdley and at other places further down river. These towns built on the flood plains create barriers to the flow of the river especially in times of high rainfall when the streams and tributaries can take no more. The rivers rise and we have seen much flooding over the past couple of winters. This of course, especially when affecting our highways can cause us considerable difficulties in doing our rounds. This is especially so if one's vehicle is a Vectra, not a big four by four truck.

The end of January '21 was wet. Even on the last Wednesday of the month there was much surface water on the local roads, though surprisingly not where they usually flooded. I was aware that any more rain and some routes would become impassable. I viewed my round for Thursday morning and did not envisage any difficulties until I was diverted out of my way by a car drowning in a dip in the road under a railway bridge. My destination was no more than two miles the other side of this obstruction. I would have to divert; it would take me a little longer but again I didn't think I would encounter any problems on a ten-mile diversion. That was until I arrived at the crossroads, I intended to turn left and head across country. A white van man was stranded in the middle of a flood blocking my chosen route, my ten-mile diversion turned into twenty miles by which time the farm I was going to had phoned to say I would not get down their drive because of floods, they would meet me and transport me down.

This was turning into a long day, I did the call but decided for once that I would keep my waterproofs on in the car, just in case. I did one more call then went onto my last, I thought this visit would be the easiest to get to. I turned off the A5 into a country lane, the sun now shining brightly and into my eyes. I was just five minutes away from my call when I encountered more water in my path. I put the Vectra in first and carried on slowly, but this flood seemed to be going on forever. I was thinking I should stop and reverse back up the road when it suddenly dipped, there was a huge influx of water into the engine and over the bonnet, and the car was dead. I was stranded. I could not see either end of the flood, other than a truck emerging one end, seeing me then disappearing back the way it came.

What could I do? I phoned the farm I was going to, and Pete Williams came in his tractor to rescue me. This is where I was glad that I had kept my boots and waterproofs on. If I opened the car door to get out, water would flood in, and I hoped still at this stage I may salvage the car to last me for the final now only four months of my career. I had to climb out of the window into the water now ebbing around the door sills. Pete arrived, we managed to secure a rope to the car and tow it out and back to his farm, which involved me having to climb back into the car through the window. We tried the ignition; Pete said the car would never go again. He was right, the engine was silent now forever!

I spent the rest of the day, having completed the call I was doing for him, emptying one car and loading another. A week later I had acquired another car; surprise, surprise, another Vectra and exactly the same colour as the previous three, no one would know I was in a different car! And on the Saturday, my brother and I picked the old one up from Pete's farm to take back to my home. An hour later and it was on the way to the scrap.

One last Vectra to last me my final few weeks, fingers crossed. But I soon found that I needed the rains to stop. I at last had a car which the heater worked, the windscreen wipers worked properly, but the driver's side window had a mind of its own and as you drove along. It would slowly drop down of its own accord, letting in rain and wind. Improvisation, I managed to wedge it shut by sticking hypodermic needles between the frame and the glass, it worked until I managed to get the spare parts to get it fixed. My Vectra's had caused me some troubles over the years but had provided the farming community with much amusement with their travails.

Water, water, often a necessity for my job but also at other times causing much anguish to me.

But I would be amused that in the new series of "All Creatures Great and Small" James, Tristan or Siegfried would be sent off on a calving and lambing, and with a little perseverance would deliver new offspring into the world, but they would be spotlessly clean when their hands and arms appeared out from the animals back end, even once not even bothering to roll up their arm sleeves. They must be cleaner animals up in the Yorkshire Dales!

20

THE BOYS IN BLUE

One of our chief roles, and something that has not changed over the years is our involvement in protecting the health and welfare of all animals. To that affect, our powers are enormous, especially working hand in hand with emergency services and the RSPCA. Earlier I have described my walk in the Forest of Dean at the bequest of the RSPCA in an unsuccessful attempt to find and treat a lame sheep a member of the public had reported to them. They have a duty to investigate any reports from the public of cruelty or neglect of animals, both large and small, tame and wild. Much of my involvement with the organisation has been more in small animal work when I carried out such work, but also in looking after injured wild birds and animals, though at many times you did have to take the objective view of whether in treating wildlife, could they actually survive in the wild after treatment. Could a one legged, or one winged bird or a three-legged animal survive if released. Or if not, what sort of quality of life could it have in captivity. On those thoughts I may not always have agreed with what the RSPCA officer may have thought was the best course of action.

Their officers are out there and do a very good job, even if at times in my opinion they are a little overzealous in wanting to prosecute people when a little bit of educating may be a better course of action. I think over the years I had to go to court twice for them in small animal work, once to a dog which had been neglected and once for a dog where the owner had cut its throat with a carving knife. My valiant efforts to stitch it back together again were unsuccessful, the dog died on the operating table in what would have been heroic surgery. What was interesting though was the outcome of the court cases. The neglected dog, where the owner's solicitors were trying to twist the line of questioning, but the judge allowed me to pass over his comments and tell the case as it was, was banned from keeping pets for the rest of his life. The lady who cut her own dog's throat was given a two-year ban from owning a pet, I could never quite see the logic of that!

Since then, I have had only once had to help them out in a farm case, but more on that later.

Working with the police has been more interesting over the years whether it has been on official state business, the Notifiable Disease outbreaks I have worked in over the years where sometimes they would be needed to give us a right of access onto farms. On other occasions, giving us the right to put animals to sleep where their welfare and health is too severely compromised. With their involvement in some incidents, we would also have to work closely with the Fire Brigade. It has not been an uncommon occurrence that a horsebox containing livestock has overturned on a road and working with the emergency services we as vets are required to attend and treat any injuries that may have occurred. Sadly, these at times have been severe. Opening the overturned vehicle, one has been greeted with carnage, either animals dead already where they have suffocated under their mates, or where many have broken limbs and it has been necessary to euthanase them there and then. There has been the odd occasion where there has been the loss of human life in these incidents as well. One can only praise the work of the emergency services (including the Army who I worked with in the Foot and Mouth epidemic of 2001) for the help and professionalism they give in what are harrowing, traumatic experiences for those involved and those dealing with such emergencies.

I think my first involvement with the police and Fire Brigade would have been in Devon early one summers morning when a bunch of heifers had broken into the slurry lagoon. Whether someone had not secured the gate or they had just broken in I cannot remember, but as they had charged in to see all the fresh greenery on its banks. Once they had overcommitted their entrance, then several were left stranded in, well there is no other way to describe it, deep cow shit. The slurry lagoon is where the cow muck is stored until it is spread on the fields, so can be very fluid but with a dry crust on top, giving it a false impression of its true nature below. And of course, as it ferments it smells more and more the longer it is left when undisturbed. The area should be fenced off, and gated but unfortunately these accidents do sometimes occur. A paramedic friend of mine would relate one of his most traumatic incidents would be where a toddler fell in, but sadly he could not save him.

But in this particular incident, happily there was no tragedy, of the half dozen heifers that fell in, some were able to scramble to the side and climb out themselves, we, and mainly the Fire Brigade only struggled with one who panicked and headed in the wrong direction before tiring and coming to a standstill. There is always a request from the bystanders for the vet to sedate the animal to stop it panicking but you cannot. If you sedate it then it may be even more tired and want to lay down. It would then drown. What we had to do was lay boards across the surface of the slurry until we could reach the distressed heifer, then place a noose around her neck so that we could then haul her back to terra firma. How efficiently this was done, but I guess over time the emergency services have had to deal with it many more times than myself at that embryonic stage of my career. One would only then on the successful completion of this job start to clean up and try to rid yourself of the smell you had now acquired, more than enough to clear any room if not an entire area!

We had obtained a happy ending, other than a few dirty heifers, and a hose pipe would soon sort that out. The farmer would receive a bill for calling the Fire Brigade out and would ensure the perimeter of the slurry lagoon was fenced secure, and the gate would always be shut when access was not needed.

All was well. It would only be a few days later when he, the farmer, realised that the Hereford bull which had proudly guarded his female entourage had gone missing. He thought back to the incident of the slurry lagoon, and could not recall seeing him during this incident, when all the heifers that had got themselves in had not submerged. All were accounted for. Search parties were sent out in the surrounding fields and hedgerows from where this group of animals had originated. And this was in the days where any large animal could quite easily hide itself in the surrounds of fields with overgrown hedges and dry ditches in summer where he could hide in the shade.

The search was fruitless, he had disappeared, wandered off looking for a new hareem, been abducted (rustling has been around for years), or had he gone into the lagoon as well? If so, why had we not seen him as all the smaller heifers were obvious and were rescued? A mystery and there was nothing more we could do; he had disappeared and there was no evidence of his whereabouts......

Until one day a few weeks later, he suddenly appeared again. Unfortunately, he was found in the slurry lagoon, when he had decomposed enough, the gases forming inside him floated him up through this thick layer of cow s..t, the mystery was solved. Why the heifers managed to keep themselves afloat and scramble back to safety and he couldn't? Was it just because he was far heavier and in struggling in this fetid gruel? He just drowned himself and disappeared from view.

My last experience before retiring with the Fire Brigade was a different experience. In the interim there had been other slurry lagoon experiences in the practices I had worked with, more overturned trailers on busy roads with the carnage I have previously described, and the occasional cow, sheep or horse that had fallen down a hole or were trapped amongst embankments by the river. Times were changing, and the biggest change in these types of emergency was the emergence of specially trained teams to deal with such emergencies. Health and Safety was now the key to all such incidents. Gone were the cavalier days of the eighties and early nineties when we were careful but still took risks. Though like in the incident of the slurry lagoon, we may have gone on boards across the surface of the lagoon, but we still would have ensured that we had a harness on to rescue us if necessary.

Again, a farmer had found a small group of heifers had gone missing. On searching for them, he had found most of them had managed to cross the River Severn and had been found on a neighbour's land. Still though there were two animals missing and after extensive searching, they were found still in the river, but had got themselves into a part where the banks were steep and wooded. After some cajoling one was persuaded to scramble up the bank and into a cattle trailer to be taken back to re-join her mates.

That left one, who had obviously spent some time in the water with many attempts to get out, but continually failing as the banks got more broken and slippery from her continual effort to escape. She was knackered.

The problem was now not so much getting her out of the river but getting her up the bank, which was not quite sheer, but not far from it, with the hinderance of many small trees that would not help any rescue.

Call the Fire Brigade!

They arrived, the trucks, the support teams and now a controller who would assess the whole situation, the health and safety issues. There was a time was when the vet was in charge but here, we were going to be working under his directorship. He would assess the risks; we would give our input and he would initiate his plan. We were going to sedate the heifer heavily; it wasn't a hard job to catch her as she was exhausted. It wasn't hard to bring her to the bank and then inject her with a sedative, she was soon lying down but our director wanted her flat out so we could roll her onto a canvas sheet and then pull the sheet up the bank with a tractor.

From a veterinary point of view, there are risks of a cow being flat out for too long, especially if lying on her left side. Her rumen, her stomach, would fill with gas as it was digesting forage and she would not be able to get rid of it. She would get more and more bloated, eventually it causing more and more pressure on her lungs and heart and that could kill her.

The other big problem was that it was not a straight pull up the bank because of all the trees. We had an obstacle course to contend with and the distance from tractor at top of the hill and heifer at bottom was considerable.

I was worried we were taking too long; the sedative would be wearing off and the heifer would get distressed being hauled up this slope. We were asked to give more sedative! The heifer was being very good but one wondered what distress levels she was having being hauled out of the river, placed on the canvas and being held down and hobbled while all this assessment was going on.

After some time, the team leader had reached his conclusions that was all was safe and ensuring that nobody was in any danger from the long ropes from the bottom of the slope where the heifer was to the top and the tractor, the slow haul began. It was steep and this would be a long slow process, hoping the heifer wouldn't slide off the sheet because of the gradient, especially if she started to panic and started struggling. At last, she was moving and bit by bit she was slid up the slope. From time to time, we would have to stop and make minor adjustments to our trajectory, usually because of trees in our path, but progress bit by bit was being made.

She was a quarter of the way up, she was halfway up, but then unnecessarily I thought, we had to stop and reassess the situation. The angle the tractor was pulling had to be readjusted and we could shorten the rope the sheet was being pulled with. At last, the final pull began up the last half of the slope, at one stage again having to negotiate a tree but once clear of that, the slope eased and our patient, now accepting her situation and lying still, reached flat ground in the field by the wood side. By this time, she had attracted quite an audience with the emergency services and all their helpers, some of the farm staff and the vet.

All that was now necessary to do was to release her from her hobbles, get her sitting up and comfortably, check heart rate etc, and wait for her to get herself to her feet so she could be loaded into a cattle trailer and returned to the farm buildings to recover.

A job well done, and a new degree of professionalism shown by the emergency services in ensuring human safety as well as the welfare of the stricken animal. The heifer showed no effects of her ordeal and was back on her feet in remarkably quick time and was soon back at the farm and munching hay quite happily.

For me, my duties there had finished. I was on call that night and would have to wait and see what other emergencies would follow. As for the heifer, the following morning one wouldn't have known there was anything wrong with her nor of the ordeal she had put herself through.

Experiences with the police, other than when they were assisting enforcing the law in welfare cases were few and far between. One night late in my career my sleep was disturbed by the phone, and I was asked if I could attend a road traffic emergency, where a herd of cattle had got onto the main road, and one had been hit by a car. Of course, they think that we are all based at our practice address, i.e., in Shrewsbury, but for me it was a twenty-mile journey from where I lived, I would be there as soon as I could.

I was up and dressed in no time and glancing at my watch, noting the time, it was two thirty in the morning. I was in my car and on the way on a dark night with little moon. Some twenty-five minutes later I was at the scene, or at least at the point where the police had closed the road. I explained to an officer who I was, and he directed me on and to find his officer who was in charge of the situation. I drove a short way on and stopped, got out of the car to be greeted by a sergeant and a ton of beef lying in the middle of the road. There was nothing I could do, the officer informed me he thought the animal was dead, and it didn't take the brain of Einstein for me to soon confirm his diagnosis.

Someone's prime Angus bull was lying dead blocking the A49, the only problem now was, whose bull was it? And how were we going to shift it and re-open the road? All cattle should have ear tags with a number identifying them, and from this one could find out to whom it belonged to. We had two problems, one that it was the middle of the night and the body that collates all this information would not be open until nine in the morning, and secondly, with that beloved Data Protection, would they release that information anyway.

There was little else I could do, fair play to them, the police took control of the situation and said they would deal with it all. They could not just leave a lump of dead meat on the side of the road until they could trace an owner, neither could they leave it where it was blocking a major trunk road, even if it were the middle of the night. What they did I'm not sure, they apologized for wasting my time (they needn't have done, it could have been a real emergency where something could have been done) and sent me on my way home.

The road was soon reopened, the bull's owner was traced, he had only come from a couple of fields away but sadly his escape had led to his end.

It was getting towards dusk one Saturday evening in early September and again I was on call, having had my supper and settled comfortably at home with my wife to watch TV. The phone went and it was police control asking me to attend a road traffic accident involving an injured deer. By coincidence, early on that same day I had been called to see an injured deer only two or three miles further back on the same busy A49 in Dorrington, but the young animal had been rescued by a member of the public and had brought back to their home and put in a shed late the previous evening. Sadly, for this deer its injuries were too severe to consider any sort of heroic fix and the only option I had was to do the kindest thing and put it to sleep.

But my evening call, the deer was injured and by the side of the road on a dangerous corner. I was informed two officers were in attendance. I informed control that I would be on my way straight away, but it was going to take me the best part of half an hour to get there.

To my surprise she offered to send a patrol car to pick me up and get me there under a "blue light", but I said that I needed my car as it had anything I needed in it in the way of equipment, and if another call did come in then I would be able to go to it as soon as we had finished with the deer. I set off and had a good journey, making good time to attend to this emergency. It was less than half an hour and I found the incident easily, indeed it was on a bad corner so parking my vehicle would need some consideration.

On one verge there was an ambulance, it was this that had seen the stricken animal and called the police and on the far verge was parked a police car along with the injured animal.

One deer, two policemen and a medic plus me the vet, this animal was royalty in who she had to look after her. I assessed the scene, and it was obvious without too much examination that the deer had a severe compound fracture of its left hind leg. Sadly, euthanasia would be the only option. Oh dear, this was not being a good day for this species.

Generally, the council will pick up and dispose of dead animals, road kills. But it was Saturday night, and no-one would be available until Monday morning. What was going to happen to this deer until then.

Of the two policemen, one of them seemed in charge.

I asked him, "How are we going to dispose of the body?"

Panic came across his face, he thought I meant what form of euthanasia was I going to carry out, not how were we going to get rid of the body.

"You are not going to inject it are you, I thought you would shoot it" he said.

It became obvious to me that the method of disposal had already been decided before my arrival. The medic, knowing what the outcome was left the scene with our thanks for stopping to attend to the animal and then calling the police. Some would have left the stricken animal where it was, including the driver who had hit it. (I have in the past in fairness been following a car more than once when a deer has run in front of it, with the deer crashing over the car. You would have thought it would have been fatally injured but I have seen them land on the road, and as I have slowed to see what injuries they have received, the deer has got up, and then jumped the hedge and carried on running. If it were injured, who knows!).

I went back to the car and got my gun and ammunition, always feeling uncomfortable with it especially in police presence, although I had the required Firearms Certificate to use it. A took a bullet out of the box, loaded the gun and ensuring the officers were safely out of my line of fire behind me, the deer was put out of its suffering.

My suspicions were correct, as soon as I confirmed the deer was dead one of the officers went to the boot of their patrol car and emerged with a sheet. The deer was wrapped up and placed in the boot.

"We'll be off duty in an hour or so" one of them said to the other.

"We'll transfer it into my van when we get back to the station and deal with it at my place when we get home," he said to his mate.

With that, he gave me the appropriate log number and his number which I would need for invoicing, thanked me for coming out, and with that they got back in the patrol car and were gone. I was left alone standing on this bad corner in the dark.

Yes, I had soon realised that this deer was going to be a police dinner, there was no way anything else was going to happen to it.

I picked up my gun and returned to the car and was just about to drive off when it occurred to me that I had left my box of ammunition at the "scene of the crime". I thought the police would be well impressed if I had to ring them to report the loss, or if a member of the public found the box at a later date. I returned across the road equipped with a torch and there on hands and knees I searched through the grass for my ammunition. Luckily, I found it quite quickly but what anyone passing would have thought in their cars seeing this strange man searching through the undergrowth.

The end of an eventful night, an eventful day. My Sunday lunch was up in the air as to what it might be, the local constabulary, venison was definitely on the menu.

As a farm vet, I only really had one episode where I had to attend an alleged cruelty case. It was a dull late summer day, mid-morning when the office received a phone call from the RSPCA asking if a vet could attend at a field in a neighbouring village to the town the practice was based in, less than a ten-minute drive. A member of the public had reported that there were several lame sheep in this field and had been for a couple days without any sign of the farmer, the owner coming to treat them. Was this a case of neglect or cruelty? We were called to investigate, and I was the one standing in the wrong place at the wrong time. It would be me attending and I would meet the RSPCA officers there in a short while. They had informed the office that on a cursory inspection they thought that the sheep had maggots in their feet.

Fly strike is a not too infrequent occurrence in summer months, especially in hot and humid conditions, and if the animals are dirty, are soiled with dirty back ends or coats. If there is a smell that will attract Blow Flies, they are attracted to that area and will lay their eggs on the coats. The area around the anus is a common sight where faeces have stuck to the wool, especially if the sheep's excrement is loose. Under the right conditions these eggs will hatch very quickly, and the resultant maggots will set off in search of food, i.e., their host. They will start eating their way through the skin and then eating the flesh of the animal, effectively eating them alive. The severity depends on how many eggs, and therefore maggots have hatched to inflict this ordeal on the poor animal. In all my years as a vet, if there is one thing that has always turned my stomach, then it would be the sight of maggots crawling over and through an animal's flesh, most commonly in sheep and pet rabbits, but also occasionally in cattle and dogs.

I arrived at the field to survey the scene. Two RSPCA officers and a group of eighty odd sheep, a few which were obviously in pain as they hobbled across their domain. I was informed that the officers would like me to examine every sheep so they could make their report and decide what process would then follow.

This was fine if we had somewhere we could catch them and go through them individually but they had not thought about that. I for one was not going to spend the day chasing sheep around a field until we had caught each and every one of them, before examining them and then letting them go to chase the next one. The theory was fine, the practicalities were not.

I managed to contact one of my local farmers to see if he had any mobile catching facilities we could borrow, and if so, could we borrow them straight away. He was only too happy to oblige and within half an hour we had a set of hurdles we could fit together with a small race and an exit gate. We had a pen which would hold all the sheep, and with his help and that of his sheepdog, we soon had all the sheep penned in the corner of the field, near the gate, with a stone wall on one side. I would get the sheep into the race one at a time, examine them quickly and treat any that needed attention before letting them go out through the gate and back to their pasture.

A slow and laborious process, especially for as I would have to turn each sheep up to look at its feet, pare any that needed attention and record any abnormalities. Yes, some did have Foot Rot, a bacterial infection especially affecting between the hooves. This infection with the necrosis of flesh there creates a smell that would attract Blow Flies, and indeed there were a number of these sheep that did have maggots in their feet. This would make the lameness even more severe. A stockman is obliged to observe his stock at least daily; he should have noticed the lameness occurring in his flock and done something about it, all be it that in the right conditions eggs hatch very quickly to produce the maggots, but not in less than twenty-four hours.

I laboured away at my task over the course of the next three or four hours. The few with maggots took more time as I would have to clean up the feet, get rid of the maggots, pare the feet if necessary and administer antibiotic by injection or topical spray, and give pain killers when necessary.

My support team, the RSPCA, to be honest were mere spectators as I did all the work. But at last, an end was in sight, we were down to the last five, four, three then two. That left one and this one, now separated from her mates was rather frisky and not too keen to be caught, with my assistants not too willing to assist me. The sheep was looking for an escape route which wasn't through the gate.

As I have described, the pen was against a wall on one side and on the other side of the wall was a private residence whose garage was directly the other side. The garage had a sloping roof, ridged at the top.

Our lone sheep eyed this up as a route to escape and leapt over the hurdles, getting a foothold on the wall and was soon on the roof of the garage. She was unsure now if this escape route was the best option with a sheer drop off every other side of the roof. But on it she was safe from us, there was no way we could envisage climbing onto it.

She strutted her stuff, deciding on her next course of action, we could only hope she would return the same way she came, down back into the pen and into my clutches. She obviously was not lame!

Her decision was made for her, there was aloud crack, and she disappeared through a newly formed, sheep shaped hole in the roof. We could then only observe from our position, looking down through the hole to see the ewe sitting in a classic car parked in the garage.

I took this as a sign I should now beat a retreat. The RSPCA had called me out, the sheep was obviously not injured or lame, I would leave it to them to explain to the owners of the car why they now had a sheep sitting in its driver's seat. It was time for me to go!

I never did ask them what the outcome of the car and garage were. The farmer, the owner of the sheep was traced, and it seemed from other local farmers that he did have a reputation as not the best stockman. I did have to go to court as a witness for the RSPCA and on giving my evidence, the farmer admitted his guilt and was prosecuted. A successful outcome for the RSPCA and a salutary lesson for any farmers following the proceedings.

Over the years I have had some interesting times with both the emergency services and the RSPCA, and I must not forget the efficiency of the Army when they came to assist us vets in the Foot and Mouth epidemic in 2001. To all, their professionalism in what have sometimes been difficult and heart-breaking experiences have been second to none. With that, they have made our roles as vets a lot easier than they may have been. For that professionalism, I can only thank them, they have been a pleasure to work with.

There have been tragedies, but along with those there have also been moments of comic relief, where a degree of light-heartedness has made situations a lot easier to cope with.

I hope in the future that the police will not have acquired too much of a taste for venison, and us, including me now as a member of the general public will not be rammed by too many sheep driving classic cars down narrow country lanes. We would have something then to bleat about!

21

POINT TO POINTS AND AGRICULTURAL SHOWS

There are times each year when the farming community like to get together, and those times are the times when there is the opportunity for the rural community to meet and mix with those from urban communities. These events also offer us the chance as vets to meet our clients on a more social basis. If they are interested, it also offers the chance for townies to come and chat to us about our role in the community and welfare issues that concern them. We also get to meet aspiring vets and their parents who come and talk to us about what we do and what they, the next generation of vets, need to do to try and achieve their ambitions. In essence it is a chance for us to advertise our profession to the general public away from their preconceived ideas brough about by James Herriot and the Supervet.

In my early days as a vet, I lacked self-confidence and hated such events. But over my later years, since I have got over my depression and gained a confidence in myself I never had before, I am a changed beast and have looked forward to these events. I have been only too pleased to attend shows to represent the practice.

The local point to point was my first experience of these events when I was down in Devon. We had a couple of hunts nearby and it was them that ran these race meetings, usually in the spring. As the nearest practice we would be asked to attend as "official vets", a job we would do as an honorary duty, giving up our time for free.

I was asked by the practice I worked for then if that particular year I would act as the official vet, representing them but there would be another vet from a different practice there as well. The two of us were there to attend to any emergency that may occur on the course. I reluctantly agreed, giving up a Saturday afternoon I was not supposed to be working to be there. The venue was less than ten miles from my home and my wife was quite excited at going along, getting in free with me and getting a hospitality lunch and drinks. A new experience for her as well as me!

We set off, her in anticipation, me in somewhat trepidation at what I may have to do if there were fallers or a pile up at one of the fences. The only trouble was that it was raining, and had been for some time. When we arrived at the course the ground was saturated, and as parking was on fields, the approaches to the course were getting cut up and getting muddier and muddier.

I needed to get as close to the course as I could as all my equipment was in the car, plus my firearm which I prayed would not be necessary to use. The traffic was queuing and despite giving plenty of time to get there, the time of the first race was getting closer and closer.

We reached the point where we thought we were as close to the start as we could get in the conditions. I would have to gather what equipment I thought was necessary and would have to walk the rest of the way. By now, my wife's eagerly awaited hospitality lunch was long gone. The poor lady, in her wellies was given a cardboard box to carry containing what bandages, cotton wool and drugs I thought I may need. Myself, I carried other odds and ends with a gun hanging out of one pocket.

How professional did we look!

We made our way as quickly from the car to the Secretary's tent, splodging through the mud and not really knowing where we were going. From time to time, I would bump into one of our farmer clients, but sadly didn't have time to stop and talk, especially when it was announced over the tannoy,

"Is there a vet on the course, we cannot start racing until there is!"

Our presence was now needed urgently but we were doing our best. When we did reach the Secretary's tent we were met with somewhat of a frosty reception, as it was re-iterated racing could not start without a vet there. I could only apologise for our unavoidable delay; it was not our fault with the now sodden underfoot conditions. There was no way I could have got the car any closer without further delay. My wife, burdened down with her box of goodies certainly didn't deserve this, if I had felt nervous about the whole thing before, I felt distinctly uncomfortable about it now.

And where was the other vet who was supposed to be in attendance?

We were ushered quickly to the start and the racing was about to begin. We were told to wait there until called upon. Under the wet, slippery conditions I was sure there would be fallers and that my services would be required at some stage and hopefully that would not be to have to shoot a horse in front of all these people, an ever-increasing crowd.

The first two races passed without incident and at last the other vet came and introduced himself to me, it did not seem a problem to anyone that he had arrived two races late and was completely blasé about it. He was an equine practitioner from a neighbouring veterinary practice, unlike me he was a horse specialist. He, now he was here and with no apology or excuse for being late, seemed to want to take over. I was only too pleased to hand over the reins of responsibility and go back into my shell, not that I felt I could relax until the last race was over and all runners and riders were safely back with their owners.

The rest of the racing passed without incident other than one horse that needed a quick look at, but it was one of the other vet's clients anyway, so it didn't trouble me. I did get to talk to one or two of our farmers, pleased to see me there, and appreciating me giving up my afternoon. But all this time I felt more and more sorry for my wife, standing there still with my box of bandages, getting colder and colder, wetter and wetter.

The racing had finished, now was it time for this hospitality that I had been promised. My wife and I made our way back to the Secretary's tent to check in, and to say that it looked like our day was done. We were then expecting that the two of us would be directed towards our due reward, a meal and refreshments.

Nothing, not even a thank you for our time. I was not happy. Unhappily, we got together all our equipment and plodded back through the mud to the car to join the queues now struggling to get away from the course. By now, tractors were in evidence and were required to pull some vehicles back to terra firma.

We arrived home cold and miserable, thinking of a thousand ways we could better have spent the afternoon.

That was that! I went into work on the Monday and later in the day one of the partners caught up with me to ask how I had got on. I told the tale of our wonderful day, the rain, the mud, our reception and the lack of any hospitality or thanks.

I finished by saying if they asked me to do it again, the answer would be a firm and definite NO! He sympathised with my sentiments. That I thought would be the end of it.

A few days later when in the office, he called me to one side and said he had been in touch with the Race committee, stating my disappointment with the way I had been treated and not even being offered so much as a cup of tea for something caused by the weather, my delay, which was out of my control.

The Hunt committee offered their sincere apologies and hoped that we would be free to attend the following year. We would be looked after. But the whole incident had left a bad taste in my mouth, and I promised myself that I would not be officiating as a vet at any such event for a very long time. I used to enjoy going to point-to-points with my parents when I was young, I have not been to one since that wet day in Devon.

The big show in Devon was the Devon County Show which was held not far from where our practice was based. This was a massive agricultural show, attended by many farmers and the general public, with a permanent showground just outside Exeter. The practice did attend as one of the official vets in situ, but it never fell on me to have to be involved. That is a show I would have liked to go with, but with vets at the show, that stretched our manpower at work, so I always stayed behind to do any calls for our clients. After that, the local agricultural shows passed me by until I arrived in Shropshire where there is a county show, but also several more local events such as Burwarton, far more agriculturally orientated, though still very popular with the urban community as well. We in a previous job did act as the official vets at this show. The way everyone who went spoke about the show, I wish at some stage I could have gone, whether as a vet or just to have a look around. Certainly on the day of the show, the first Thursday in August, farm work would drop to nothing other than emergencies. All the farmers had gone to the show, a real social gathering of the year for them. Even my brother who worked for a local agricultural machinery business looked forward to attending this show, he didn't to many of the other local shows! It seemed that most of south Shropshire turned out that day, a real meeting of town and country. I wonder if I will get to go one day, though it would not be the same now that I am no longer part of that community, though no doubt I would bump into many familiar faces.

We as vet practices had got used to hosting evening events for the farmers, usually supported by a drug company who would have a vested interest in selling a new product they were about to bring out. These evening meetings would offer the incentive to the farmers of a free meal and free beer, always a sure way of bringing in an audience. Arranging these evenings did play some part in bringing back a little confidence to myself as I would often have to give a small presentation as well. I did seem to put a curse on the speaker's computer equipment though, which would often seem to pack up after my talk. Being a technophobe, I would just speak but the modern way is PowerPoint, that is unless I had put a jinx on it.

Depression set me back, but when I was coming out of it, I looked forward to doing presentations with a new-found confidence in myself. It was with this that in my last practice outside Shrewsbury I at last got to go to one of these local shows again. We would attend two local shows as I have mentioned earlier, The West Midlands Show at the County Show Ground in town on the banks of the Severn, and Minsterley Show just up the road from our base in late August. We shared veterinary duties at both shows with neighbouring practices, especially at the county show where there would be serious equine competitions, and we were not an equine practice. The Kings Troop one year as the main ring attraction, they would not want a bunch of amateurs treating their horses, we left it to the experts. But we were happy to treat farm stock that needed attention. Having said that, there was always a rush not to be duty vet, so it usually fell upon the shoulders of the vet who was on second call that weekend. I managed to avoid it every year!

The county show always seemed to fall between two hurdles to me, not being an agricultural show, nor catering for the town which was a stone's throw away. I guess that is why I never really enjoyed it that much, although I did go a couple of times and it was always a pleasure to bump into and chat to our farming clientele, plus many old acquaintances from years gone by. There would always be a farmer somewhere who would get you on a stand and get you a free snack or drink, greatly appreciated by my other half. One would cast an eye towards the farm animal competition rings just to see how our clients were doing in the stock classes, and there would always be the country craft tents to look at as well.

But for me the show that I really enjoyed and made a must on my annual calendar was the most local, Minsterley. A show organised by many of our local farmers and on the fields just outside Hanwood, this really was the local show where the countryside came out to enjoy all that it offered. August is obviously harvest time and getting the corn in would always be a priority in our varying weather. Attendance by the farming community depended on the state of the harvest, but if they could get there, then they would be there, even if for a couple of hours.

Once I had been the first time, I didn't want to miss it again. This is the show where we as the practice would give our clients hospitality, a snack and a beer, cup of tea, whatever. Though a G and T was never on offer.

The first time that I attended I had been working for the practice for a few years, having gone from part-time to full time working. With my depression and if I were on call then I was to begin with, reluctant to get out of my comfort bubble. But when I was getting better and more assured of myself, I finally decided to give it a go.

The show ground had a large central ring, probably too large for many of the events that took place in it, but large enough if the big attraction were monster trucks or such like. Around the ring would be the craft tents, the exhibition tents and the hospitality tents. Ours would always be near the entrance to the ring (and handily close to the toilets). In the early years we would hire a small tent that would be big enough to house us, a table for a few brochures, and a table to have some drinks and a few biscuits, crisps etc on. We were still a young business and couldn't afford to spend a great amount of money on hospitality even if this show would be our best form of advertising.

Sadie and Sally, our receptionists and well known in the farming community, would set the stand up and provide refreshment. A couple of the other vets and I would chat to any passing farmer who happened to be passing, taking it in turns from time to time to go for a stroll around the showground and have a look at some of the other stands if they were of interest. Roel and Kerry would have photographs entered in competitions in the exhibition tent and would await anxiously as to when they could go in to see if they had won any prizes (yes, they had).

Slow going to start with, as we stood on the stand and waited for people to appear. The occasional cup of tea or coffee was consumed but at my first outing to the show it was a cold and wet day, and many may have decided to stay at home. In the afternoon things did get busier and it was nice to chat to farmers including some I knew from previous practices I had worked for in the area. Good to catch up with them and now at least they knew where I was if they wished to re-join me and an expanding practice. I had arrived mid-morning and by the time I left late in the afternoon I had thoroughly enjoyed the experience, even if I hadn't had the chance to explore the rest of the show. It had been a wet day but a worthwhile one, and with the mud after I left, some farmers would be employed towing cars off the car park back to the main road.

My next trip to the show was a very different experience, I had climbed a mountain a couple of months previously and this would be a chance to thank those many farmers who had sponsored me. I had climbed the mountain because it was a lifetime ambition but when a friend had suggested to me that if I was doing it, why not try and raise some money for charity. An experience that changed me as a person and made me so much more self-confident having raised nearly two thousand pounds for a local hospice. Both they and I had gained from my efforts.

Unlike the previous year, we were blessed with proper summer weather. The sun shone, and it was definitely shirt sleeve orders for the day. Would farmers come or would they be combining; we would have to see what the day brought.

The previous year, it had been crowded in our tent, especially with people seeking shelter from the rain. This year we had opted for a bigger tent to accommodate our visitors, whatever the weather may bring, plus we had this time brought a bit more in the way of refreshment with us. Again, I arrived mid-morning and again we had a slow start but as the day drew on, we got busier and busier. The farming community had come out to enjoy a day of viewing, catching up with their peers, just having a day away from their labours.

To many I recalled my climb up Kilimanjaro, the days and nights on the mountain, altitude sickness and would I do it again. For me it was a chance to show my appreciation to those who had supported me and who were willing to share my triumph. I chatted all day, now a far more confident person than I had been, and once again did not get the chance to view the rest of the show. If I had set myself a time that I would wind my way home, that passed and as the show was coming to an end, our stand was still busy.

And we were soon to discover that we need not worry about taking any booze back to the office with us, once the Young Farmers Club floats had finished parading in the main ring, they would join us for a drink, and they weren't going to leave until it was all finished!

I was beginning to develop a love affair with this local show which would carry on until I left. We were expanding fast as a practice, more clients over a bigger area but it was surprising how many of them from far and wide would still make their way to this local show.

We decided that our tent was still not big enough so the next year we bought our own, thinking it would get used year after year, and for other events as well if people wanted to borrow it. Friday evening, the day before the show would be tent erecting night, blending ours in amongst all those others professionally erected. Alas that year, though we had much amusement putting it up, the day of the show the rains came again. The good thing was we could entertain without our clients getting wet, the downside was that we would have to take it down again, but worse, we would have to get it dry before we could fold and pack it all away until it would be required again.

We took it down, carted it back to the office where we had a large, boarded loft space used for storage. There we would suspend the tent over a rope hanging across the room and wait for it to dry. It took a long time! A great plan but the practicalities told us that in future we would go back to hiring a tent, but larger. All we needed to do was to arrive on the previous evening to a fully erected tent and deposit whatever we needed for the stand the following day. Easy!

If I wasn't on holiday, over the coming years it was always in my diary to go, to represent the practice on their stand. We had more vets, more support staff but I was always keen to volunteer ahead of the queue. With increasing popularity, our hospitality expanded as well. Along came a hog roast. Would we seriously get through this whole pig through the day? Had we enough bread rolls to make up sufficient baps? My first job on arrival, could I go to the nearest baker and get as many bread rolls as they had? And get some ice. They wanted it to put in buckets of water to cool the lager and cider, when the Young Farmers arrived, they would want a cold drink. One of us would be carving, one making up the baps, another serving drinks. But as much as I could, I would be there to serve our clients, to chat to them and obviously if there was the opportunity to drum up a bit of work, that would be pursued.

We improved the hospitality, tables and chairs outside the tent. We even bought a big model cow and calf to display outside, along with one of those tall banner things that flap in the wind and can be seen some way off. People would know where our stand was! Provided the weather was fine, we now had space, food, drink and a place where especially some of our more elderly clients could sit down and rest.

Come wind, rain or shine, every year was the same, a slow start but by the time the pig had arrived mid-morning the stand would begin to get busier and busier. It was strange how every year you almost saw the same people in the same order, the early birds coming for a coffee and then by midday it would be time to start dishing out the beers, the lagers and the ciders along with opening the wine. The stand would start to flow, and we would be busy servicing the demands of our clients as well as finding time to chat to them as well both on a social basis and about work.

Importantly to me, I would always try and find time for some of our smaller clients, those that were not our biggest source of income but were loyal and always had a good word to say about us when talking to their neighbours and friends. It wouldn't just be the farmer, but his wife and often children as well. These are the farmers of tomorrow, so it was always worth looking after them.

And then with modern marketing, we would start offering free mugs with our logo on, pens, balloons and all that goes with this way of doing this. There would be competitions, one of the girls in the office made a huge papier mache model of a cow's head and there was a prize if you could get the correct name of the cow. The stand was getting celebrity status and it was a pleasure to be on it.

As the afternoon progressed, we would get busier and busier as more people arrived and would stop on their circuit of the trade stands. There would be the constant serving of food and drink with the pig quickly diminishing in size, as he sat proudly on his tray head to the fore, tail pointing to the rear and in between disappearing into people's baps. People would stay longer at this time of day, chatting amongst themselves and to us the vets. A meeting of friends having the chance to catch up with each other away from their busy home lives.

We would review the success or not of the stand every year, could we do anything better? After a couple of years of the pig, we alternated years between that and supplying beef roles, meat supplied by a local farmer who reared Longhorn beef.

But the problem we soon found was that we were starting to feed the whole show. Well not literally, but once it was known there was food on offer, then anyone passing by would stop, try and take a couple of cans of beer, a meat roll and then proceed on their way, whilst also pocketing a few pens, a couple of mugs and anything else they could pick up. You would then see these same people come back again an hour or so later with their friends, ushering them towards the pig and a free meal.

I found this frustrating. We were serving anybody rather than looking after our own clientele, but I suppose the modern human being will take whatever they can! How could we stop this? Do we issue vouchers to our clients? Hand them out when wandering around the show, put them in our newsletter, or just politely ask people we didn't recognise as to whether they were clients or had any interest as us as a veterinary practice. A difficult one, and what could you do about the kids who would take a couple of mugs and then return later and pick up some more? Grin and bear it!

We built ourselves a bar out of wooden pallets, we would now serve drinks from it and would be perfectly in our rights to ask if they were of age to drink, and if they were clients. Very often the drink came before the food and if they had been unsuccessful in the drinks department, then they didn't stay around for the food.

The next addition was the "Team Building Cider", bottled and served up as "Staggers" and "Toe Curler", and our first efforts at it, it was potent stuff. Some of our clients who boldly tried it in year one wouldn't touch it again, remembering what they felt like twelve months previously, despite our assurances that it was not so strong. Others risked it, few risked a second, others took a bottle home to drink when driving would not be an issue. But the cider became part of "our" show, with the addition of a little elderflower cordial it made for more than a very pleasant drink on a warm summer's day.

We still had farmers arriving late, and the Young Farmers finishing their afternoon in the tent. These are our future clients when they took over from dad, and especially for the younger vets, these would be the farmers they would be working with up to their retirement.

All in all, it was a good day out and it is something I will miss in retirement. To meet the clients, and their families on an informal basis away from work was fantastic. A chance to renew old acquaintances, catch up, have a laugh, offer help if needed. It was a pleasure to see farmers bring their young families to the stand and then a few years later see those same children exhibiting a calf or sheep they had reared themselves in young handler classes, with mum and dad in the background offering moral support. If at times one wondered where the next generation of livestock farmers was coming from, so many in the past wanting to stay on the land but more interested in the easier life of arable farming. But these youngsters offer hope that there is a next generation to carry on the job of food production for our nation.

A great show, and at the end of the day for us to take home a little bit of hog roast, a bit of beef and best of all some crackling! My last show would have been 2020, but like so much else it was cancelled because of Covid. I missed that. I thought it would be the chance to say goodbye to many clients properly though I still had a few months to go. The show had become part of my life, something I looked forward to and something I will have many fond memories of.

After years of practice, we got very slick at putting everything up, and taking it all down again and packing it quickly into a white van to return tables, chairs, cows, calves, etc, etc back to the office.

I did go to the show in 2021 briefly. Another wet one and it was after all those years the first time I and my wife did have the chance to look round the whole show, catching up with several of the farmers, especially those showing their stock in livestock classes. Perhaps I will get there one last time before I depart the area, one last chance to be at something which over time has meant a lot to me. In the future, I cannot envisage going to other local shows would have the same meaning for me.

But having said that, long may this type of show go on. It does offer the next generation of farmers to tread their early steps into the industry with the rearing and showing of their own calves and sheep. It gets them to meet other like-minded children. It offers the younger generation to see the fun and the involvement the Young Farmers Clubs have in the community, it is not just an exclusive farmers club, but open to anyone who wants to be involved. In that community they can have fun, they can learn skills that perhaps they would not have in day-to-day life. They can learn from the experiences of their peers, especially for those who do see their future in farming. And that is on top of the enormous amounts of money they raise for charity every year.

Most of all, this type of show allows town to meet country, and for the man in the street to learn a little bit more about where his or her food comes from. Our dietary habits change as more people become vegans, vegetarians or just prefer organic produce. Farmers have to change their methods to accommodate the preferences, but at the end of the day food comes from the land whether it is produced in this country or from abroad. Some farmers will develop their own little niche markets in certain produce, the number of local cheeses now produced would be an example, and these agricultural shows allow them to advertise and sell their "niche" products.

It is important that people do understand where their food comes from, whatever their tastes and I would hope that this type of show will continue long into the future so everyone can have a better understanding about their own food production.

22

OUT OF HOURS, OUT ALL HOURS

I was talking to a senior vet in another practice on one of the trips I had to Girona and were discussing our wind down to retirement. The difference between him and me was that he had been a director in the partnership he was in, whereas I had left partnerships and now worked as an employee in my final job. Nearing retirement, he could negotiate his terms for slipping out of practice. Cutting out night and weekend duties some years before he finished, and slowly reducing his hours was the plan he had arranged for himself.

Myself, I was bound by my employment contract to what hours I worked. Nearing the end of 2018, I approached the Directors to see if I could reduce my rota for 2019 to half of the out of hours I was doing, with a reduction in salary to compensate them for my fewer hours worked. In 2020 I asked if I could cramp all my weekend and night duties into the first nine months of the year and then would work no more out of hours duties.

Back in Girona, Bill was telling me how much he was enjoying his increased leisure time and his wind down to finishing all together. Was I envious? Especially as I was older than him? Yes, I was! And so it was that I worked on until the end of September 2020 in what seemed rather a bizarre rota that a couple of months, I seemed to be working virtually every night, and other months like August I worked one first and one second call.

September was to be one of those busy months and I was to work the last weekend of the month. After that, no more nights and no more weekends. Expecting the worst, because fate seems to work that way, I started the weekend expecting it to be busy. It would be just like the last couple of my week night duties had been.

The Friday evening started quietly, just a call to see a sick calf as the office was closing. That finished off a hectic afternoon. I returned home hoping for a peaceful evening. I got that and went to bed only to be called out to a calving near Oswestry, a forty-mile drive for me from home. Me and the farmer, the cow now recumbent through her exertions and what felt like a rather large calf that didn't want to come out into the world. With a struggle and a bit of manoeuvring of the calf, I managed to squeeze it out with the pleasure of getting a live calf. I returned home happy whilst reflecting on all the calvings I had done over the years. Bed was a welcome sight until the next call at breakfast time, but again nearly forty miles away. The calls continued to come in, I was busy but coping without having to call my back-up out. Late morning produced another calving, but not at the farmer's main farm, I struggled to find it but got there eventually to find that the cow was down the field, and I wouldn't get my car there. I had to guess all the equipment and drugs I may need, loaded them all into the back of the farmers truck and went off to find the cow. It was a long drive across a couple of fields, but we found her prostrate across a muddy gate way with a calf partially out. This calf was enormous, but we eventually managed to get its enormous hips through her birth canal. Right from the start we knew the calf was dead, so the cow was the important consideration.

And we had no water to clean up with. I had finished giving her the appropriate drugs she needed. Filthy, we loaded the truck up again and returned to the farm buildings, where thankfully we found a hose for me to clean off with, though it took me sometime as the rewards of my labours were drying quickly on me!

My day got quieter until early evening when I had to visit another sick calf, and then on the way home I was called to another calving. This time it was relatively straight forward, delivering a nice heifer calf from a young suckler cow. Always nice to see when the calf is soon up on its feet and trying to suckle mum.

The rest of my evening was quiet, being disturbed again Sunday morning to go to another calving a long way from home. Sadly, the calf was dead and decaying inside the cow, whose birth canal was closing back down again. The calf wasn't going to come out and a caesarean wasn't a feasible option with the chances of peritonitis almost one hundred percent. The cow would have to be slaughtered.

I would have two more calls that day. One which didn't really need a vet in attendance, the other a stock bull that had broken his leg and had to be put to sleep, though he defied the powers of my firearm for some time before at last giving up the ghost.

The rest of Sunday evening passed, then the night into Monday morning. My duty would finish at eight and thankfully I had no more calls. As my clock struck eight, that was the last duty I would ever have to do. After all those years it was if a great weight had been lifted from my shoulders, a strange feeling in that I hadn't realised how relieved I was to at last have reached this point.

I had given a final finishing date by now to my bosses, eight months to go and no more nights and weekends. Wonderful, my me time was my own from this day forward.

Of course, when I knew I wanted to be a vet and when I qualified and left university I knew out of hours work was part and parcel of the job, the career I was about to commence. As the Bristol year of '77 departed to search for employment, while perusing the jobs column in The Vet Record, one thing we would all be looking at was what was the out of hours rota. One in three, one in four nights and weekends on call was acceptable. Less than that was far too much for a new graduate in his or her first job and probably with no back up. If no rota was stated, then it was probably bad. There was one interview I went to that I was told basically you were on call every night and the calls would be designated to whoever lived closest. That was a definitely "no thank you very much"!

Times have changed with out of hours work over the years to give the modern vet a better work/life balance. It has had to, to look after the well-being of the modern vet, something I have alluded to earlier. This is especially so in small animal practice where now there are specialised out of hours services covering several practices, working out of one base. You can volunteer to work for one of these services to earn extra money, otherwise, your free time is tour own. Farm practice is different and hasn't adopted that system. They largely look after their own at night and weekends, partly because of the practicalities of covering large areas, and farmers do like the continuity of seeing their own vet. I think also that what you see small animal vets pay for out of hours services, there is no way a farmer would pay that sort of money.

Throughout my career I have done the out of hours work for the clients of the practice I have worked for. The only exception has been when neighbouring single-handed practices have asked the practice to cover for them while they have been indisposed or on holiday.

The other thing that has changed over the years is the number of call outs you get in an evening or at the weekend. In my early days, less than three calls before bedtime was a quiet night. Certainly in my early days in Devon, at the weekend when on first call, I didn't expect to spend any time at home as one went from one call to the next. My first Sunday on call there I remember treating thirteen cows with Milk Fever, holding bottles of Calcium Borogluconate high in the air as it was slowly administered first intravenously then a second bottle under the skin. This was very tiring on the arms which were not used to this sort of treatment, but a great experience in how to find the cow's jugular vein if you had any previous doubts and rewarding in giving the cow a slap she would miraculously get up and search for her new-born calf to attend to. Oh, that they would respond so quickly these days, but modern feeding seems to add its complications.

But over the years, calls have decreased more and more especially in the summer months when very occasionally we may not get a call out at all. Perhaps one or two phone calls, farmers or small holders looking for advice. The reasons for this, probably several.

Certainly, over my time in the profession there has been a marked decrease in the number of dairy farms. Those are the farms you mainly get called out to out of hours other than during the lambing season. Those small family farms, next door to each other when I was in Devon are now few and far between. In my early days the call may have been for one's expertise but there would also be an element especially if it was a calving one was being called out to that it was an extra pair of hands. The vet may have been the one doing the calving and the farmer the helper, but two extra hands just made the job a lot easier, and if one was honest, a lot of those calvings were not particularly difficult anyway.

There has also been a marked reduction in the number of cow numbers especially in the national dairy herd which has diminished through poor profitability, poor return on investment. Labour issues have also been significant as well as succession issues as a farmer nears retirement, the farm or the milking herd can be a farmer's pension fund.

Once I had to go out to a calving in the middle of the night. The farm was nearly thirty miles away, a long drive in the dark and I knew when I got there, there would only be myself and Pete, the cowman. Staff, help would be in short supply. I guess I have always thought through possible scenarios on the way to calls, especially at night, also wondering what time I would be back in my warm bed as I would be working the next day. At night it took the best part of an hour to get to the farm, only to find no signs of life, no lights on in the calving boxes, a scene that did not look very conducive to a quick return to bed.

Pete eventually appeared and informed me the cow was still down the field, we would have to calve her there. We gathered what equipment that I thought we would need, even some water and with arms laden we set off in the dark down the cow track. Our only light being that of a large torch. We eventually reached her standing quietly in the corner of the field, and as always in these cases a load of brambles and a large bunch of stinging nettles close by.

If you are quiet, a lot of cows are quite thankful for the chance of some help. They don't bolt off into the distance or in this case the darkness, meaning we would have to find her again, and possibly walk her back up to the farm where we could restrain her adequately. This cow was quiet and allowed me to walk behind her, gently placing an arm into her birth canal to feel what presentation the calf was in. I could feel two legs, and just behind was the head of the calf. It looked as if it was straightforward if the cow remained quiet, we should have the calf out in no time. Pete quietly passed me the calving ropes and I managed to place first the blue rope over the foot of the left foot, tightening the noose as I did so, then the red rope over the right foot, again tightening the noose when placed over the foot. If the cow stood still, then I could start applying gentle traction. Often at this stage we would use a calving jack to apply pressure, slowly easing the calf out into the world.

This time, as I applied gentle traction just using my own strength, the cow was quite happy to stand and start to strain as I pulled. The calf seemed to be progressing easily through the birth canal, a quick check while I stopped pulling just to make sure the head was following the legs and had not turned back on itself. It was coming even without Pete's help in pulling and it was only a short while before we had a live heifer calf born into the world as with only my meagre strength and a little help from mum, the calving progressed easily.

A quick check to make sure there was no twin still inside, and my job was done. I washed as best as I could by torchlight, we collected our equipment and started the walk back to the farm buildings for a proper wash off. Mum was left happily licking her calf all over. Her maternal instincts to the fore, she was attending to her new offspring, passing us a thankful glance as we set off, leaving her to attend to her maternal duties.

Having washed off, I was back in the car and heading home to my bed. The actual calving can have taken no more than ten minutes from start to finish, a successful outcome but probably very much where just another pair of hands was needed.

Another significant factor in the reduced number of calls we receive would have to be attributed to how much more skilful the modern fulltime herdsman is. He is now a highly accomplished professional in his or her own right with a thorough knowledge of milking techniques and of animal husbandry. Over the years, through initiatives run by the Agricultural Training Board and through classes run by veterinary practices, we have educated farmers and their workers so that they now have a high ability in dealing with a lot of situations. Though unlikely to be an out of hours call, we have taught lameness and how to deal with it, use of medicines, lambing courses and many more. Emergencies such as lambings the skilled shepherd will be able to deal with him or herself, and especially with their smaller hands, women can be very adept at this.

Some emergencies would be classed as needing to be treated by a veterinary surgeon, such as any intervention into a body cavity, abdominal surgery, caesareans and such like, that is governed by law. But even when carrying out surgery in the middle of the night, some of these stockmen are more than adequate assistants with the likes of caesareans. Whereas in olden days we would generally operate as a pair of vets, now the assistance will come from on-farm unless we do feel we need further professional assistance. Not everything is straightforward! They have even learnt not to put their grubby hands into the surgical sight when removing the calf from the cow's uterus while we have scrubbed up meticulously. They may not wash as long as we do, but it is a step in the right direction. They are more than competent, with the required knowhow, of how to revive the offspring once it is delivered meaning we as the operating vets can attend to the cow or sheep, closing the womb incision and then the flank wound. This is a great help and time saver when a cow is heaving to push anything else out through the wound that she can, an inflated rumen, handfuls of guts or the uterus. You don't have to abandon her while attending to a calf that is struggling for life.

Of course, the fact we have to obtain first is that our assistance is not squeamish. More than once the big, tough farmhand who can cope with the sight of anything, when it actually comes to it, he can't, and he has had to be caught before he hits the floor. Not so easy when your hands are inside a cow trying to get on with the operation and then you have to scrub up again. I think over the years I have learnt those who are a great help and those who cannot stand the sight of an operation. It wouldn't be very long before I retired that I was doing a caesarean on a cow which the farmer's son had spent some time trying to calve. I soon realised after trying myself that this calf would have to come out of the side and proceeded with the operation with his and his fiancée's help. She was a great help, but he from the start to the end of the caesarean, was my help, restraining the heifer, keeping her still for me. The whole time he faced in the opposite direction until I was able to assure him that the side was now all neatly stitched up and there was nothing gory to see.

Some of our farmers were well attuned to the process of a Caesar. This is especially so with breeders of high genetic merit pedigree beef cattle, knowing if there were foetal oversize in the presentation and knowing the best outcome was an elective caesarean. These were the people who knew the process inside out and would often have the cow restrained and clipped up before you had even arrived at the farm. Just a quick check, feeling the calf per vagina and you were ready to proceed. The saving of this time causes less stress to the calf waiting to imminently enter this world, but also in the middle of the night, a return to bed for all would be far quicker!

The other attributing factor to night calls would be economics, farming, like many other industries goes through highs and lows in terms of economic returns. Economics governed by the price of the final product being produced, beef prices, milk prices, they can all vary so much so that there are good years and bad years. Have the seasons been kind meaning there is plenty of forage? Has the harvest been poor meaning supplementary feed prices are high? We as vets just become another expense, so the farmer may try a bit more (and not always with great results) to solve the situation himself.

As the years have gone on, as I have said earlier, duties have certainly got quieter. There is the odd day, night in lambing season where I have just gone from one to the next and then onto the next, not stopping all day. But there have also been odd weekends which have been so quiet you are almost willing the phone to ring, just to be able to escape from the house for an hour or two.

But if I have already mentioned my final weekend on call, I drove over five hundred miles that weekend to get to calls. Far more than in olden days. Farms are farther apart, there is more driving and that is one thing that I will not miss.

But even if throughout my career I have never had settled nights or weekends on call, never being able to relax fully if not out or in bed sleeping uneasily conscious that the phone may ring at any time. I think I have never found it a chore (except for the driving). Some of the more challenging and interesting cases will be seen out of hours, the real emergencies and getting a good outcome is always so rewarding. I wondered to myself as my career drew to an end, how many more calvings would I do in my final year, eighteen months, and how many lambings. As it turned out, not so many lambings but I still did nearly fifty calvings in that time. As I got older, they did seem to be the more difficult ones, those that skilled stockmen could not manage.

But throughout all those years, while driving home in the dark, analysing what you did well, what you may do differently next time. I would always take great satisfaction and joy if there had been a successful outcome and cow and calf were left getting to know each other, and the calf would be getting its first feed of that so essential colostrum.

But as well as the outcome of the case, there would also be the joys of nature that you see at night. Driving down the A5 towards Shrewsbury at sunset, initially with the sun in your eyes so that you are almost blinded, but then as it falls behind the Welsh Hills in the distance such a magnificent sky full of yellows, reds and oranges. Similarly in early morning those same colours as the sun rises from behind the Wrekin, stopping at Atcham Bridge over the River Severn as the sun rises for a new day to begin. One of my iconic views of Shropshire.

Driving down narrow back roads and meeting young badgers scurrying along the side of the road about on their business.

One night, one of my final nights on call, passing Attingham Park to see a brilliant full moon over the Wrekin and in its light first to see a fox trotting along the side of the road and shortly afterwards to see a barn owl in full flight swooping down to investigate the latest roadkill, an easy meal. The joys of nature, ever present all around and a real experience to be able to see the likes of these that so many people would miss out of.

For us farm vets, out of hours work will never go away but it is far less than it used to be. Will I miss it? No. But I will miss the satisfaction of good outcomes, and what nature has to offer in night-time hours.

23

CHARITY BEGINS AT HOME, AND ABROAD

A new series of Herriot's "All Creatures Great and Small" starts on TV and we again see the role of the vet in society. Perhaps not as we once were the pillars of society especially in the rural communities, but there has always been someone around asking us to help in charity events or raising money for local and national causes. In days gone by it may have been donating prizes at the local ball as a fund raiser for nearby charity or donating or sponsoring the Young Farmers in one of their events, but there would always be a request somewhere., "Could you support our charity?" As the year progressed the number of those requests would go up and up. There are so many good causes, and it is hard to support them all, plus of course the animal charities that are around. The RSPCA, the Blue Cross, the Dogs Trust, Donkey Sanctuaries, local animal sanctuaries and the Guide Dogs for the Blind to name but a few. How many of them can you keep supporting?

There would also be many calls for us to talk to different local bodies, talking to the local Women's Institute was a common request. Along with invitations to attend schools career conventions, talks to the local Young Farmers Clubs and many more. For these, we always gave our time happily and freely, only too pleased to give our support to the local community. Some vets loved doing this and if a volunteer was asked for, there would always be a small band of ever eager participants. The time they gave up was always much appreciated as were the demonstrations of some of the "tools of the trade" we use or used in the past when they were taken along to show the audience.

Even at Veterinary Congresses there would be a raffle or a whip round for a charity, often the Royal Agricultural Benevolent Institute or the Veterinary Benevolent Fund (charities supporting those involved in agriculture of as a vet whose lives may be going through difficult times) at cattle vet events. For these I was always happy to dip my hand in my pocket and give what donation I could afford, to help those in my associated professions going through less well times than myself.

In my shy early days as a vet, I always felt uncomfortable asking people to donate to a charity, it was definitely something outside my comfort zone. But in my latter years I have found a change of heart and have made huge efforts to support specific local charities plus one abroad. As in your school days when you were asked to raise money, it was always the same people you ended up asking for support to the given charity. Though I would have to admit at school when every pupil was asked to raise ten pounds towards buying a property in very rural Wales to use as an outward-bound centre, mine was raised by putting a quid on Highland Wedding to win the Grand National. Thirteen to one was the price I got so I was able to keep a couple of quid myself and it did not interfere with my earning money for myself, helping dad on the farm.

Other vets I have worked with have joined their local Rotary club to participate in the local community, but me, I preferred keeping myself to myself.

We as a Practice joined a group called XLVets along with many other Practices throughout the United Kingdom. This was primarily a group of practices joined together to share ideas, knowledge, training etc as well as there being some financial advantages in buying goods and services although we all worked independently.

It became part of their ethos to help agriculture related charities and so it was through them that I came out of my shell in term of being a fund raiser. Through the group I had heard of trips to Africa, namely Mozambique, to send pairs of vets over there for a fortnight to teach the local smallholders more about farming and how they could get more out of their limited resources especially related to livestock farming. Through teaching, it was hoped that they could improve themselves financially as well as providing more food for the local community, helping everyone become more food sufficient. I had always had a love of Africa and this, despite my lack of self-confidence, was something that appealed to me. Perhaps I should start supporting some of their fundraising, get more involved?

XLVets organised a fund raiser whereby each member of the group would ride a bike from their closest fellow member practice to the next one, effectively a relay across the country combining all the practices. Our part, to cycle from Llansantffraid where the Cain Veterinary Group were based to Whitchurch where Lambert, Leonard and May were based, a ride of about fifty miles with our base about half distance.

This was 2009 and I was fifty-five and had not ridden a bike since I don't know when, probably since my school days. But I was a frequent visitor to the gym, so this appealed to me to test my fitness. A charity event I was actually going to participate in, especially as we as a practice decided we could only do it in an evening after work so would have to split the ride into its two parts, from Cain Vets to our base, then on another day from us to Whitchurch. I had a challenge, one to ride a bike, and secondly to raise some sponsorship. I was amazed that so many of the farmers I asked were happy to support the old boy. Perhaps they thought I wouldn't make the distance, even though on the dates arranged I could only do part one. I think in total I raised nearly as much money myself as the rest of the practice put together, somewhere around seven hundred and fifty pounds.

With that support, I was going to have to do it. So, one summer evening after work a group of about fifteen of us loaded bikes into a horse trailer and set off to Llansantffraid to start our ride. Welcomed by the practice there, we were sent on our way meandering towards the Severn and following its course some of the way back towards Shrewsbury. One of the other vets had lent me a mountain bike and to my dismay it had multiple gears. The last time I had ridden a bike there were only three. The first part of the ride was relatively flat and so there was no great need to change gear but as we got onto more undulating roads there did seem to be the need to change, I didn't seem to get the grasp of doing this so did the whole twenty-five miles in two gears, the last couple of miles which were a steady but not too steep a climb were hard work!

But it was a very enjoyable evening cycling through some lovely Shropshire scenery and of course finding, okay we knew it was there, a country pub to have a beer to quench our thirst. One of those picturesque pubs on the side of the river, the Royal Oak at Melverley was a welcome rest stop.

Even despite the sore backside the next day it had whetted my appetite for fundraising, though it was another three years before I would undertake such a task to raise money again. For those who know me, my depression was now severe. But having realised that the only person who could cure me was myself, I at last decided to attempt my lifetime ambition of climbing Kilimanjaro, the "Roof of Africa". I won't repeat myself on this story as I wrote my first book, "*Kilimanjaro. My Story*" on this expedition and on the lasting affect it had on me as a person, the new me! But again, I was indebted to all those who supported me both emotionally and in sponsorship as well when I decided to try and support a local hospice in Shrewsbury while doing the climb. Another couple of thousand to the good and to a very worthwhile cause.

I had got the fundraising bug. The practice decided a couple of years later it would enter a crew in a charity day run by the same hospice, Dragon boat racing on the Severn in the middle of Shrewsbury. Severn Hospice run this event annually (Covid allowing) where many crews race against each other in these Dragon boats. I had witnessed this racing a few years earlier at Evesham when on a visit to my mate Dave on his canal boat. We had the previous night moored up on the banks of the Avon in town and gone to bed after watching an open-air theatre production. We woke up to find a lot of commotion as this racing was being set up and we were moored on the finish line. We moved the boat a few yards along the bank and spent a pleasant day watching this event take place. It whetted my appetite to have a go and so when we saw it advertised in Shrewsbury, we decided we would put in a work team. We had to guarantee that we would raise at least two hundred pounds for the hospice.

A team would consist of sixteen rowers and one person beating the drum, seated at the rear of the dragon, setting the rhythm for our pulling our oars/paddles through the water. Could we manage to get a full team from work? We may struggle! We managed to rope in a couple of farmers, my mate Dave and even managed to get a couple of "ringers", a couple of ladies who rowed as their sport in town so with a squad of eight women and eight men we were ready to go. We would have three races against other teams, two boats in each race and the fastest times would then go into a final race where four boats would race together.

Again, my farmers were only too pleased to support "the old boy", especially as it was for a local charity, and I was able to surpass the financial requirement to participate quite easily.

We would meet up by the river, bringing along both food and liquid refreshment and have a good time while raising money for a very worthwhile cause.

But this particular Sunday turned out to be one of the hottest days of the year, and in our wisdom as we were farm vets, we had decided we were going to race as many others were doing in fancy dress. Our chosen attire, cow onesies with our drum beater, Pablo in a fluorescent green tutu, very much the part.

We were called for our first race, eight divine maiden heifers and eight burley bulls seated in our Dragon paddling up to the start, trying to find some sort of rhythm to our rowing. We were pitted against a team from a club I had been involved with before so there was a little rivalry in this race.

The starting gun went off, we were racing and surprisingly we were pulling in front, I think helped greatly by the experience of our proper rowers in the bow of the boat. We were lined up with the fair maidens at the front with the beefier representatives at the back, the stern. We won quite easily, but in these cow outfits were feeling the temperature, time for some refreshment, liquid of course.

Over the course of the afternoon, we would have two more races. But looking at some of the other teams, they looked a bit serious and professional, they were there to win the day with sixteen burley men in their outfits. Much to our surprise we also won our next two races, we were undefeated though the third race was a tight affair with us pulling away for our win literally over the last few yards of the course. Pulling hard, by the time we were reaching the finish line I would have to admit I was knackered and was quite grateful to find that although three out of three, we were not one of the four fastest. We would not have to race again.

A couple of beers and we would head home, thoroughly entertained and again money had been raised for a good cause. Since then, a couple of the farmers have frequently asked, "Are we going to enter again?", they had enjoyed it so much they fancied another go. And my cow onesie, it ended up as a teaching aid in Kenya, another story!

We would have charity events in the Practice, sweep stakes for the football and rugby World Cups, the Olympics, the Grand National and there would be a consensus on who this time we would donate the proceeds to. Mental health was coming more and more to the forefront so for several of these events *Mind* was our chosen charity. A little in-house fun but again raising money for a good cause.

By this time XLVets and the Cattle Veterinary Association were supporting a charity *"Send a Cow"* who were trying to improve livestock farming in East Africa, more specifically Kenya, Uganda and Rwanda. A project whereby local small holders would be taught how to use their limited land better to be more productive. If they were showing themselves to be compliant, they would then receive a calf or a goat which they would rear and then produce milk for themselves. The offspring of the cow would be returned to the charity so it could be given to another farmer to start the process again.

After Kilimanjaro, I had fallen in love with Africa. I wanted to go back and if my return could mean that I could be involved in a project like this, even better. I had decided that five years after my climb of Africa's highest, I would return and fulfil a lifetime ambition to see its wildlife. In 2017 I returned, this time to Kenya to firstly climb Mount Kenya for charity, then to spend a week on safari. XLVets had now started a project whereby two vets would go out in turn to each of these three countries to teach farming practices to the charity facilitators on the ground, so that they could then go and educate their small holders. I was only too keen to use my mountain climb as a way of raising money for *"Send a Cow"*.

Again, this tale is documented in another book, but again I was very grateful to the local support I had in raising another two grand plus for the charity. Farmers were only being too keen to ask me what my next climbing project was to be.

I had got the bug for raising money, and now especially for this in my mind very worthwhile cause. I had put my name forward to go on one of these training trips with my newfound confidence in myself and so knew when I climbed Mount Kenya that the following year I would be returning. I was given the choice of Kenya in May or Rwanda later in the year. It was an easy choice. A return to Kenya, because I wanted some continuity in my visits, and I had found on that visit that I wanted to find out more about the wonderful people of that country.

I therefore was going over to Kenya to work for the charity rather than raising money for them. My gift was my time. So in May 2018 I boarded a flight to Nairobi along with my veterinary companion for the trip, Anna Patch from the Shepton Mallett practice. We would spend ten days teaching a large group of delegates, not only from the three participating countries, but also from Ethiopia, Zambia and Burundi (one of the poorest countries in the world). We were the fourth pair to go out, this being the second visit hosted on Kenyan soil. We were based just outside Busia in the southwest corner of the country. Teaching so many at first seemed very daunting but once we broke the ice, it was an exhilarating experience. Again, I have written about this visit elsewhere (*"Kenya: My Privilege" in 2022* still to be published) so I won't dwell on it too much. But this was one of the best experiences of my life, and to think at the end of it that it would hopefully benefit so many poor people and hopefully develop for them better nutrition and create a little wealth. Anna and I had three days on safari in the Aberdares at the end of our teaching and saw some great strides in rhino conservation first-hand.

It was a real privilege to go out there and offer something. I am pleased to say that I am still in contact with some of my newfound Kenyan friends, still offering advice from time to time as well as keeping an interest in what they are achieving. Areas in the world that have not created global warming but are desperately suffering from the effects of climate change.

My fund raising would continue but now with a firm commitment to *Send a Cow*. Retirement was fast approaching, and if I wanted to go out with a bang, then it would be one last fundraising event. I signed up for one of these Action challenges and for me and a developing love of Dorset, then my challenge had to be the Jurassic challenge. This was a marathon length hike along the Southwest Coast Path from outside Wareham to Weymouth. This was due to take place in May 2020 and I was starting to train for it when along came Covid. It was postponed hopefully until September or there was the option to transfer to the 2021 event. This I decided to do, but with lockdowns, restricted working etc it was difficult to see people to get to sponsor me. I always felt the personal touch of speaking to people face to face to explain what you were doing and what the charity would do with any funds raised. People knew of my previous efforts for *Send a Cow* and of my work for them, so I did receive some good donations but nowhere near the target I had set myself.

I was committed to doing it, the weekend before I retired, May 22nd,2021 and so set off down to Dorset. Accompanied by my wife, Jane, my driver to drop me off at the start and retrieve me from wherever I ended up finishing. Yes, I was a little disappointed that I wouldn't be raising as much money as I hoped but it would be something.

As the day of the event drew near (for those really fit people who wished to, they could undertake the 100km challenge over two days) I kept an eye on the weather forecast. We would be walking for seven to ten hours along a very exposed part of the coast, and I would want to have the right clothing etc with me. The forecast got worse and worse the closer the time got to the start date. Gales from the Southwest, the direction we would be walking into, rain, rain and more rain. The organisers cancelled the tented village for those hikers who would camp (we went Airbnb) because of Health and Safety and offering hikers to compete in another event later in the year if they were put off by the weather. We had just got Covid clearance for this sort of event to take place so I was doing it come rain, wind or shine.

But as we drove down on the Friday, it was awful, wet and very windy and as we approached Wareham, the weather was far from welcoming. Trees were swaying, leaning in the wind which was blowing at 60mph. The weather was horrendous, the only blessing being that the forecast was slightly better on the Saturday, hiking day! We found our accommodation and then went into Wareham for our first meal out since the lifting of lockdown. A couple of photos on Facebook of the conditions and the donations came flooding in. Thank you everybody! I was only a stone's throw from the two grand I was hoping to raise.

And the wind seemed to be relenting!

Jane dropped me of near Corfe Castle the following morning at eight. This would be early enough to go through the Covid protocols, register and be ready to start my hike at nine along with many others. The wind had dropped, there was just a dampness in the air with light drizzle. It was time to start we were off, those of us doing a marathon hike. Though at some stage we would be joined and passed by those doing the whole challenge starting earlier from this point, doing a circle towards Swanage and back before continuing on our course, some of them running so far quicker than us walkers. A gentle stroll around Corfe Castle before we started to climb, and I was surprised how dry the path was. I soon found that a charming lady called Charlotte and I walked at about the same pace, so we continued on as hiking buddies. We talked about our respective jobs, Covid experiences and much more. This turned out to be a great distraction from thinking about the miles ahead. We talked and walked, eventually joining the coastal path with magnificent views over some of the Jurassic coast with its cliffs, small beaches and rocky promontories. We were after a couple of hours approaching Lulworth and its famous cove, and here I was grateful for Charlotte's company, without her I would have taken a wrong path.

We had found though that I did uphill's a lot faster so at the Lulworth checkpoint I left her and went on alone. The old man felt if he stopped, he may not start again and as soon as we had passed Durdle Door we would have the three steepest climbs of our trek. But her company had certainly made the time pass quicker and she had been very interested in both my work and the charity I was raising money for.

The walk up to and past Durdle Door was very familiar. I had done it numerous times to stand over one of England's iconic view. But now I would have three serious climbs. I was just about to start the second when my phone rang, it was Peter Davies, one of my farmers and he was interested to know how I was getting on. He had supported me in previous events I had done, and I hope it was a sign of the relationship I had built up with my clientele that he was interested in my progress. We chatted briefly, me giving a rough time at which I expected to finish but the second climb was now facing me. I could walk or talk, not both. He would check in with me later.

Two very tough climbs followed before the path levelled out as Portland Bill and Weymouth got closer and closer. Here the path did get muddier as we came off the cliffs and walked more through woodland and pasture. The path led through a pub beer garden. It would have been lovely to partake in some liquid refreshment, but I had to press on with just a touch of cramp beginning. As I entered the outskirts of Weymouth towards Lodwell Park, the finish, a quick stop to put on my charity t-shirt and then onto the end.

A welcome sight. The end of a long walk, and for an old bloke the thirteenth fastest time as I would find out later. A glass of Prosecco, a medal and a meal before my wife picked me up to take us back to our accommodation. I did get to speak to Charlotte again after she finished some forty-five minutes after me.

A great experience for which again I had raised a lot of money for *Send a Cow*, and that was to be my last charity event, and maybe the hardest.

I guess over the years, doing different things I have helped raise well over ten thousand pounds for various causes. This along with what work I have done for the RSPCA, PDSA and in giving my time to help a couple of ladies who rescued hedgehogs.

It is important we as a profession are seen to be participating in the community, but time continues to be an increasing pressure! But we must make the effort.

For me it has been very important. I hope I have done my bit, and it has certainly developed me as a person and helped me get through depression. I finished the walk at Weymouth and said never again.

I think I said that at the bottom of Kilimanjaro. I have just signed up to do a fifty-kilometre hike on Exmoor in August 2022, and again I will try and raise money for *Send a Cow!*

24

THE GOOD, THE BAD AND THE....

On passing your final exams, before one is allowed to practice one has to give a Hippocratic Oath to the Royal College of Veterinary Surgeons. Stating your intention that throughout your career as a vet you will abide by their rules and the health and welfare of animals is always a precedent to you. What it was all those years ago, I cannot remember. But on the payment of a suitable sum of money you acquire the letters MRCVS after your name, and you are then allowed to practice as a vet. This is of course as long as you pay your annual retention fee. I have obviously dutifully done this.

The other important organisation to join on qualification was the British Veterinary Association (BVA), if for no other reason than because its weekly journal, *The Veterinary Record*, had all the new available job listings in it. But the journal was also full of clinical and scientific papers on up-to-date research, a lot of which was far too technical for a new graduate like me.

But the thing with the BVA was that it did represent its membership whereas the Royal College purports to look after the general public, regulating the veterinary profession like the British Medical Association does for doctors. It acts as the eyes of the profession and has the power to discipline members of the profession if they have done wrong, been negligent or their work has not been up to the required standards they deem fit for one to continue to practice. Of late they have also set requirements as to the amount of professional development each vet is required to do annually. They set practice standards so that now you can have approved Royal College premises. They are essentially in their eyes our watchdog.

I qualified and I paid my subs for both, and for some years continued to do so for both organisations. Thankfully after qualifying, the BVA then also produced another journal, *In Practice*, on a bi-monthly basis which contained far more practical articles than *The Vet Record* and was a far more valuable source of further education with a far more practical approach to what we may meet in the field. I still have many of what I considered to be good and relevant articles, kept for posterity (but for how much longer we shall see as more and more gets shoved into the loft!). What the BVA also offered was an umbrella that consisted of different types of vet practice as associations were set up for cattle vets (BCVA), for equine vets (EVA), for small animal vets (BSAVA), for pig vets (PVS) and more latterly for sheep vets (SVA), incorporating caprines as well. These individual associations, under the BVA umbrella, now have important roles in how their parts of the profession develop. They offer valuable support to their members both in terms of educational and continuing developmental needs, and in adopting policies which will shape the future. I joined the BCVA firstly after I had been qualified some years. My tutor when seeing practice in Aylesbury, Ian Baker, was one of the founder members and an early president of the society. When I did join it was great to be able to see him, catch up with him again as he was always keen to see how my career was progressing. There would be regular meetings and an annual congress which varied its destination each year, there would be more than one occasion where the spring meeting was held at Harper Adams College/University just down the road from home but where I would pack a suitcase and disappear for a couple of nights. Cattle vets do drink, and it is surprising how much good information one picks up just chatting to other farm vets in the bar, even at two o'clock in the morning.

At some stage I left the BVA, but continued my membership of the BCVA, and I suspect that I will continue that membership for years to come, just to keep in touch with the part of the profession that I have been involved with for so much of my career. I did in my brief small animal career attend their annual conference in Birmingham, again picking up valuable new ideas as well as at last seeing the sights of my nearest city. This included the canal network near its centre and yes, some great bars where we would be entertained by pharmaceutical companies. More latterly I have also joined the Pig Veterinary Society, partly out of interest and partly because it is a requirement for me to be a member to be able to carry out Red Tractor farm assurance visits to piggeries that are signed up to the scheme. But again, the association produce valuable information about the ever-increasing science involved in the pig industry plus important information about disease status in the country and indeed the world, African Swine Fever tries to edge itself ever closer in Europe.

But these Associations also have an important role in national disease control. Initiatives from the BCVA on the control of Johne's Disease, on TB in cattle, on Bovine Viral Diarrhoea have given us as farm, cattle vets more expertise in going out and trying to control these diseases which it would be nice to say that one day we could eradicate, are examples of where they are trying to move the industry forward. They are helping us to meet the requirements that the food purchasers are now demanding from their farm sources, ever increasing standards.

They have become a stakeholder at national level in such things as TB control and policy. In my time their biggest role was in the help and direction they gave to both government and to us at the "coalface", working with the 2001 Foot and Mouth epidemic. Their daily bulletins were a great comfort to us working in the field, giving advice, progress and direction. To me in my time, all those involved in the hierarchy of the association helped get us through the outbreak, applying common sense, not always evident in those with higher authority.

That help, advice, support has been important as they have been involved in other novel disease outbreaks such as Blue Tongue, BSE and Schmallenberg (hey, I spelt that right at the first attempt!), again acting as a stakeholder where national decisions have had to be made.

The BCVA has been an invaluable and important asset in my career and has always been a friendly and helpful organization to be part of. The good....

The Royal College, that would be another story! I can see the need for regulation, but as was said in The Life of Brian, "What have the Romans ever done for us?", then I would question the same of the college, other than put our fees up every year. I was bemused a couple of years ago how they could justify an increase of over twenty percent because of Brexit, but of course I was obliged to pay.

When I first qualified it seemed an organisation run by old duffers, the elderly part of the profession who just got themselves re-elected year after year and were very much old-school. I have been a good boy and religiously voted every year on who I would like to be regulating me, always choosing people who had some empathy with general practice, i.e., they had to be in it and preferably young. Of late I have looked at the manifestos as to what they were saying about well-being and offering some support to the new young graduate who now faces so many stresses when entering practice. They need the colleges support, not a big stick waved at them. If there were not in my eyes enough suitable candidates, then I would not use all my votes. I wonder how many do likewise or does the establishment have enough core votes that the same people get re-elected again and again. Not many of my colleagues bother to vote, I think that says a lot about people's feelings for the college.

A colleague of mine, Andy Bartholomew has recently published a book on his memoirs in practice, "It DID Happen to this Vet", and owning his own practice in Oxford he wonders whether the added regulation we are now burdened with offers any great advantage or value to the general public. Other colleagues I have spoken to would be of the same opinion. We have had regular updates on policy, on what we should be doing through this Covid pandemic, I would have to say I would read an oracle from the BCVA, but the Royal College briefs I would give just a cursory glance!

The bad? I will be grateful when I no longer have to part with my hard-earned cash to give to them!

Again, "What have the Roman's ever done for me?"

25

.... AND THE UGLY

I wonder just how many calvings and lambings I have done in all my years in farm practice? I lost count a long time ago. It would certainly run into the hundreds if not thousands, especially as the number of caesareans I have performed in both species would be in the hundreds. As I have said in the past, there is nothing more satisfying, especially when you have got up in the middle of the night to see a calf or lamb taking its first breath, a shake of its head then in a few minutes it is trying to get to its feet. Clumsy looking to start with as it tries out those four appendages it has never had use of before (other than a vet pulling on them to ease the neonate through the birth canal), raising its body above four shaking limbs, probably then toppling over only to then try again. Success, it stands there, legs pointing outwards to support its weight while it gets used to this new world it finds itself in. Mum by this stage is licking furiously, cleaning the coat of the newborn, sometimes knocking it back off its legs only for it to rise again. Once it has sorted out its bearings it is off to find mums teats to suckle that all important colostrum so rich in nutrients and antibodies. This is even more rewarding if it has been a caesarean that you have performed to get too this end, a great result with mum and offspring united and bonding together. Again, amusing to watch in sheep when it has often been twins that have been delivered, like myself a twin, then the race to see who will be up first and suckling or seeking mum's attention. The bringing in of new life to this world has always been one of the most rewarding parts of the job.

Being brought upon a dairy farm I started early I learning to calve cows. Unlike some of my contemporaries at university I was well used to rolling up my sleeves, feeling inside the birth canal of dad's cows and delivering a calf. Some of them were straightforward and may have calved by themselves, others, having had a feel inside I may have left to dad to calve. But at least I had felt inside a cow and had felt was right and what may be wrong, all I needed was a little more experience and to develop my scrawny arms.

One of my first experiences was with mum, calving a cow in one of our loose boxes. With a little patience and gentle traction, I delivered a healthy heifer calf who was soon trying to stand up. We named all our cows and calves, as well as them having the necessary ear tag numbers as required by legislation.

"Thump'er," mum suddenly said.

I was attending to the calf, making sure her airways were clear, she was breathing well and quite lively. I wasn't sure why I had been given this command, but mother knows best so I did, I thumped the calf!

"What did you do that for?" asked mum.

"You said thump her," I replied quickly.

"No," replied mum, "I meant we shall call the calf Thumper."

The cow's name was Bunty, Thumper was an appropriate family name. Thumper in time became one of my favourite cows, a real character who always sought me out when in the yard, thinking I may just have a tasty extra morsel for her. She was often right and would stand there while I scratched her head.

Lambings I would have to admit I was naive about until I went to university, but what was the problem, they were only small cows! I went down to Salisbury Plain in my second year to help the son of the famous landscape painter, Lionel Edwards, with his lambing. This was being dropped in at the deep end.

"There are the sheep, let me know if you have any difficulties," he said.

I soon learnt how to catch and then lamb a ewe single handily in the middle of a large field. It was great experience and stood me in good stead for the rest of my career.

The rewards are new life. But nature is cruel and sometimes even after all your best efforts, blood, sweat and toil, the end result is a dead calf or lamb. The mothering instincts are still there as mum frantically licks the newborn waiting for that first breath and then it getting to its feet. Even in death, that instinct to mother is preserved. It is even more heart-breaking when you get the calf or lamb out alive but after a few desperate breaths, there is one final gasp and that is it. You can see the heart still beating but there is no chance of revival. Premature births and abortions more often than not one end up with dead foetuses because they have died inside the uterus, or they are not physiologically capable of surviving at this stage of their development.

One also finds that over large calves and lambs don't seem to have the get up and go to live for long after birth. Is it too much of a shock to the system, to their heart, that having lived on their lifeline, the umbilical cord, for so long that when they need to survive themselves, they are not capable of doing so? Jumbo was a massive calf I delivered naturally not long before I finished. He had to be the biggest calf I had ever managed to get out of a cow, especially through the backend. When I first put my hands inside the cow and felt his feet, they were enormous but with gentle traction on my own, I got him out and with a little persuasion, got him breathing. He would have weighed nearly a hundred kilos, far too big for his own good.

How we struggled with him over the next few days, got him drinking and on his feet, but he just had no fight in him and after three weeks of struggle he died. So much hard work for nothing, so disappointing but my experience of these massive calves told me right from the start we were probably on to a loser.

There are certainly highs and lows!

But nature throws up many surprises. How many times would I have been asked to examine a cow who either should have calved some time ago, or the farmer would report that the cow was acting strangely, walking around with her tail raised slightly. A rectal examination would reveal a mass in her vagina. A vaginal examination would reveal a small bag of bones, a mummified calf which had probably died in the third or fourth month of gestation, the cow had expelled it this far and then it had just sat where it was now causing slight discomfort. The cow would often stand with her tail slightly raised. With a little lubrication it would be possible to remove the foetus, and in time the cow would breed again.

On more than one occasion I have been called out to cows calving where there has been a complete change in their behaviour. Buttercup was for three hundred and sixty days of the year a very placid cow. But now with the hormonal changes going on in her body as she approached parturition, she was willing to take on the world, show her a matador and she would take him on. What was a quiet cow was now a raging bull, pawing the earth in front of farmer and myself who now had to try and calve her! The dangerous part of our profession! On one occasion we managed to trick the cow into the cattle crush after an hour of trying to get near her, in that hour all we saw was her front end coming towards us. We eventually managed to deliver twins, make them comfortable, release the head yoke in the crush and then exit the pen rapidly before she had got herself fully out. No one got near for a couple of days, but eventually she did settle down again to be a proud mother showing off her new calves.

On another occasion, late one Saturday night, a similar occurrence happened. A suckler cow wanting to calve but was not letting anyone get near her. When I arrived, she was in a large barn with far too much space to be able to do anything with her. Sedation was out of the question, we needed to get near her to do that so again a long time was spent trying to trap her in a smaller space so that I could examine her. We only succeeded in the end when in her anger she went for one of the farm hands who was outside the pen but near a big metal stanchion. She charged him and, in the process, got her head stuck between the stanchion and the wall. We leapt into the pen quickly and I managed to calve her successfully. The calf was alive, we cleaned it off and left it in some clean straw to await mum. We retreated, she had got herself there, she would have to get herself out, and she did.

It would not be uncommon to get a call in the morning that a sheep or cow had produced an offspring the previous night and they thought that she had finished giving birth. We were always taught from an early stage, and I especially learnt it on Salisbury Plain, always check there is not another. You would not want to be catching the ewe twice, but farmers often think when one was out, that is it. We would be called to then try and remove a second, in the case of sheep often a third and by then the offspring would have died through delayed parturition. Here was where the outcome would be known to be disappointing before you started, and often difficult as the womb and birth canal were starting to close down. But sometimes a miracle would occur, and a live offspring would be produced.

Again, the vagaries of nature. In my early days in Devon I was called out to calve a cow, the call telling me it would be twins as there was a tangle of legs and heads the farmer could not sort out. On examination I managed to find which head and which legs belonged to which calf and then by repelling one and pulling gently on the other I was able to calve a first twin and then the second. A successful outcome as both calves were alive and mum was keen to administer her maternal instincts.

Always check for another I remembered. On inserting my arm back into her birth canal I indeed could feel something else, something furry. After a little manoeuvring, I managed to extract what I had been feeling, a furry ball with an eye in it. My first sight of triplets in cows and if this was just a little grotesque it was also just a little bit interesting, the intricacies of foetal development. It did always remind me though and reinforce that advice of "always check for another".

Triplets in cattle have been few and far between in my career but I did deliver a set of three back in 2006, three fine heifer calves, one black, the other two grey resorting to some Charolais blood somewhere in their lineage. All three in 2021 are still going strong. Over the years pairs of twins have been produced by them and going forward two of them have now been retired, they can spend the rest of their lives happily grazing and chewing over old times with each other.

We had been told in our university lectures of some of the abnormalities you can get especially in cattle, deformities, some grotesque to look at. This is where nature can be cruel. Some of these deformities are developmental, some will be genetic, others caused by infection by certain viruses infecting the cow and foetus at the wrong time of pregnancy, often mid-gestation. My first experience of a schistosome, a calf that had developed so that it was inside out, bent back on its spinal column, was a gruesome sight.

These calvings will be presented as either four feet coming out together, where you having to decide whether there are two calves, or is it this deformity? Or you will be presented with a load of intestines coming out through the birth canal and feeling in deeper you may feel the spine of the calf. Invariably they turn out to be caesareans, although through embryotomy, I have managed to cut the calf up inside the cow and remove it per vagina. They are usually born dead, but my first experience was with George again, performing a Caesar but this time when we got the calf out it was still very much alive. Our first consideration at his stage was to get the cow sown up, the wounds closed so she could go on to be a healthy cow again. But the memory of this moaning mass of legs and guts with a beating heart was something I will never forget, at the first opportunity we put it out of its misery.

There have been other deformities encountered over my years, and usually again they do involve caesareans. The domed foreheads one sees with calves and lambs with Hydrocephalus, deformities of spines and ankylosis of limbs mean that unless it is possible to perform an embryotomy, then the damage that could be caused by applying traction to deformed limbs would cause too much damage to mum.

In 1986 I was working in Gloucestershire on the southern side of the bank of the Severn. It was the year of the Chernobyl disaster and we wondered whether we would see any effects of it in this country. Was it coincidence or not? But certainly in the spring of 1987 I saw more deformities in lambs, and a few in calves than I had ever seen before in my career. Spinal deformities underdeveloped rear ends, with ankylosis of the hind leg joints, things I had never seen before and did not see again for a number of years. Whether these were the effects of radiation carried from winds blowing over from Eastern Europe I will never know, but that was the experience that I had.

Schmallenberg is a village some eighty kilometres east of Cologne. Why is that of any interest to me? In 2013 we saw the emergence of a new viral disease which was first seen in this village; hence it being named after it though shortened to SBV, no-one could spell Schmallenberg! This was caused by an Orthobunyavirus which I only mention because it is a nice name, but more importantly it was transmitted by biting midges of a certain species. Blue Tongue virus had been transmitted a few years previously also by biting midges, carried over from the continent on prevailing winds.

Some acute disease was seen in cattle, milk drop, fever and sometimes diarrhoea but what we did see at a later stage were still births and foetal deformities. It was found that if cattle were infected between sixty two and one hundred and eighty days of gestation, sheep between twenty-five and fifty days, then these effects on the foetus could occur. The virus attacked the developing nerve tissues causing deformities of the brain and spinal cord, and then to muscular and skeletal development. We as vets were seeing the same sort of deformity as I saw in 1987 after Chernobyl, something effecting foetal development at a crucial stage in foetal growth. This made for some difficult lambings and calvings, again with disappointing outcomes.

A vaccine was quickly developed. Some used it, others didn't. In time the disease died down only to re-emerge again in 2016 when it was not so serious, perhaps there was still some natural immunity in our grazing stock. As I write, do I hear of the possibility of another re-emergence with herds of cattle testing antibody positive again. All I can say is that I won't be around this time to be calving or lambing them.

We have been aware of other viruses causing deformities, Bovine Viral Diarrhoea effecting a foetus differently if infecting at different stages of gestation. It can cause cataracts, hydrocephalus and stillbirth. Border disease in sheep, a similar virus to BVD again causing similar effects or with lambs being born as "hairy shakers". Not a retro rock band of the eighties but a syndrome where the lamb tremors and has an abnormal coat.

Vaccination programs will prevent some of these diseases and therefore foetal abnormalities, but not all so sadly the "ugly" will still be presented to us for calvings and lambings.

And here, I have not even mentioned yet those foetal presentations where you put your hand in and feel two heads and it soon dawns on you that they both belong to the same calf. Quite a challenge!

Nor the one time, after much head scratching over a ewe I thought was having twins as I had three hind legs presented but eventually figured out that they all belonged to the same lamb. I delivered it alive, a good-sized lamb but with two perfectly normal and developed right hindlegs, though one was only loosely attached. A lamb which would provide an extra joint for the table, but the farmer didn't want to persevere with it.

Not all lambings, nor calvings are straightforward, the end results of some are not pretty. Nothing changes over the years and no doubt my colleagues in the future will continue to see these freaks of nature.

I can only say again that what a joy it is when everything turns out right and I leave the farm with a contented farmer, contented cow or sheep and the pleasure it has brought me of bringing new life into the world successfully. I will miss that.

26

PIGS and SAUSAGES!

Throughout my career, then our porcine friends have been the main farm species I have had least to deal with. This has not so much been by choice but more in the areas I have worked there have been few pig farms. Certainly, in my early days as a vet when I was attending small family farms, and in some of the "backyards" of small holdings when I worked in the Forest of Dean, then it was not uncommon for these holdings to have a couple of sows and to rear a couple of litters of piglets from these each year.

An example of this would take me back to my childhood when mum and dad were starting their own farm with just a few milking cows, gradually expanding when they could. In the farmyard there were four pig sties, offering for the modern pig sheer comfort with a large indoor lying area and an even bigger outdoor area where the sow could exercise, eat and drink. Piglets were reared up to weaning, in those days when they were about eight weeks old then they would be off to market, bar one or two which would stay for future home consumption. They would be fed waste food and milk, a very traditional method of producing pork using these livestock "garbage" eaters. They did very well on the waste from vegetables, old fruit and bread etc plus a bit of supplementary feed. Sows would often be seen with their front legs on the wall at the front of the pen, looking at what was happening in the yard, or more likely wondering when their next meal would appear. They had their own characters, but one of them signed their departure tickets when she managed to open the gate to her pen and then make her way to the house where me and my two brothers were sitting down to lunch.

"Food", she thought, and finding the front door open made her way into the dining room, much to our horror. A chase ensued; three young boys being chased around the table by a rather hungry pig, who would have been quite happy even with a ham sandwich. Mum and dad's arrival saved us, but the dear sow did take some persuading that this was not a restaurant for pigs.

Us boys stayed; the pigs departed, and the pig sties became very good pens for rearing calves. When they got too big, the opportunity arose for us boys to earn some money mucking them out for the princely sum of seven and sixpence each. On reflection, this was slave labour!

The young piglets would be castrated when big enough. Mum swinging the piglet between her legs, head pointing backwards. Then while securing the piglet firmly held upside down with hindlegs parted, dad would with a couple of deft cuts and a pull, quickly perform the required operation.

Relatively painless unless mum felt the teeth of said piglet biting her leg, registering his protest.

Starting in practice then this situation would be repeated on small holdings, a couple of sows rearing a couple of litters each year. These pigs may have been kept inside or outdoors, especially in orchards where in autumn they could gorge themselves on windfalls, and root and wallow to their hearts content.

In those days they, if they were ill, they had good old fashioned pig diseases which we had been lectured on at university or you could find described in any pig husbandry book. These were relatively easy to diagnose and easy to treat with often a couple of jabs of penicillin being enough to cure their ailments. Erysipelas, a bacterial infection causing diamond shaped skin lesions was common, but easy to treat with the pig returning to normal in a couple of days. Meningitis was an alarming disease to see with piglets laying on their sides, legs flailing and with a characteristic twitch in the eyes. But again, though an acute disease, with prompt treatment, again a couple of jabs with penicillin and they would soon be back to normal.

The sows would have their litters, piglets reared or sold and occasionally we would get to sample them. I was always taught that if you had time, never turn down hospitality, it shows that you have time to listen and to get to know your client and also is a sign that they are showing their appreciation of a job well done.

Early in my career in Devon I had been called by Conrad Snook to calve one of his cows. A short dumpy man in his late middle age, balding but with a very defined grey moustache. He also was a colleague of one of my best friends who by coincidence had used to work for him and was there to assist with the calving. I successfully calved the cow along with Anthony's assistance and in gratitude, Conrad asked us in for breakfast.

It would have been rude to say no! Out came the frying pan and soon we had a full English in front of us, much of it home produced. This included the thickest rasher of bacon I have ever seen with a layer of fat on it which would have sent your cholesterol levels through the roof. Of course, it would have been rude to have left any of it, I didn't, including the rind. Home produced bacon, gorgeous. The perfect start to another day's vetting out on the farms!

If there was one problem with this extensive stock keeping of pigs, then it would be one of restraint. Sows are solid animals and if they have a mind to, they are very hard to stop in their tracks when they have the freedom of the wide outdoors, whether it be in an orchard or as were so many pig herds, kept in a field with their mates, a big acreage and through their wallows and rooting, often very muddy or wet. Even in large sties the pig would be king or queen of their own domain.

A quiet sow, more a farm pet, would be quite happy with the farmer's wife scratching her head while you examined her, maybe not so happy when it came to injecting her (the pig that is, not the farmer's wife!). But most pigs would either be restrained by looping a noose behind their top canines and applying pressure, she would normally pull against the wire and then stand peacefully (other than the noise she would make, deafening), or with a board you could keep her penned against a wall or fence, her thinking it to be more solid than it was. This was fine until it came to examining a sow in an ark in a field, a corrugated iron shack, arched so it was tall in the middle but then curved down to ground level at the sides. But when I say tall, even someone of my height would be leaning over to get in. If the pig you were examining were lying near the sides, then me, the poor vet, would be on all fours. Plus, the fact that a few of her mates may also be in there sleeping, it made an examination a rather hazardous occupation. We usually managed, just, and then would have to wade back through the mud to get whatever treatment was required hoping that in the meantime the pig had stayed where she was and was still accessible past her mates.

Back in Devon all those years ago, I accompanied my colleague George to see a boar that had a lot of abdominal discomfort. We had gone with the intention that we would do an exploratory laparotomy, abdominal surgery, though quite what form of anaesthesia we were going to use I wasn't sure. I guess as usual we would have made it up as we went along as we did in those early days of my career! However, on our examination, we found that his condition was too severe to warrant any intervention and that the kindness outcome was euthanasia there and then. He was in his boar pen, a breeze block and concrete building. George would shoot him, manfully disappearing into the pig house.

Was I worried? Yes, I was. Pigs, and boars especially have skulls like rock, and it would take an accurate shot to put him out of his misery. I had seen in the past large sows shot with a captive bolt and it have no effect on them, other than having a gun stuck in their forehead and being rather annoyed about the whole process. For now, supposing the boar turned aggressive, supposing there was a ricochet in this enclosed space, this situation was fraught with complications. Yes, I was very worried about George and sighed a huge relief when after a loud bang, a few seconds later he emerged safely stating the boar was now dead.

Over the years we have had pig sedatives introduced to our shelf of different drugs. But I personally have never had any great faith in them as their dose rate was so wide per kilogram of pig. Having said that, I did find a good combination of drugs not long before I retired when I had to do some dental work on Clem, more a pet pig whose canines (tusks) where growing too long and starting to cause problems. The combination worked very well as he quickly went to sleep, and some twenty minutes after I had finished attending to his teeth, he was starting to come round again, regaining full consciousness. All we had to do while he woke was to drink a cup of coffee and to keep him warm. The downside is that Clem was a small pig, probably a hundred kilos at most. Sedating him was expensive with using a Ketamine combination, for the average sow or boar in production being far heavier, the cost would be prohibitive!

The greatest time for some sort of restraint is at farrowing and when she is suckling her pigs. Though maternal, the sow is a clumsy oaf and can frequently lie on her newborn piglets. Years ago, before farrowing, sows would be tethered in stalls in big pig units, rows of sows restrained in lines with little ability to be able to move. Thankfully in this country, this practice has been banned with freedom to move classed as one of the essential requirements of any animal.

Farrowing crates do still exist though. These offering the sow the space to stand, lie, defecate and to eat while providing an area either side of her where the piglets can suckle her, exercise and develop their behaviour. A heated area will be provided for them as temperature is a challenge for these hairless neonates. Also, on the plus side now, the piglets would be weaned at about three weeks of age against the eight weeks in the past, so sows would not be restricted in these crates for too long. For us vets, they do offer good restraint of the sow especially if we are required to assist in the farrowing process. Sows have long tortuous uterine horns, and some will have over twenty piglets in one farrowing. Farrowing can be a long process if there are difficulties, requiring patience, along arm and a bottle of Oxytocin by your side to get enough uterine contraction to bring the next piglet into reach of your arm extended deep inside the pig. A large piglet or one coming sideways, so blocking the passageway, is the usual cause of labour difficulties but thankfully it is not that common an occurrence and I have never had to perform a caesarean on a sow.

There are still the big outdoor pig herds, I have worked with a few in the past. But throughout my career there have not been the pig numbers in the Southwest, and in Shropshire for me ever to have to become a pig specialist. Not like the huge numbers in East Anglia, Yorkshire and some of the Home Counties. They have always been of interest to me but never a great part of my working life. But as the years have rolled on, pig husbandry and their veterinary needs have become far more of a science. Now there will be pig specialist practices looking after huge numbers of pigs from neonates up to breeding stock. I learnt a lot of the science, not at university, but when I spent two weeks at the Veterinary Investigation Centre in Reading when I was in my final year. Watching post-mortems was the way to learn about the different pig diseases now taking over as herd problems rather than the old-fashioned diseases that I have already mentioned affecting more individuals. Pneumonia outbreaks, different forms of enteric disease caused by both viruses and bacteria, herd problems which now require herd solutions whether in terms of management changes or mass medication.

A fast-changing industry requiring different needs. These large pig practices become more consultants, doing some visits, especially in the case of serious disease outbreaks but a lot of their work will be done from post-mortem and lab results and telephone consultations. There work becomes advisory, looking after huge numbers of pigs on different units as well as producing health plans for high health status breeders who act as a pyramid nucleus for supplying high genetic merit breeders to other pig farms. The pig industry has evolved a lot over the years, and probably in terms of science, more than most in the farming sector. It is an intensive farming system requiring top quality veterinary input, even more so as the meat purchasers, the supermarkets have ever exacting welfare standards, all good for the pig. The abolition of tethers already mentioned, and there will be changes to farrowing crates as well in the pipeline in the near future. The welfare of the pig in these modern systems is an always monitored and ever advancing benefit, especially as the general public are more and more interested in how their food is produced. The modern pig vet is an important stakeholder in progressing the industry in the right direction, for the good of the pig and the public perception of how their upkeep is maintained for the benefit of their welfare.

I have stayed in contact with the industry mainly through a couple of farms requiring regular quarterly farm assurance visits. I have also seen the odd pig belonging to small holders and those people who have decided that a pig is a good pet, not realising that Kune Kunes do grow from being cute cuddly little piglets into a large and forceful presence in the home environment. A little hairy piglet sitting next to you on the sofa snuggling down to watch Peppa Pig is one thing, a hundred and fifty kilo adult pig is another, or one needs to get a bigger sofa.

Clem and his family would give me visits in the glorious scenery of the Shropshire Hills below the Stiperstones. There would be other visits here and there and the other vets in the practice would be reluctant to see their porcine friends. But most of my work would be on one farm, Warwick Farm, where I would be the nominated vet to carry out their farm assurance and any other disease control measures that were necessary. I was told before my first visit that the buildings left a little to be desired and that a strong puff of wind may be the end of some. On my arrival on farm, I found these warnings to be true. I wondered how, certainly from an external perspective, how some of them still stood. But despite their appearance they were functional and what internal modifications had been made to the buildings made them more than comfortable for those pigs calling these sheds home. It was a compromise between welfare and economics, the comfort of the pig being paramount. Over the years when money allowed then some of these sheds have been modified or replaced with more modern building designs, especially for growing pigs allowing the modern technology of climate control in the houses to be utilised.

I think Peter, who had wanted to be a pig farmer all his life with Warwick Farm at last allowing him to pursue his dream, put in a lot of hard work in developing his unit over the years that I acted as his vet. The reward was that he started producing better and better results. When I started, like so many pig units then, livestock had antibiotic incorporated in their diet on a daily basis. Enzootic pneumonia was endemic on the farm along with a couple of other pig herd diseases. But over the years, through improved management and targeted vaccination programs, Peter and I have reduced in-feed medication to nil. A success story which has happened in a lot of pig herds throughout the country, meaning the industry have succeeded in meeting the reduction in antibiotic use targets that had been set for them very easily. This has to be good for the consumer and for human health.

It is sad that as Peter has reached this success, the pig price has collapsed. Feed prices have gone through the roof and spaces in abattoirs are greatly reduced. The industry is in crisis at a time when in my opinion we should be supporting a food industry, producing more home-grown British meat. This at a time when Peter's thoughts were turning retirement and to following his other love, horse racing over fences, and becoming part-owner of several horses. Wanting to hand over of a legacy to the next generation while he and his wife enjoyed a retirement at the racecourse, a rethink has been necessary and as I retire then he has to rethink his pig farm future, economically unviable to continue as it is. Through triumphs and tribulations, it has been a pleasure to do his work for him. We have watched through changing times how we have between us improved productivity while not compromising the health and welfare of the pigs, even improving it. A successful team approach, which will be happening commonly throughout the pig industry.

A very rare occurrence, but I did once have to TB test a small herd of pigs, a rare breed herd. This was an unusual case brought about by meat inspectors finding on a regular basis TB lesions in the pigs which had been sent to slaughter for meat. The surrounding farms had been down with the disease in their cattle, but these pigs would not have gone on "cattle" land. Pigs root in the soil, and one of the areas they rooted was over a badger sett.

It was decided by Animal Health that the pig herd would be tested, and they needed a volunteer to do so. Guess who? This was something that in all my years I had never had to do, but I was going to have to! I read up what to do and set off to the farm on a hot summers day to carry out the test on the forty pigs. The farmer was there to help me, deciding I could test the three sows in a crate, easy, but he would have to catch the piglets one by one, and I would test them while he held them, me then marking each one numerically when it was done. Half the piglets were about ten kilos, easy. The rest were nearer forty kilos and as you can imagine, it was hard work for the farmer to firstly catch and then hold them while I tested them. He sweated a lot more than I did, it was a struggle, but we succeeded in completing the test, pigs running everywhere. It was lucky we had marked the ones we had done as they got out and mixed with their mates several times while we were doing it all.

Sadly when I returned three days later to read the test, again having to catch each pig one by one, the results were a disaster. You could see even at a distance that they all bar two sows had huge reactions, they were all infected and even on post-mortem it was found that the two sows had lesions on their brains as well.

A one off in my career and with a disappointing ending.

But another one off was having to go and inspect a farm that reared wild boar. As their name suggests, if kept in captivity they are classed as wild animals and subsequently fall under the Wild Animals Act. They would need a licence to be able to be kept. Again, I was volunteered and set off to see these pigs, accompanied by a couple of ladies from the licensing authority. My mission, to ensure the health and safety, and the welfare of the wild boars, and to ensure that their premises were secure. We did not want wild boar escaping and running wild in Shropshire. It was an interesting afternoon, seeing boar for the first time and they were not as big as I expected, and these chaps actually seemed quite docile in their habitat, a well (double) fenced enclosure where they could root around amongst the trees and shrubs to their hearts content. They are diggers and so along with an electric fence, a wire mesh fence was sunk some eighteen inches into the ground to ensure they would not get underneath.

They are reared to supply a niche market, one often finding wild boar chops or steaks on restaurant menus now, and these pigs were valuable. Most staggering was that the off cuts, the cheek muscles etc that weren't saleable in their own right would be made into sausages or chorizo, and these were sold for a fortune. The diversification of farming these days!

And what of sausages? Well firstly, at Jane's wedding party we did enjoy one of Peter's pigs for a hog roast to feed our guests. And it fed us for quite a few meals after that as well. But more than one farm does still rear the odd litter, some finding that said offspring when old enough, then mate and there are even more pigs on the farm. These were meant for the freezer, and I cannot deny that the odd kilogram or five of sausages have made their way to me.

And they have been delicious, keep them coming!

27

THE FUTURE

So, what of the future for farm veterinary practice? As mentioned before, Bob Dylan sang, "The times they are a changing". My forty plus years have seen many changes. For the future, well do I care? It will no longer affect me!

Yes, of course I care! I have been involved in farming all my life whether as a farmer's son or as a farm vet. If my interests diversify, I will always have half an eye on what is happening in my profession, even if then I will be an outsider.

But I guess here that I must state that these views and opinions are mine and mine alone, they are only what I think should or may happen.

The future of farm vetting very much runs hand in hand with that of livestock farming, maybe even all farming because the different forms are linked in one way or another. And the future of farming depends very much on the consumer and the food production industries. I suppose when I voted to come out of Europe, I did so because I had a vision where our island would become far more self-sufficient in producing her own food. Although I have always been against subsidies, any industry should have to survive on its own two feet, I saw a country where manufacturing would be encouraged and supported so we became less dependent on China. But most of all I thought there would be some sort of food policy where we became far more self-sufficient in producing food for our ever-growing population. We have a great diversification in types of farming and of different types of food we can produce. If I accept that we cannot grow everything (our climate is just not suitable), then with a bit of thought and encouragement and a fairer price paid to home production by the supermarket buyers, then that goal could be achievable.

The country, the World, has challenges for the near and distant future. Climate change, conservation, an ever-increasing population and in time just a pressure on natural resources are problems that need to be dealt with head on.

Farming in this country certainly has and is having a role in conservation. Guardians of the land, I have already described how some farmers take this role very seriously. Farming gets blamed a lot in climate change arguments with the poor ruminant being harangued for burping and releasing amounts of methane into the atmosphere and affecting the ozone layer. But seriously is this that significant when you consider the vast amounts of fossil fuel burning carried out in China, in India? And although they are recognising the risks post-Trump, in the United States as well. One should not forget that valuable commodity that come out of the other end of a cow or sheep or a goat, not milk or offspring but faeces and urine. Certainly, in my time in East Africa this was considered as valuable a product to start with as milk, being a valuable fertiliser to improve the quality of the soil where they produced other food stuffs, vegetables and fruit. People in this country may not enjoy the smell of muck spreading, when rotting manure and slurry is returned to the land providing humous, and important minerals to encourage good future growth and fertility off the land. Without this, what would we have, human manure, would we be keen on eating food produced from our own excrement?

People have become more particular about their diets. The vegans, the vegetarians getting more front-page press about their causes than the majority of the omnivores like myself who enjoy a good mixed diet of meat and vegetable. Is there enough reporting about the difference between dairy (milk) allergies and intolerance so that people are put off or deprived such an important nutrient source as milk, being such an important source of Calcium amongst other things? I believe I have read that the carbon footprint of producing milk alternatives such as almond or coconut milk are far higher than that of cow's milk.

One of the challenges that farming faces is that it has never been very good at marketing itself, banging its own drum about what it does well and the value it adds to the country.

We as farm vets (though obviously not me now) have to encompass some of these changes. Helping the livestock farming industry to move forward, tackling these challenges while staying efficient while remaining guardians of the countryside and ticking all the boxes on the ever-increasing demands of animal welfare.

The beef and sheep industry will carry on as it is, there will be a place for intensive feedlot systems producing a saleable carcass in a very rapid time. The traditional grass-based systems of fattening lambs and cattle will also survive with some of the older traditional native breeds coming to the fore in these systems. Much will come down to consumer choice. I personally like my beef with some marbling, coming from slower fattening processes, i.e., grass. But the likes of MacDonalds and other fast-food chains have their own choices of which will types of beef they want and as long as the cost of living doesn't make these premium joints and steaks too expensive, there will always be a market for them.

The pig industry is going through its own problems related to spiralling costs and difficulties in processing the number of pigs ready for slaughter. A shortage of slaughter men has exacerbated this problem and one wonders how long the industry can survive in this present climate. The pig farmers have become more efficient, more productive and have made giant strides in reducing antibiotic usage. Pork is by far the cheapest joint yet, there isn't the capacity to process it. Welfare standards increase, but they have costs. The industry is struggling. A lot of things are cyclical, but one wonders how long it will take for things to turn around and in what state the industry will be in when that happens.

It would be nice to think at some stage in the not-too-distant future as one wanders around the supermarket looking in the meat counters, that picking any packet up it would say "Produced in Great Britain". A dream of mine that probably will not happen but should.

The dairy industry, which has taken up most of my time in practice, faces its own challenges against a background of a milk price that does not alter that much over the years while costs have spiralled. Feed, bedding, fuel costs have all gone up but perhaps the greatest challenge now is labour. When I started there would be men and women who had worked the land all their life, probably working on the same farm as their fathers and their fathers before. These people knew the land, they could tell you all about local nature. What blackbird had nested in which hedge year after year, how the landscape had changed and would always have some farming yarn for you. Their likes are now few and far between and now trying to find people to work the hours necessary on a dairy farm is becoming increasingly more difficult. Before Brexit there were many Eastern Europeans, Polish, Romanians and Latvians who came over to do this work. But now many have returned home. They were hard work for a vet, or so I found, as when you asked them anything or required some help, they suddenly didn't speak any English. A herdsman works long hours. Milking can start at four-thirty, five in the morning and evening milking finish late at night, especially if a farm is on three times a day milking. People don't seem to be prepared to work those hours anymore, so it is becoming harder to staff your farm. I was recently on a farm and was having breakfast with the farmer and his helper, a very well-spoken gentleman. In conversation, he told me he had just moved into and was looking for part-time work for no better reason than just to occupy himself for a few hours.

"What was his previous job," I asked.

He replied, "I am a retired nuclear submarine commander."

Farming for the short term was a novelty for him, for others, trying to get fresh faces into the industry and for the hours they have to work is difficult.

Many dairy farms need investment, modernising, but if this is done is there ever going to be the return if costs go up. The milk price stays flat and most of all if you cannot get the staff to milk your cows, the business is unviable.

The large milk producing farms with massive herds will continue. A few of the small family farms will also continue on a less intensive farming system, more a traditional grazing system rather than one using high yielding Holsteins who need more sophisticated diets than just grass and a bit of corn. Which system does best in the future time will tell?

The answer, back to Bob Dylan, is blowing in the wind.

And the vet's role in all this.

My years in practice have seen many changes. Mostly for the better but one always thinks, yearns for the good old days, seeing them as far better than modern day. Certainly, those days in Devon were far more relaxed even if the number of calls in a day were significantly higher than now. But different situations have different needs. Farms are far bigger, stock numbers are far higher, farming is more intensive and farm economics more exacting.

Where do we fit in?

If the bulk of our work is now centred on fertility work, much time spent on Routine visits, then we have to involve ourselves more in the economics and management of the farms we tend. We become part of a team, along with farm advisors and nutritionists, breeding advisors and agronomists. We become important in designing breeding protocols, in disease management, In herd health planning and ensuring Farm Assurance requirements are met. We have partly become consultants. There are still the day-to-day fire brigade calls, and the emergency calls such as lambings and calvings but that side of practice brings in less of a proportion of income than when I started out. We have trained farmers to do more and more themselves, which has reduced our workload in certain areas. That is where I would say that the job is not as interesting as when I started, purely for the greater variety of calls I saw all those years ago.

We have seen disease eradication schemes set up such as those for Johne's Disease and for BVD and I'm sure over the years these will develop further so that we can say as a country we are as free of these economically damaging diseases as we can. Bovine Tuberculosis is another, though we have been trying to control this disease for many years now and what progress we are making is questionable. It worries me that at some stage the Government of the time is going to throw it back at the farmer and say it is your problem, sort it out yourselves. Deadlines are set for its control, whether they are achievable then in some respects it is up to us as a profession to make sure it happens. If I do not mention badgers, an emotive subject, all I will say is to meet some of the farmers whose lives have been affected by their herd going down on a TB test, the economic and even more the emotional upset it causes, I don't think the general public can appreciate the effect it has on them. Farmers, their wives brought to tears by the loss of what seem good healthy cattle having to be destroyed and their farms closed down until it is deemed clear again some months later (if they are lucky).

There is much pressure on farming to reduce the amount of antibiotic used in food production, not just nationally but internationally as well. The World Health Organisation wants us to stop using certain categories of antibiotic in food production in the hope that it can reduce the chance of possible drug resistance in human medicine. As one goal is achieved, the bar will be raised again to even more reduced target levels of antibiotic use. We dispense the drugs, the antibiotics and we have to police this. Try to improve management, the environment as well for livestock so that health is achieved not through drug use, but more from good practice.

Again, this emphasises our role in Farm Assurance and herd health planning.

We have more and more vaccines available to help us in disease management and control, but vaccines alone cannot control disease.

But we must not while attending these large herds and flocks ,forget those smaller holdings. The small family farms, the small holdings and those that have just wanted the odd sheep or pig, looking for "The Good Life". Even those herds of a thousand cows, it may be a large herd, but that herd is made up of a thousand individuals and that to me is something we must not forget.

Over the coming years, like farming, then farm vet practice will be a challenge especially if the economic fortunes of farming do not improve. We have to remember that whatever we decide to give in advice, if it goes wrong then it is not us who loses financially, it is the farmer.

There has been a trend to evidence-based medicine. The modern idiom and with that in mind it is a sadness to me that that good old-fashioned thing called clinical judgement has gone out of the window. I was always taught by my late tutor at Bristol, common things occur commonly and they do. With that in mind, to me it is not always necessary to dive in with a scalpel at first instance or to run up huge lab fees for what you already know.

There will always be a decision to make between the science of vetting and the art of vetting, I hope that the two can work in conjunction with each other. It is important to look at the cow or sheep or pig, it will tell you a lot, and by all means what other data you have to help you with diagnosis and control. The other important party is the farmer. If you blast him with science, you may well lose him and in so doing, lose his ability to comprehend and act on any advice that may be given.

Building trust and a personal relationship has and always will be an important consideration in initiating disease control, in vetting in general.

Farm vets will move with the times, but I hope they do not forget some of the old ways which made us such a revered profession in the past.

The times they are a changing!

THE QUIET VET

My retirement date was set at May 31st.2021.

 I had originally decided to go at the end of the tax year, 2020/21 which conveniently fell over the Easter break. I was counting down the months, the days which seemed to be dragging interminably with Covid and Lockdown. But in the end, I had a slight rethink. I guess I fancied one last spring lambing and hoped by then that some restrictions would be lifting and that I would get the chance to say goodbye properly to those clients I had served over the years. The end of May it would be.

My countdown had reached twelve more months, then I had to reset. It was back to over four hundred days, not that I was counting. How slowly they seemed to pass, twelve months, nine months, two hundred days, one fifty then a hundred. Then they seemed to race by and all of a sudden, I was in my last month, it was the beginning of May, my days were numbered.

May 31st.was actually a Bank Holiday, Whit Monday so my last day was actually the 28th., a Friday. It was a bizarre feeling after those forty-four years to get up one last time to go to work. Except I couldn't because of Covid, I would have to wait until a call came in.

Fiona and Jim had given me a send-off tea and cakes, a party at Binweston on the Tuesday after my last Routine visit there. It was lovely to hear the appreciation they had for the work I had done there for them on one of our biggest dairy units, working together to forward the health of the herd. Jill at Drury Lane had also produced a special cake for me at my last Routine there, with the promise of a leaving present to remember the farm by when it was ready. It turned out to be a wonderful picture, a print of a view from just up the road from the farm, looking across the valley and towards the Stiperstones, a lovely reminder of many happy days spent there on her farm.

I knew I did have things to do on my last day. My final stock take, finish my bookings, empty my car of the firm's drugs and equipment and of course, submit my final expenses. But that would have to wait until I went into the office later, all I could do now was to wait and see what calls came in. It would be ironic that when that call came, it was to go and see a calf with pneumonia at Fairview below the Wrekin. The irony, this was one of the first, if not the first farm I had to visit when I started work in Shropshire and as the day would turn out, it would be the last. Time to chew over old times with an old friend and client.

I had received a call from Alistair that he and Tim would like to take me out to lunch on my last day. This was where it had all begun all those years ago when we had had an informal lunch in Shrewsbury with them enquiring if I would like to join them on a part time basis, and here we were again on my final day.

I went into the office before my lunch appointment to start my clearing up. I had not been there long in the area that up to four personnel could enter when one of the girls came and asked if I could meet her outside the building in about five minutes.

I went out and there were Tia, Siobhan, Laraine, Hannah, Heather, Charlotte, Susan, Jules and Chloe all waiting for me. Socially distancing of course. All came out to say their goodbyes and presented me with a box of goodies. It was an emotional moment for me, a great team who had made working through the isolation of Covid a lot easier and who had been so helpful in their time working with me. I would be sad to be saying goodbye, but it was the end of my road.

I went for lunch with my bosses, reflecting on old times but also being well aware that I couldn't eat too much as a group of farmers were taking me out that evening for a meal as well. Discussions on what I thought I had achieved over all those years? What was my greatest achievement? How did I view the future? All very light-hearted and lastly a big thank you for all that I had done for the practice over the years.

Then I was asked by the office if I could go and pick up one of the TB testers from where he had left his car to be repaired after an accident and back to the office. This was the one member of staff I did not know and here I was chatting to him on my last day, finding him to be like me, a United fan. I also found one of the things I would not miss, the congestion on the by-pass around Shrewsbury, it was quicker for me to drive through the centre of town than to take the "quick" route.

I tidied up, did my stocktake, emptied my car, I was done. Sean arrived and I was moved when he also presented me with a leaving present, a compass for my walking. I was done.

It was a strange feeling just to get into the car and go, that was the end of my working career, one last drive through the gates of the practice onto that suicidal turn onto the main road, something else I wouldn't miss, blind turns are no fun, and thoughts back to that battered Opel back in Devon all those years ago!

It was time to reflect on one last drive home from work.

I had a lovely evening being entertained by a group of farmers and their wives, and one of my other bosses, James who did call into the Mytton and Mermaid during the meal to say his goodbyes, and thank me for my past contributions. It was nice to be appreciated by so many, a reward for my past efforts. It was my leaving party, Jane said she would drive so I could have a drink, she managed to get us lost half a mile from home!

The Saturday night was my own private end of term do and it was a pleasure to take Jill, Dan, Cristina and Alex to The Walrus in Shrewsbury for one of the best meals out I have ever had. Even if at one stage I was choking on a piece of rather rare lamb while no-one realised, it could have been a very brief retirement!

We had planned to go away straight after my retirement day. After a couple of days in Bala with Dave and Lisa over the bank holiday, we were to set off to Dorset for the best part of a fortnight. My plan was that I would be on holiday rather than being at home and getting up on a working day, only not to go into work. It was a lovely few days away, blending into village life, relaxing, walking, reading, cooking and going to the pub. Life like I hoped it would be in retirement! My son joined us for twenty-four hours and it was fantastic to spend some real downtime with him, walking, chatting on the beach over a beer or two. Chatting to the locals, watching the sunset over the Jurassic coast from the top of Colmer Hill. This is what I dreamed retirement would be like, except we were in Dorset, and I would never be able to realise my dream of retiring here, it was too expensive.

Partly through divorce and depression, but vetting for me had never been the lucrative profession that people think it is. If in my original plans for life had been that I would have earned enough to retire at around fifty-five, that had not happened. My career had been a vocation, not a cash cow.

From those early days in Devon, through a few years in Gloucestershire and many years in Shropshire, I had now reached the end of my road. I could look back on great days, admiring Devon from the top of Hembury Fort, watching the Severn Bore, those mornings watching the sunrise at Atcham, and the ruggedness of the Shropshire Hills. Happy times with many fond memories.

Did I achieve everything I wanted to in my career? I guess the honest answer to that is no and that would probably be down to a lack of confidence in myself for so much of my career. I lacked confidence then I became partially deaf and then suffered from depression. They made me quiet and subdued, and I guess unless people knew then they would have found me rather aloof.

My parents pushed me when I was young to achieve what I became, a qualified vet and I would have to thank the contributions Ian Baker made when I was a student in Aylesbury, and George Dart in Cullompton in developing my career. The Foot and Mouth outbreak of 2001 had a severe effect on me, the start of my depression from where life seemed to be going wrong for me. When I had started to find the answers myself to overcoming this, Jayne Weaver encouraged me to write. This was firstly when no-one else would contribute to the monthly practice newsletter and then to writing my account of Kilimanjaro, she pushed me into finishing the book. Articles I wrote which I hoped were practical but not boring in the newsletter plus my Christmas special which I tried to make pure comedy. Perhaps somewhere Jayne saw there may be an author lurking somewhere inside me, but even if as I write this, I am still only using two fingers to type.

Years ago, I had ideas about drug usage and control. But I did not have the technical ability to pursue them, or the communication skills to get someone else to. Health monitoring schemes, likewise, but again people want digital formats, not paper like me. These ideas have come to fruition but not through me and have happened sometime after I thought about them. Wasted opportunities because I was too quiet.

I got there in the end but would have to reflect on why I didn't find myself until late in my career. Where after now having a new confidence in myself, I would speak up in meetings, ask pertinent questions, develop ideas, champion well-being in the workplace. The quiet vet suddenly (though still quietly spoken) had a voice. The relationship I built up with farmers was I think always a positive for me. Reaching decisions between us so we had a clear direction in the way forward. Was one of my fortes that of knowing how to build these relationships? One doesn't have to be loud and forceful to succeed in this area, just patient and be able to listen and understand the needs of your client. That was the help I could give to younger vets and students seeing practice, it may be vetting from the old school, but it does work.

I cannot deny that along the way I made the odd mistake, don't we all. But I have always tried to do my best for client and my patient. I suppose I would always stop and analyse where I think I may have gone wrong to do better next time.

I have worked with some great people over the years, too many to mention here but to name two in my later years. Siobhan so quietly efficient but always so helpful especially in these strange times of Covid. To add to her, Charlotte, to me such a talented artist. She has had so many comebacks at the practice between her Art Degree and who has now blossomed in her new career. But again she was always so helpful and one never begrudged the time to help her and make her job easier in the pharmacy. If she has one fault then it is apologising all the time, even to the extent that she says sorry for saying sorry. People like Roel, where perhaps we always misunderstood each other, and at times he made my life difficult. But, in the end, I think we had a mutual respect for each other and our individual abilities, such that in the end, I always enjoyed having a chat with him.

And I have met some great characters as well, true country folk and chatting to them, talking of their lives and livelihoods is something I will miss. As I grew in confidence in myself post-Kili then I have chatted far more to these people, to me it is part of building that special bond between vet and farmer. Some of those chats would be about their surroundings, listed buildings they lived in and some of the social history that this environment provided.

Not long before I finished my career, I was sent to do a small TB test on the Staffordshire/Shropshire border. I thought this could be interesting as it was at an old mill in a hamlet called Somerford. I had fifty cattle to test on a place I had never been to before, though the first person I would meet was a farmer I had met at another premises, he was helping out. The test went smoothly and when we were done, I asked if the Mill was still operational. It wasn't but John, the farmer, said when I returned three days later, he would show me around what remained of it.

He would be happy to.

A clear test and then onto the mill. It was really interesting to see how the millstream went under the house, to see the millpond and where the wheel used to be. Over a cup of tea, he showed me old pictures of it as it used to be. Fascinating!

Then John showed me some photographs of the previous spring, it had rained heavily and there was much flooding in the area, including the mill pond. Water levels had risen and risen until water was entering the house.

Photographs of the flooding and there was John sitting in his living room in his favourite chair with his wellies on. The lower twelve inches of his boots submerged in water but that wasn't going to stop him having his creature comforts.

A great character and the sort I will miss.

It may be that looking back, my successes were in Africa. Climbing Kilimanjaro was an ambition achieved and the positivity I received from my success changed me as a person, as a cure for depression and bringing so much positivity to me. Back to Kenya some years later and finding more of the real me, making positive and important decisions that have stood me in good stead ever since. Returning the following year to work for *Send a Cow* in Kenya was a real privilege and showed me that this quiet person could stand in front of unknown people and pass on knowledge he had gained over his career for the benefit of others.

My life will now move on, almost certainly not in Shropshire. I hope in time North Wales will give me the environment to develop those other interests that have been shelved during my career, more walking, writing, landscape drawing, gardening, cooking and even rediscovering golf again. I have in those months since retirement still kept my hand in a little with vetting and have enjoyed it without the commitment to being full time. I will continue to do a little more probably in 2022 and then it is goodbye.

If I have shown frustration at times, it has never been with my patient. More through being given an impossible schedule to complete or because my helpers have not been that helpful.

Not so long ago, feedback to the practice was that I had been a pleasure to work with, really efficient and quick and that the farmer had really enjoyed my company. I have on many occasions been complemented on my patience, on my quietness with the animals I have been there to help.

I hope that I have built trust and confidence with my clients, and hope that even if being rather old school, that quietness and patience with animals will be my epitaph. Don't we like a lot of TLC when we are ill.

Its Christmas eve, my first Christmas in retirement, and once again I settle in front of the television to watch the new Herriot Christmas special, *"All Creatures Great and Small"*. Is this not where I started?

THE QUIET VET!

Acknowledgements:

Firstly I would have to mention my parents, Tony and Sylvia for the encouragement and support given to me when needed.

I have mentioned persons who have had a significant affect on my career, namely Ian Baker and George Dart.

To Sam Ellis for her continued support in liking after my website.

To Siobhan for the time she gave going through my manuscript.

To the Directors of Shropshire Farm Vets for allowing me the time to go to Kenya to work for *Send a Cow* in 2018.

To the many colleagues and support staff who have worked with me and helped me throughout my career, but too numerous to mention all by name.

And of course the farmers who I have strived to help throughout my career, again too numerous to mention all by name, but a few with special thanks, Jill and Dan, James and Gill, Peter and Julie, Peter and Fiona, James and Fiona, Alan, James and Chris, Bob, Paul and Christine, you will know who you are. A special thank you, the memories of you all will last forever.

www.ingramcontent.com/pod-product-compliance
Lightning Source LLC
Chambersburg PA
CBHW022003090426
42741CB00007B/871